INNOVATION TOGETHER

T0189228

Innovation Together
Microsoft Research Asia
Academic Research Collaboration

Edited by

Lolan Song,
Representing University Relations
Microsoft Research Asia
Beijing, China

 Springer

Editor
Lolan Song
Microsoft Research Asia
Beijing, China

ISBN: 978-1-4614-9790-5

© 2008 Microsoft
Softcover re-print of the Hardcover 1st edition 2009

Chapters 1, 2, 4, 6, 9, 14 and 15 reprinted with kind permission from ACM
Chapters 3, 7, 8 and 13 reprinted with kind permission from IEEE
Chapters 10, 11 and 12 reprinted with kind permission from Elsevier

Printed on acid-free paper

springer.com

Foreword

When I read Chris Buckley's article, *Let a Thousand Ideas Flower: China Is a New Hotbed of Research* (New York Times, September 13, 2004), I had just returned to Beijing after living abroad 19 years and joined Microsoft Research Asia (MSRA). "The Chinese are going to become sources of innovation"; Chris Buckley had quoted Denis Fred Simon, a specialist in Chinese science and technology. Soon, I too had become a believer of this prediction and wanted to contribute to its realization.

Innovation is the new national strategy of China. In 2006, China issued the Outline of National Medium- and Long-term Science and Technology Development Plan (2006-2020). The Outline identifies innovation as China's new national development strategy and a main engine for driving development. To build an innovation-oriented country, China will invest more than 2.5% of its GDP in research and development by 2020[1]. Meanwhile, China has invested more than 3% of its GDP in education[2]. In 2006, China graduated more than 1.5 million college students who majored in the fields of science and engineering[3]. With a large number of highly trained technology graduates, China is transforming itself from a manufacturing center to one of the fastest growing innovation centers of the world.

I joined MSRA to lead University Relations (UR). In this position, I have witnessed the rapid economic growth in China and a much improved environment for higher education and basic research, which have brought challenge and opportunity to my work. I have thought much about how to identify more opportunities for col-

---

[1] Refer to *The Outline of National Medium- and Long-term Science and Technology Development Plan (2006-2020)* announced by Ministry of Science and Technology, China and the vice minister's talk at the press room:http://www.most.gov.cn/eng/pressroom/200608/t20060829_35696.htm.

[2] Refer to *The educational development during the 10th 5-Year Plan* announced by Ministry of Education, Chin and Education in China news report: http://www.edu.cn/20060228/3175654.shtml.

[3] See 2007 China Science and Technology statistics Data Book at http://www.most.gov.cn/eng/statistics/2007/200801/P020080109573867344872.pdf.

laboration with academia, how to design programs to foster innovative research, and how to advance education by partnering with universities.

The MSRA UR Program was created at the start of MSRA to nurture strong and mutually supportive partnerships and collaboration with the academic community. Since its establishment, MSRA has partnered with as many as 100 universities and research institutes of the Chinese mainland, Hong Kong, Taiwan, Japan, Korea, Australia, New Zealand and Singapore. A collection of research papers in this book demonstrates a slice of the results of collaboration with universities over the past decade.

To foster a healthy academic environment, MSRA has built a close partnership with universities, research institutes, and governments. In 1999, MSRA partnered with the National Science Foundation China (NSFC) to setup the NSFC-Microsoft Joint Program. Over thirty projects have been funded to support fundamental research at Chinese universities and research institutes. Articles in this book by Prof. Hujun BAO of Zhejiang University and Prof. Weimin ZHENG of Tsinghua University introduce part of their work sponsored by the NSFC-Microsoft Joint Program Grant.

MSRA has also established corporate-university joint research labs to carry out research and development in specific areas. Since1999, ten joint labs have been established; with eight of them recognized by the China Ministry of Education as key labs (the other two are in their initial stages of development). These labs have published hundreds of academic papers in prestigious academic journals and others have been presented at highly respected conferences. Some of them are part of this collection. You will also find papers about research work in search and data mining technology by the Microsoft-Shanghai Jiaotong University Joint Lab, as well as those about system and networking research at the Microsoft-Hong Kong University of Science and Technology Joint Lab.

Research collaboration extends across the Asia-Pacific region. In 2005, the Microsoft Institute for Japanese Academic Research Collaboration (IJARC) was established in Tokyo, Japan to enhance linkage with Japanese academic communities. In February 2007, the Microsoft-Queensland University of Technology eResearch Centre in Brisbane, Australia was opened.

To develop the next generation of researchers and IT professionals, MSRA offers a variety of research programs for both students and new faculty. Talented students are awarded an opportunity to work as interns at the "World's Hottest Computer Lab", as referred to by the MIT Technology Review. Promising new faculty are supported by the Young Faculty Special Fund or Professorship Award in their research career at an early stage. This book presents several papers of the Fellowship and Professorship winners. The first author, Guojun Qi, a PhD student at the University of Science and Technology of China, won the Best Paper Award in ACM Multimedia 2007. Another student, Zhijie Yan, from the same university, won Best Student Paper Award in IEEE International Conference on Acoustics, Speech, and Signal Processing 2007. Dr. Sanjiang Li, a young associate professor of Tsinghua University, who won the 2007 Microsoft Research Asia Professorship Award, has published more than 20 articles for top international conferences and journals. One of his articles published on Artificial Intelligence 2007 is selected for this book.

"We have a wonderful partnership with Microsoft Re-search Asia," said Dr.Gu Binglin, President of Tsinghua University when he awarded Bill Gates an Honorary Doctorate Degree on 19 April 2007. "Such a relationship has set up a role model for the industry, the universities, and research organizations to work together to accelerate innovation and talent fostering." This kind of feedback from a well-respected scientist and educator is the best reward for our work and motivates us to do better.

This book is a gift to celebrate MSRA's 10th anniversary in November 2008. It is the product of team work by University Relations at Microsoft Research Asia. I wish to express my deepest appreciation for the contributions of Gao Zhang, Xiangwen Liu, Xin Ma, Miran Lee, Gang Guan, Bernard Oh, Joseph Shih, Bei Li, Tingting Huang, and especially to Lihua Tang, the project manager who led the effort and made it a success. In addition, I am grateful for technical expertise provided by Baining Guo, Jian Wang, Wei-Ying Ma, Shipeng Li, Frank Soong, Zheng Zhang, Jian Sun, Xin Tong, Feng Wu, and Zhouchen Lin. And finally, many thanks for the great leadership provided by Dr.Harry Shum and Dr.Hsiao-Wuen Hon, the former and present Managing Directors of MSRA.

Looking back, we have accomplished much in the first decade as partially demonstrated by this collection. Looking forward, we, at Microsoft Research Asia, are confident that much more will be achieved by cooperating with our academic partners in the next decade.

Lolan SONG
Director, University Relations
Microsoft Research Asia
August 8, 2008
Beijing, China

Preface

Happy Birthday, Microsoft Research Asia (MSRA)! You are ten years old!

Since the very beginning, I have served on MSRA's Technology Advisory Board. This has given me a unique and enviable position to observe the development of the Lab up close and personal. Over the last decade, I have visited the Beijing office on numerous occasions, attending the TAB meetings in which the most recent innovative research results were showcased. I have also participated in the annual Computing in the 21st Century conferences and the Faculty Summits, and visited many universities in China that are a part of the University Relations program - from Xian to Hangzhou and from Hong Kong to Harbin. Above all, I have had the great pleasure of interacting with some of the most brilliant and earnest student interns anywhere in the world. No wonder the Technology Review magazine in 2004 called it "the World's Hottest Computer Lab!"

Innovation has been the hallmark of MSRA - not just in a slogan, but as a way of life. The leadership of MSRA has created an environment that enables its researchers to invent new ways of doing things and to create value - whether it be multimedia, networking, user interface, or search. Over the last decade, hundreds of such innovations have been transferred into Microsoft products. In addition, countless papers describing the research results have been published in top-tier computer science conferences and journals, thus directly benefiting the research community at large. One would be hard pressed to find another commercial research lab anywhere in the world that has created as much in so little time. MSRA has become a "must stop" for leading researchers around the world when they visit Asia. In fact, 2008 witnessed the first computer science faculty member from MIT, Prof. Frans Kaashoek, to spend his sabbatical leave at MSRA - a testimony of its prestige and international standing.

This, of course could not have been done without a close collaboration with the academic community in the Asia-Pacific region and beyond. MSRA runs one of the most comprehensive University Relations program in the world, with far-reaching outcomes. For example, MSRA (in partnership with National Science Foundation, China) has jointly funded over thirty research projects in Chinese universities. Eight of its ten corporate/university joint research labs have attained National Key Lab status. In terms of talent development, MSRA has hosted more than 2,500 student interns from more than 100 universities worldwide, and it has offered more than 250 Fellowships to talented students. In fact, the highlight of my annual pilgrimage to MSRA has always been the interactive sessions that I conduct with these talented interns and fellows. As a faculty member from MIT running one of the leading academic computer science research labs, I can say that we have been the direct beneficiary of the development of this talent pool. Having been an MSRA Intern/Fellow makes an applicant for graduate admission stand out among his/her peers; it means they are among the best of the best. At this writing, about a dozen MSRA Interns/Fellows are pursuing their PhD in our department. In reciprocity, some of our own students are beginning to spend their summers in Beijing as MSRA interns.

It is therefore fitting that MSRA would mark its tenth anniversary by publishing a book highlighting a collection of innovative research papers, all of which have been authored or co-authored by faculty members and/or students through collaboration with MSRA members, or with financial support from MSRA. These papers have previously been published in top-tier international conferences and journals, such as the IEEE International Conference on Computer Vision, the IEEE International Conference on Computer Vision and Pattern Recognition, SIGGRAPH, and Speech Communication. The topics range from computer vision and graphics to speech-based interfaces and search. As impressive as these papers are, they represent but a small subset of the academic research accomplishments of MSRA's University Relations program.

Congratulations on the first ten years of your life, MSRA! I look forward to witnessing equally stunning research accomplishments in the coming decades.

Victor Zue
Delta Electronics Professor, Department of Electrical Engineering and Computer Science, and
Director, Computer Science & Artificial Intelligence Laboratory Massachusetts Institute of Technology
Cambridge, Massachusetts, USA
2008

Acknowledgements

1. Jiaya Jia, Jian Sun, Chi-Keung Tang, Heung-Yeung Shum, *Drag-and-Drop Pasting*, ACM Transactions on Graphics, Volume 25 , Issue 3 (July 2006) , in Proceedings of ACM SIGGRAPH 2006, Pages 631-637, 2006 ©2006 Association for Computing Machinery, Inc. Reprinted by permission.
   DOI: http://doi.acm.org/10.1145/1141911.1141934
2. Kang Hoon Lee, Myung Geol Choi, Jehee Lee, *Motion Patches: Building Blocks for Virtual Environments Annotated with Motion Data*, in ACM Transactions on Graphics, Volume 25 , Issue 3 (July 2006) , Proceedings of ACM SIGGRAPH 2006, Pages 898-906, 2006 Copyright ©2006 Association for Computing Machinery, Inc. Reprinted by permission.
   DOI: http://doi.acm.org/10.1145/1179352.1141972
3. Takaaki Shiratori, Yasuyuki Matsushita, Sing Bing Kang, and Xiaoou Tang, *Video Completion by Motion Field Transfer*, Computer Vision and Pattern Recognition, 2006 IEEE Computer Society Conference on, Volume 1, 17-22 June 2006 Pages:411 - 418 Copyright ©2006 IEEE. Reprinted with permission.
   DOI: 10.1109/CVPR.2006.330
4. Guo-Jun Qi, Xian-Sheng Hua, Yong Rui, Jinhui Tang, Tao Mei, Hong-Jiang Zhang, *Correlative Multi-Label Video Annotation*, Multimedia 2007, in proceedings of the 15th international conference on Multimedia, Pages: 17 - 26, 2007 Copyright ©2007 Association for Computing Machinery, Inc. Reprinted by permission.
   DOI: http://doi.acm.org/10.1145/1291233.1291245
5. Guofeng Zhang, Wei Hua, Xueying Qin, Tien-Tsin Wong, and Hujun Bao, *Stereoscopic Video Synthesis from a Monocular Video*, IEEE TRANSACTIONS ON VISUALIZATION AND COMPUTER GRAPHICS, VOL. 13, NO. 4, JULY/AUGUST 2007 Pages:686 - 696 Copyright ©2007 IEEE. Reprinted, with permission.
   DOI: 10.1109/TVCG.2007.1032
6. Tai-Pang Wu, Chi-Keung Tang, Michael S. Brown, Heung-Yeung Shum, *ShapePalettes: Interactive Normal Transfer via Sketching*, in Proceedings of ACM SIGGRAPH2007 Article No.44, 2007 Copyright ©2007 Association for Computing Machinery, Inc. Reprinted by permission.
   DOI: http://doi.acm.org/10.1145/1275808.1276432
7. Wenpeng Ding, Feng Wu, Xiaolin Wu,Shipeng Li,Houqiang Li, *Adaptive Directional Lifting-Based Wavelet Transform for Image Coding*, IEEE Transactions on Image Processing Feb. 2007 Volume: 16, Issue: 2 Pages: 416-427 Copyright ©2007 IEEE. Reprinted, with permission.
   DOI: 10.1109/TIP.2006.888341
8. Yanmin Zhu, Yunhuai Liu, Zheng Zhang and Lionel M. Ni, *Low-Power Distributed Event Detection in Wireless Sensor Networks*, in Proceedings of IN-

FOCOM 2007, Alaska, March 2007. 26th IEEE International Conference on Computer Communications. IEEE 6-12 May 2007 Pages:2401 - 2405 Copyright ©2007 IEEE. Reprinted, with permission.
DOI: 10.1109/INFCOM.2007.289

9. Hongliang Yu, Dongdong Zheng, Ben Y. Zhao and Weimin Zheng, *Understanding User Behavior in Large-Scale Video-on-Demand Systems*, in ACM SIGOPS Operating Systems Review, Volume 40 , Issue 4 (October 2006), Proceedings of the 2006 EuroSys conference, Pages: 333 - 344, 2006 Copyright ©2006 Association for Computing Machinery, Inc. Reprinted by permission.
DOI: http://doi.acm.org/10.1145/1217935.1217968

10. Sanjiang LI, *A representation theorem for minmax regret policies*, Artificial Intelligence, Volume 171, Issue 1, January 2007, Pages 19-24 Copyright ©2007 with permission from Elsevier.
DOI: 10.1016/j.artint.2006.11.001

11. Yunlei Zhao, Shirley H.C. Cheung, Binyu Zang, and Bin Zhu, *A Note on the Cramer-Damgård Identification Scheme*, Internet and Network Economics, Volume 3828/2005, Pages 385-390, Copyright ©2005 Springer Science+Business Media, Inc. Manufactured in the United States.
DOI: 10.1007/11600930

12. Zhenyu Xiong, Thomas Fang Zheng, Zhanjiang Song, Frank Soong, Wenhu Wu, *A tree-based kernel selection approach to efficient Gaussian mixture model-universal background model based speaker identification*, Speech Communication, Volume 48, Issue 10, October 2006, Pages 1273-1282 Copyright ©2006 with permission from Elsevier
DOI: 10.1016/j.specom.2006.06.011

13. Zhi-Jie Yan, Frank Soong, Ren-hua Wang, *WORD GRAPH BASED FEATURE ENHANCEMENT FOR NOISY SPEECH RECOGNITION*, In proceeding of Acoustics, Speech and Signal Processing, 2007. ICASSP 2007. IEEE International Conference on Volume 4, 15-20 April 2007 Page(s):IV-373 - IV-376 Copyright ©2007 IEEE. Reprinted, with permission.
DOI:10.1109/ICASSP.2007.366927

14. Dou Shen, Jian-Tao Sun, Qiang Yang, Zheng Chen. *Building Bridges for Web Query Classification*. In Proceedings of the 29th ACM International Conference on Research and Development in Information Retrieval (SIGIR 06) Pages 131-138 Copyright ©2006 Association for Computing Machinery, Inc. Reprinted by permission.
DOI: http://doi.acm.org/10.1145/1148170.1148196

15. Xiao Ling, Wenyuan Dai, Gui-Rong Xue, Qiang Yang, and Yong Yu. *Cross-Domain Spectral Learning*, To appear in Proceedings of the Fourteenth ACM SIGKDD International Conference on Knowledge Discovery and Data Mining (KDD 2008), Las Vegas, Nevada, USA, August 24-27, 2008 Copyright ©2008 Association for Computing Machinery, Inc. Reprinted by permission.

Contents

Part I
Next Generation Multimedia

Chapter 1
Drag-and-Drop Pasting*

Jiaya Jia, Jian Sun, Chi-Keung Tang, Heung-Yeung Shum

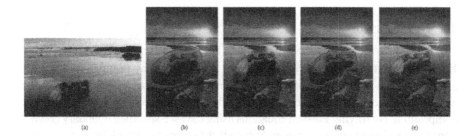

Fig. 1.1 Drag-and-Drop Pasting. Given a source image (a), the user draws a boundary that circles the wood log and its shadow in the water, and drags and drops this region of interest onto the target image in (b). The result from Poisson image editing (c) is however not satisfactory. Structures in this target image (e.g., the dark beach) intersect the source region boundary, thus produce unnatural blurring after solving the Poisson equations. Our approach, called *drag-and-drop pasting*, computes an optimized boundary shown in (d), which is then used to generate a seamless image composite (e).

Abstract In this paper, we present a user-friendly system for seamless image composition, which we call drag-and-drop pasting. We observe that for Poisson image editing [Perez et al. 2003] to work well, the user must carefully draw a boundary on the source image to indicate the region of interest, such that salient structures in source and target images do not conflict with each other along the boundary. To make Poisson image editing more practical and easy to use, we propose a new objective function to compute an optimized boundary condition. A shortest closed-path algorithm is designed to search for the location of the boundary. Moreover, to faithfully preserve the object's fractional boundary, we construct a blended guidance

Jiaya Jia
The Chinese University of Hong Kong

Jian Sun and Heung-Yeung Shum
Microsoft Research Asia

Chi-Keung Tang
The Hong Kong University of Science and Technology

* Source: ACM Transactions on Graphics, Volume 25 , Issue 3 (July 2006), Proceedings of ACM SIGGRAPH 2006, Pages 631-637, 2006 Copyright ©2006 Association for Computing Machinery, Inc. Reprinted by permission. DOI Bookmark: http://doi.acm.org/10.1145/1141911.1141934

field to incorporate the object's alpha matte. To use our system, the user needs only to simply outline a region of interest in the source image, and then drag and drop it onto the target image. Experimental results demonstrate the effectiveness of our "drag-and-drop pasting" system.

Key words: Image processing, Poisson image editing, Image compositing

1.1 Introduction

Image composition is the process of creating a new image by pasting an object or a region from a source image onto a target image. Poisson image editing [Perez et al. 2003] has been proposed recently as an effective approach for seamless image composition. By solving Poisson equations using the user-specified boundary condition, Poisson image editing seamlessly blends the colors from both images without visible discontinuities around the boundary. Poisson image editing not only has an elegant mathematical formulation, but also appears to be easy to use.

The effectiveness of Poisson image editing, however, depends on how carefully the user draws the boundary. As shown in Figure 1.1, Poisson image editing may not always produce good results. Given source and target images in Figures 1.1(a) and (b), and the blue boundary casually drawn by the user, Figure 1.1(c) shows that Poisson image editing may generate unnatural blurring artifacts at places where the boundary intersects with salient structures in the target image (e.g. the dark beach at the top). To obtain seamless composition, we observe that the user needs to take the target image into consideration before drawing the boundary for Poisson image editing.

In this paper, we propose a method to optimize the boundary condition for Poisson image editing. With the optimized boundary shown in Figure 1.1(d), we again apply Poisson image editing to obtain seamless composition as shown in Figure 1.1(e). We note that in Figure 1.1(d) the optimized boundary avoids as much as possible salient image structures on both source and target images.

To optimize the boundary condition, we propose a new objective function which is iteratively minimized using a shortest closed-path algorithm. We search for the optimal boundary in between what the user casually draws (the region of interest) and what the user really cares about (the object of interest). Compared with the original Poisson image editing, our system allows the user to easily drag the region of interest from the source image and to drop it onto the target image, without the need for careful specification of the optimal boundary.

Often, the optimized boundary may intersect with the object of interest. In this case, fine structures of the object may be missing after blending with the target image through Poisson equations. We introduce a blended guidance field to integrate an alpha matte into Poisson equations to faithfully preserve the fractional boundary of the object and produce more natural image composite.

1.2 Related work

Image matting is a common way to extract an object from a source image which can then be pasted onto a target image naturally using an alpha channel. Most matting methods require a trimap in order to estimate the alpha channel and foreground color. There has been a lot of work on natural image matting using a single image [Berman et al. 2000; Ruzon and Tomasi 2000; Chuang et al. 2001; Sun et al. 200]. Other techniques [Smith and Blinn 1996; McGuire et al. 2005] employ a controlled environment or a special device to reduce the inherent ambiguity of the matting problem, thus produce higher quality results.

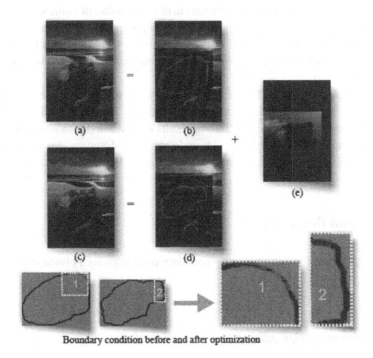

Boundary condition before and after optimization

Fig. 1.2 Comparison of the boundary conditions. (a) and (c) are results by solving Poisson equations with different boundary conditions. They are equivalent to adding (b) and (d) to the source image f_s shown in (e) respectively. (b) and (d) are results by solving the corresponding Laplace equations. The red curves are boundaries while the rectangular shaded areas are caused by the difference of the source and result images. The bottom row shows the boundaries in (b) and (d). Note that the color variance along boundary 2 is smaller that along boundary 1.

In image composition, the multi-resolution spline technique [Burt and Adelson 1983] has long been used to seamlessly blend two different images through interpolations at different levels of Laplacian pyramids. Poisson image editing [Perez et al. 2003], on the other hand, blends two images through Poisson equations with a guidance field and a user-specified boundary. Image stitching in the gradient domain

[Levin et al. 2004; Jia and Tang 2005] has also been proposed to reduce the artifacts caused by structure misalignment, and to correct color discrepancy.

Image compositing can also be done by piecing together multiple image patches from a single image or from multiple images. Graph-cut textures Agarwala et al. [2004], for instance, stitch textures or natural images by finding the best seams using the graph cuts algorithm [Boykov and Jolly 2001]. Interactive digital photomontage [Agarwala et al. 2004] combines different regions of a set of roughly aligned photos with similar content into a single composite. Graph cuts are used to minimize the binary seams between the combined regions, and followed by Poisson image editing to reduce any remaining artifacts. In comparison, our method has the following advantages. The experimental comparisons are shown in section 1.5.

1. Agarwala et al. [2004] require the user to draw a number of strokes to initialize the graph-cut. For complex examples, the labeling requires a number of strokes be drawn iteratively. One example is the thin parts of the object, the user has to carefully draw lines inside them. No strokes are required for the same examples in our method.

2. Our method optimizes for the new boundary energy based on the minimum-error property in solving the Laplace equations and uses iterative optimization, thus can produce smooth and natural blending results even when the source region and the target images differ largely in color and structure. Moreover, our method can handle fine and transparent structures while solving the Poisson equations.

1.3 Optimal Boundary

We address the problem of optimizing boundary conditions for Poisson image editing in this section.

1.3.1 Poisson image editing

To paste a region of interest from the source image f_s to the target image f_t, the following minimization problem [Perez et al. 2003] is solved using the guidance field $v = \nabla f_s$ given the boundary condition defined on the user-drawn region of interest Ω_0:

$$\min_f \int_{p \in \Omega_0} |\nabla f - v|^2 dp \text{ with } f|_{\partial\Omega_0} = f_t|_{\partial\Omega_0}, \quad (1.1)$$

where f is the resulting image, and $\partial\Omega_0$ is the exterior boundary of Ω_0. We denote $f' = f - f_s$. Since the guidance field $v = \nabla f_s$ is a gradient field, Eqn. 1.1 can be written as:

$$\min_{f'} \int_{p \in \Omega_0} |\nabla f'|^2 dp \text{ with } f'|_{\partial\Omega_0} = (f_t - f_s)|_{\partial\Omega_0}. \quad (1.2)$$

The associated Laplace equation is:

$$\Delta f' = 0 \text{ with } f'|_{\partial\Omega_0} = (f_t - f_s)|_{\partial\Omega_0}, \tag{1.3}$$

where $\Delta = (\frac{\partial^2}{\partial x^2} + \frac{\partial^2}{\partial y^2})$ is the Laplacian operator and f' is a membrane interpolation inside Ω_0 for the boundary condition $(f_t - f_s)|_{\partial\Omega_0}$.

Eqn. 1.3 is simply a different interpretation of Poisson image editing by solving alternative Laplacian equations instead of Poisson equations. As illustrated in Figure 1.2, the result from Poisson image editing (a) can be obtained by first solving the corresponding Laplacian equations using the boundary condition $(f_t - f_s)|_{\partial\Omega_0}$ in (b), and then adding back the original source image (e). Similarly, with a different boundary condition, (c) can be obtained from (d) and (e). Both images (a) and (c) are taken from Figure 1.1.

Eqn. 1.2 leads to the following important property. The variational energy $\int_{\Omega_0} |\nabla f'|^2$ will approach zero if and only if all boundary pixels satisfy $(f_t - f_s)|_{\partial\Omega_0} = k$, where k is a constant value [Zwillinger 1997]. In other words, the membrane interpolation is constant if and only if the boundary condition is constant.

As illustrated in Figure 1.2, the boundary conditions $(f_t - f_s)|_{\partial\Omega}$ determine the final results. At the bottom left of Figure 1.2, the color difference between the source and target images, $(f_t - f_s)$ along the user-drawn boundary $\partial\Omega_0$ (on the left) and another new boundary $\partial\Omega$ (on the right) are shown. From the zoomed-in views at the bottom right, we can observe that pixel colors along the boundary $\partial\Omega$ have much less variation than those along $\partial\Omega_0$. A smoother boundary condition produces smaller variational energy in solving the Laplacian equations, thus improves the quality of the resulting composite.

Where is the optimal boundary? Obviously it should be inside the region of interest Ω_0 that the user has drawn. It should also be outside of the object of interest Ω_{obj} which is what the user really wants to paste onto the target image. However, an ordinary user would prefer not to carefully trace Ω_{obj} but only to casually specify Ω_0 instead. Fortunately, recent interactive segmentation techniques such as Grab-Cut [Rother et al. 2004] and Lazy Snapping [Li et al. 2004] can be used to produce Ω_{obj} once Ω_0 is given. For most results in this paper, Ω_{obj} is automatically computed by GrabCut using Ω_0 as initialization.

The question now is how to construct a color-smooth boundary condition $(f_t - f_s)|_{\partial\Omega}$ in the region $\Omega_0\backslash\Omega_{obj}$, where $\partial\Omega$ is a closed boundary to be estimated, as shown in Figure 1.3 (a).

1.3.2 Boundary energy minimization

The optimized boundary $\partial\Omega$ should lie in between Ω_0 and Ω_{obj}. To reduce the color variance along the boundary, the following objective function or boundary energy is minimized:

$$E(\partial\Omega, k) = \sum_{p\in\partial\Omega} ((f_t(p) - f_s(p)) - k)^2, \text{ s.t. } \Omega_{obj} \subset \Omega \subset \Omega_0, \tag{1.4}$$

where k is a constant value to be determined. Note that in all our experiments, we take the value of each color pixel $f(p)$ as a ternary set in $\{r, g, b\}$ color space. $(f(p) - f(q))$ is computed as the L2-norm in color spaces. $(f_t(p) - f_s(p)) - k$ represents the color deviation of the boundary pixels with respect to k.

Iterative optimization Since the optimal boundary may pass through all pixels in $\Omega_0 \backslash \Omega_{obj}$, simultaneously estimating the optimal k and the boundary $\partial \Omega$ is intractable. In the following, we propose an iterative optimization algorithm to optimize them.

1. Initialize Ω as Ω_0.
2. Given the current boundary $\partial \Omega$, the optimal k is computed by taking the derivative of Eqn. (1.4) and setting it to zero:

$$\frac{\partial E(\partial \Omega, k)}{\partial k} = 0$$

$$\Leftrightarrow k = \frac{1}{|\partial \Omega|} \sum_{p \in \partial \Omega} (f_t(p) - f_s(p)), \tag{1.5}$$

   where $|\partial \Omega|$ is the length of the boundary $\partial \Omega$. So k is the average color difference on the boundary.
3. Given the current k, we optimize the boundary $\partial \Omega$.
4. Repeat steps 2 and 3 until the energy of Eqn. 1.4 does not decrease in two successive iterations.

The convergence of the above algorithm is guaranteed in step 4 by constraining the energy defined in Eqn. 1.4 to be monotonically decreasing.

In step 3, computing an optimal boundary is equivalent to finding a shortest path in a graph $\mathscr{G}$ defined in $\Omega_0 \backslash \Omega_{obj}$ (in short, the band).

1.3.3 A shortest closed-path algorithm

The nodes in $\mathscr{G}$ are pixels within the band while the edges represent 4-connectivity relationships between neighboring pixels. The cost $((f_t(p) - f_s(p)) - k)^2$ is defined on each node as the color difference with respect to k. The accumulated cost of a path sums up the costs of all nodes on the path. For a single object, the estimated Ω_{obj} in our method can be regarded as genus-0 region and $\Omega_0 \backslash \Omega_{obj}$ is of genus-1 type, as shown in Figure 1.3 (a).

Unlike a standard shortest path problem, $\partial \Omega$ is a closed curve enclosing Ω_{obj}, which complicates the optimization. To make it tractable, we first change the type of region $\Omega_0 \backslash \Omega_{obj}$ from genus-1 to genus-0. This can be done by breaking the band connectivity using a cut C, as shown in red in Figure 1.3 (a). In the corresponding representation in graph $\mathscr{G}$, we remove all edges crossing the cut. In the following, we show how to compute a closed shortest-path using 2D dynamic programming.

A shortest closed-path algorithm

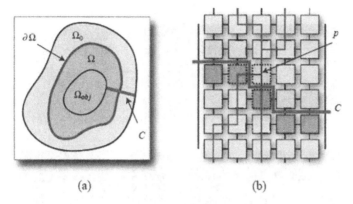

Fig. 1.3 Boundary optimization. (a) The region of interest Ω_0 is pasted onto the target image, which completely encloses the object of interest Ω_{obj}. The optimized boundary $\partial\Omega$ lies inside $\Omega_0 \backslash \Omega_{obj}$. The cut C is shown in red. (b) Zoom-in view of the cut C. The yellow and blue pixels are on different sides of C. The dashed yellow pixel p is adjacent to two blue pixels. Two shortest paths, shown as blue lines, are simultaneously computed.

- As illustrated in Figure 1.3(b), for each pixel p on one side of the cut C (shown in yellow), we compute the shortest paths to all adjacent pixels on the other side of the cut (shown in blue). Since graph $\mathcal{G}$ is a 2D grid, computing the shortest path from any node to all others in the band can be achieved by 2D dynamic programming [Dijkstra 1959; Mortensen and Barrett 1995] with a complexity $O(N)$, where N is the number of pixels in the band. Among all the shortest paths starting from pixel p and ending at the neighboring pixels on the other side of the cut, $Path(p)$ is the one with minimum cost. In Figure 1.3(b), for two dashed blue pixels that are neighbors to p in the image plane, their corresponding shortest paths are computed and shown as blue lines.
- We repeat the previous computation for all pixels on the yellow side of the cut C, and get a set of $Path$. The optimized boundary $\partial\Omega$ is assigned as one that gives the globally minimum cost. Suppose that there are M pixels on the yellow side of the cut in graph $\mathcal{G}$, the overall computational complexity is $O(MN)$.

If the optimal boundary passes the cut C only once, the above algorithm will reach the global minimum of the energy defined in Eqn. 1.4. Indeed, the path with the minimum accumulated cost seldom twists in our experiments.

The cut C intersects the band at two pixels on $\partial\Omega_0$ and $\partial\Omega_{obj}$ respectively. There are many possibilities how it is initialized. In our method, to achieve better performance, we compute a shortest straight line segment among all pixel pairs connecting $\partial\Omega_{obj}$ and $\partial\Omega_0$ by computing the Euclidian distance. This line segment is then rasterized into a pixel list in a 2D image plane. The cut C is drawn adjacent to the pixel list on any side. There are two benefits in computing the shortest cut C. First, the short length reduces the probability that the optimal boundary passes the cut more than once. Second, with fewer pixels adjacent to the cut C, the value of M will be small, which speeds up the computation.

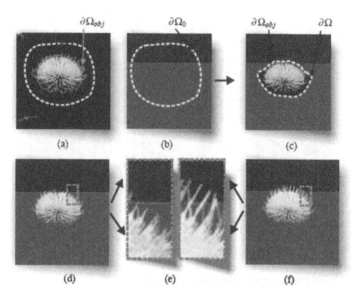

Fig. 1.4 Preserving fractional object boundary. Given the input source image of a flower in (a) and target image in (b), the optimized boundary $\partial\Omega$ snaps closely to the top of the flower's silhouette $\partial\Omega_{obj}$, thus intersects the fine details as shown in (c). Using the optimized boundary to solve the Poisson equation, as shown in (d), the fractional boundary cannot be well preserved as depicted in the zoom-in view (e). Our approach integrates the object's alpha matte in the Poisson equation, and faithfully preserves the fine details and produces an improved composite of the flower shown in (f). The corresponding zoom-in view is shown in (e).

1.4 Fractional boundary

An optimized boundary condition reduces the variational energy in solving the Laplacian equations, and avoids unnatural blurring in the composite. However, the optimized boundary may intersect with the object with a fractional boundary and break up subtle and fine details. Figure 1.4 depicts a scenario where $\partial\Omega$ is close to $\partial\Omega_{obj}$ and breaks the hairy structures (shown in (c) and (d)). To faithfully preserve the object's transparent boundary, we propose to incorporate an alpha matte in a blended guidance field for Poisson equations, by detecting the regions where alpha blending should be applied along the boundary.

1.4.1 A blended guidance field

Our goal of introducing transparency is to preserve precise fractional boundary of the object of interest from the source image when it is composited onto the target image while being capable of blending the color of the object seamlessly with the target image. Conventional alpha blending techniques cannot modify the color of the source object. To combine alpha blending with Poisson image editing, we define a binary coverage mask M to indicate where alpha blending should be applied

($M(p) = 1$) and vice versa, which partitions the image into regions. However, when directly applying the blending techniques in separate regions, the pixels in adjacent region boundaries may have color discontinuities since they are processed by two methods respectively without an appropriate spatial transition. To eliminate the artifact caused by the color discontinuity, we integrate the alpha matte in the blended guidance field in the Poisson equation.

We denote $\Phi = \{p | 0 < \alpha(p) < 1\}$ as the fractional object boundary, where α is computed automatically within a few pixels surrounding Ω_{obj} by coherence matting [Shum et al. 2004]. Comparing to Bayesian matting, coherence matting cooperates a prior of the alpha value in its formulation. In our method, we model it as a Gaussian distribution with respect to the median axis of Φ. Taking Figure 1.5(b) as an illustration, Φ is of the shape of a narrow blue belt. The blended guidance field is $v' = (v'_x, v'_y)$. For each pixel $p = (x, y)$, $v'_x(x, y)$ is defined as:

$$v'_x(x,y) = \begin{cases} \nabla_x f_s(x,y) & M(x,y) = M(x+1,y) = 0 \\ \nabla_x(\alpha f_s + (1-\alpha)f_t) & M(x,y) = M(x+1,y) = 1 \\ 0 & M(x,y) \neq M(x+1,y) \end{cases} \qquad (1.6)$$

$v'_y(x,y)$ is defined in a similar way. It shows that, depending on whether the alpha matte is applied, $v'_x(x,y)$ is defined as the alpha blended gradient or source image gradient in regions $M = 1$ and $M = 0$ respectively. However, in between these two regions, the gradient has no exact definition in image space. So we assign value zero to these pixel gradients to smoothly fuse the two regions and eliminate color discontinuity.

Given the new blended guidance field, we minimize the following variational energy:

$$\arg\min_{f} \int_{p \in \Omega \cup \Phi} ||\nabla f - v'||^2 dp \text{ with } f|_{\partial(\Omega \cup \Phi)} = f_t|_{\partial(\Omega \cup \Phi)}, \qquad (1.7)$$

where $\Omega \cup \Phi$ includes pixels either within the optimized boundary or inside the fractional object boundary, and $\partial(\Omega \cup \Phi)$ is $\Omega \cup \Phi$'s exterior boundary.

Based on the above analysis, to solve the boundary problem, we construct the binary coverage mask M within $\Omega \cup \Phi$ before solving Eqn. 1.7. Consider the pixels inside the object where $\alpha(p) = 1$, *the guidance field v' will always be ∇f_s regardless of the values of $M(p)$*. Therefore, we do not need to compute M in these pixels.

Figure 1.5 illustrates how we estimate M. In Figures 1.5(a) and 1.5(b), $\partial\Omega$ penetrates into the fractional object boundary in two segments 1 and 2, where some pixels with fractional alpha value are left outside Ω. This breaks the structure of the object boundary. Around segments 1 and 2, matte compositing is applied in the blended guidance field and M is set to 1. In the following, we list the main steps to construct the mask M:

- We first compute the head and tail intersections between $\partial\Omega$ and the belt Φ in each segment, indicated as red dots in (c). Two segments that contain the intersections are indicated by arrows 1 and 2 in Figures 1.5(b) and 1.5(c).

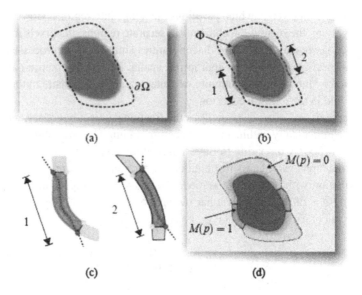

Fig. 1.5 Construction of the binary coverage mask M. (a) A source object with fractional boundary is pasted onto a target image. The dashed curve is the optimized boundary $\partial\Omega$. (b) The blue belt shows the region $\Phi = \{p|0 < \alpha(p) < 1\}$. As indicated by arrows 1 and 2, $\partial\Omega$ penetrates into the belt where matte compositing should be applied. (c) Zoom-in views of segments 1 and 2, around which the region $\{p|M(p) = 1\}$ is computed. (d) The resulting binary coverage mask where $\{p|M(p) = 0\}$ and $\{p|M(p) = 1\}$ are shown in yellow and green.

- To get the region where alpha blending should be applied, we compute the nearest points on the other side of the belt Φ, as shown by the yellow points, and connect the corresponding red and yellow points by straight line segments. Thus, the belt Φ is partitioned into blue and green in Figure 1.5(c).
- We set the green region in Figure 1.5(d) as $\{p|M(p) = 1\}$, and set $M(p) = 0$ for the remaining pixels p in $\Omega \cup \Phi$.

1.5 Experimental Results

We apply drag-and-drop pasting on a wide variety of source and target images, and compare it with Poisson image editing, matte compositing, and digital photomontage. The results are automatically computed by applying boundary optimization and the blended guidance field consecutively.

Sand pyramid. If the source and target images vary significantly in color and structure, as shown in Figures 1.6(a) and (b), Poisson image editing method cannot produce satisfactory results (Figure 1.6(c)). When applying "digital photomontage" [Agarwala et al. 2004] using the user-drawn strokes in Figure 1.6(d), the result still does not faithfully preserve the object structures (Figure 1.6(e)). Our approach computes an optimized boundary around the sand pyramid (Figure 1.6(f)). No blurring,

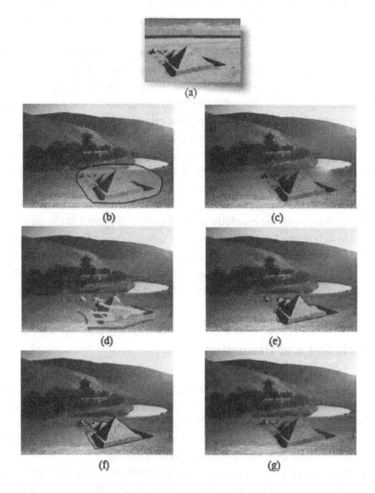

Fig. 1.6 Sand pyramid. (a) Source image. (b) User drags a region of interest to include the pyramids, and drops it onto the target image. (c) Poisson image editing result using the user-drawn boundary. (d) The user-drawn strokes used to initialize segmentation in [Agarwala et al. 2004]. (e) The refined boundary using the method in [Agarwala et al. 2004]. (f) The optimized boundary from our method. (g) Our blending result. No unnatural occlusion or broken structures are observed.

color mismatches or broken structures are produced (Figure 1.6(g)), even though the top of the pyramid intersects with the river in the target image.

Motorcycle. In Figure 1.7, the pasted motorcycle touches the cars and the Toyota sign in the target image. Figure 1.7(d) shows the result using Poisson image editing with a user-drawn boundary. It is not surprising that the result looks unnatural, because the pasted region does not match well with the target image. Figure 1.7(e) is the matte compositing result. Note that the alpha matte between the two wheels in the source image is difficult to be extracted automatically. In addition, the color of the source object does not match well with the target scene. Our automatically optimized boundary is shown in Figure 1.7(f), in which the alpha blending is appropriately applied to faithfully preserve the fractional boundary of the source object. Note that the optimized boundary preserves the inherent structure of the target image as well, as shown in Figure 1.7(g).

Chimney. Figure 1.8(a) and (b) show a chimney pasted into a sea line image where the alpha matte is needed at the intersection pixels. Figure 1.8(e) is the alpha matte automatically computed. Note that the matte of the smoke is not accurate. Both Poisson image editing using the mixing gradients and matte compositing cannot produce good results. Our method does not rely on the entire matte of the object, but only part of it where the optimized boundary snaps close to the silhouette of the object. Figure 1.8(g) shows the satisfactory result produced using our method.

Surfing. We show in Figure 1.9 a difficult surfing example. Poisson image editing using the user-drawn region cannot avoid boundary misalignment (Figure 1.9(b)). "Digital photomontage" requires the user to draw a number of strokes to initialize the graph-cut. Even with the carefully marked strokes (Figure 1.9(c)), their method is susceptible to labeling errors due to the thin arms of the surfer. Our method using the optimized boundary and the blended guidance field works well in this difficult example. The optimized boundary passes through a highly textured area while not breaking any salient structure in the target image, e.g., the body of the lower surfer.

1.6 Conclusion and Discussion

In this paper, we have proposed a user-friendly approach to achieve seamless image composition without requiring careful initialization by the user. Compared with the original Poisson image editing, our system is more practical and easy to use. Moreover, our approach can also preserve fractional object boundary by introducing a blended guidance field that incorporates the object's matte.

Our method uses GrabCut and image matting methods to automatically compute Ω_{obj} and α respectively. The alpha matte is only used in the region where $M = 1$ as described in section 1.4. Therefore, we do not require precise alpha value for all pixels. Only if the automatically computed Ω_{obj} and α contain large error, the user interactions are needed.

We propose future research directions are as follows: 1) Investigating the degree of diffusion or color change controlled within the Poisson image editing framework. When the source and target images differ significantly in color, solving the Poisson equations changes the source object's color in the composite. This may not be always desirable. An example is to paste a dog from a white beach onto green grass. The dog's color in the composite will have a green shade after solving the Poisson equations. 2) If the target image has complex structures, no matter how we refine the pasted region boundary, the structure of the source region and target scene cannot be precisely aligned. One possible solution is the modification of the boundary conditions.

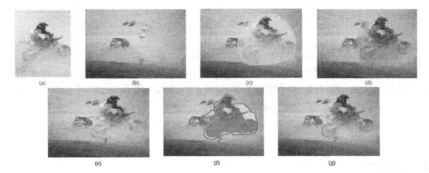

Fig. 1.7 Motorcycle. (a) Source image. (b) Target image. (c) The user-drawn region on the source image is overlaid on the target image. (d) Poisson image editing result with the user-drawn region. The boundary intersects with salient structures in the target image. (e) Matte compositing result. The color of the motorcyclist does not match well with the target scene. (f) The optimized boundary and the binary coverage mask to preserve fractional boundary. The color code is the same as Figure 1.5 (d). (g) Our result. The object is naturally blended into the target image without unnatural blurring.

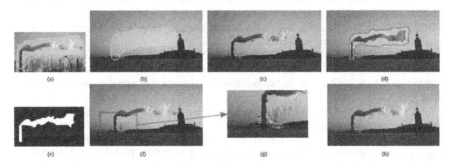

Fig. 1.8 Chimney. (a) Source image and the user-specified region of interest. (b) The user-specified region on the source image is overlaid onto the target image. (c) Matte compositing result. Note the color of the chimney does not match well with the target scene. (d) Optimized boundary and binary coverage mask. The color code is the same as Figure 1.5. (e) The alpha matte computed by the matting method. (f) Poisson image editing result using mixing gradients in seamless cloning [Perez et al. 2003]. (g) Zoom-in view of the mixing gradients result. It is noted that the unwanted tree branches and the occluded sea-line can be seen because of their strong gradients. (h) Our result. The chimney is seamlessly blended with the target image without structure and color mismatch.

Fig. 1.9 Surfing. (a) Source and target images of surfers. (b) Poisson image editing result using the user-drawn boundary, showing unnatural occlusion and other obvious artifacts. (c) The user-drawn strokes used to initialize graph-cut in [Agarwala et al. 2004], and the refined boundary from graph-cut. The thin parts of the object, e.g., the arms of the surfer, are missing. (d) Our optimized boundary where the object structures are faithfully preserved. (e) Our blending result. The two surfers look natural in the final composite. The matte is applied around the surfboard to faithfully preserve the fractional boundary.

Acknowledgements

The authors would like to thank Michael S. Brown for providing his voiceover in the video and Ruonan Pu for her help in preparing the paper. Jiaya Jia's research was funded by the grant from Microsoft Research Asia and Research Grant Council of Hong Kong special Administration Region, China.

References

AGARWALA, A., DONTCHEVA, M., AGRAWALA, M., DRUCKER, S., COLBURN, A., CURLESS, B., SALESIN, D., AND COHEN, M. 2004. Interactive digital photomontage. Proceedings of ACM SIGGRAPH 23, 3, 294C302.

BERMAN, A., VLAHOS, P., AND DADOURIAN, A. 2000. Comprehensive method for removing from an image the background surrounding a selected object. U.S. Patent 6,134,345.

BOYKOV, Y., AND JOLLY, M. P. 2001. Interactive graph cuts for optimal boundary & region segmentation of objects in n-d images. In Proceedings of ICCV.

BURT, P. J., AND ADELSON, E. H. 1983. A multiresolution spline with application to image mosaics. In ACM Transactions on Graphics, vol. 2, 217C236.

CHUANG, Y., CURLESS, B., SALESIN, D., AND SZELISKI, R. 2001. A bayesian approach to digital matting. In Proceedings of CVPR01, vol. 2, 264C271.

DIJKSTRA, E. W. 1959. A note on two problems in connexion with graphs. Numerische Mathematik 1, 269C270.

JIA, J., AND TANG, C.-K. 2005. Eliminating structure and intensity misalignment in image stitching. In Proceedings of ICCV.

KWATRA, V., SCHODL, A., ESSA, I., TURK, G., AND BOBICK, A. 2003. Graphcut textures: image and video synthesis using graph cuts. Proceedings of ACM SIGGRAPH 22, 3, 277C286.

LEVIN, A., ZOMET, A., PELEG, S., AND WEISS, Y. 2004. Seamless image stitching in the gradient domain. In Proceedings of ECCV, Vol IV: 377C389.

LI, Y., SUN, J., TANG, C., AND SHUM, H. 2004. Lazy snapping. Proceedings of ACM SIGGRAPH, 303C308.

MCGUIRE, M., MATUSIK, W., PFISTER, H., HUGHES, J. F., AND DURAND, F. 2005. Defocus video matting. In Proceedings of ACM SIGGRAPH, vol. 24, 567C 576.

MORTENSEN, E. N., AND BARRETT, W. A. 1995. Intelligent scissors for image composition. Proceedings of ACM SIGGRAPH, 191C198.

PEREZ, P., GANGNET, M., AND BLAKE, A. 2003. Poisson image editing. Proceedings of ACM SIGGRAPH, 313C318.

ROTHER, C., KOLMOGOROV, V., AND BLAKE, A. 2004. grabcut - interactive foreground extraction using iterated graph cuts. Proceedings of ACM SIGGRAPH, 309C314.

RUZON, M., AND TOMASI, C. 2000. alpha estimation in natural images. In Proceedings of CVPR00, 18C25.

SHUM, H.-Y., SUN, J., YAMAZAKI, S., LI, Y., AND TANG, C.-K. 2004. Popup light field: An interactive image-based modeling and rendering system. ACM Trans. Graph. 23, 2, 143C162.

SMITH, A., AND BLINN, J. 1996. Blue screen matting. Proceedings of ACM SIGGRAPH, 259C268.

SUN, J., JIA, J., TANG, C., AND SHUM, H. 2004. Poisson matting. Proceedings of ACM SIGGRAPH, 315C321.

ZWILLINGER, D. 1997. Handbook of Differential Equations, 3rd ed. Boston, MA: Academic Press.

Chapter 2
Motion Patches: Building Blocks for Virtual Environments Annotated with Motion Data*

Kang Hoon Lee, Myeong Geol Choi and Jehee Lee

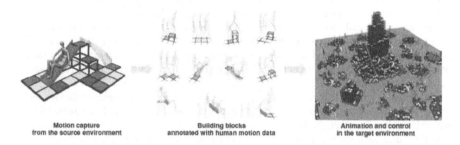

| Motion capture from the source environment | Building blocks annotated with human motion data | Animation and control in the target environment |

Abstract Real-time animation of human figures in virtual environments is an important problem in the context of computer games and virtual environments. Recently, the use of large collections of captured motion data has added increased realism in character animation. However, assuming that the virtual environment is large and complex, the effort of capturing motion data in a physical environment and adapting them to an extended virtual environment is the bottleneck for achieving interactive character animation and control. We present a new technique for allowing our animated characters to navigate through a large virtual environment, which is constructed using a set of building blocks. The building blocks, called *motion patches*, can be arbitrarily assembled to create novel environments. Each patch is annotated with motion data, which informs what actions are available for animated characters within the block. The versatility and flexibility of our approach are demonstrated through examples in which multiple characters are animated and controlled at interactive rates in large, complex virtual environments.

Key words: Interactive character animation, human motion, motion capture, virtual environments, path planning

2.1 Introduction

The real-time animation and control of human figures in complex virtual environments have been an important problem in computer graphics. A number of techniques have been developed for animating human figures: the motion of the figures may be keyframed, simulated, procedurally defined, or live captured. We are particularly interested in the last technique using a database of

Kang Hoon Lee, Myeong Geol Choi and Jehee Lee
Seoul National University, e-mail: {zoi,mingle,jehee}@mrl.snu.ac.kr

* Source: ACM Transactions on Graphics, Volume 25, Issue 3 (July 2006) , Proceedings of ACM SIGGRAPH 2006, Pages 898-906, 2006 Copyright ©2006 Association for Computing Machinery, Inc. Reprinted by permission. DOI Bookmark: http://doi.acm.org/10.1145/1179352.1141972

recorded motion. This data-driven approach can create a rich variety of natural human behavior from a large data set recorded from live actors. However, applying data-driven approaches to human figures in a complex environment is still challenging because a large motion set must be searched in real-time in order to select motions appropriate to given situations, and the selected motion must be adapted to match the environment.

The virtual environments we intend to design are often too big to be physically realized and accommodated in a motion capture studio. Motion capture in such a large environment is certainly difficult, if not impossible. One approach is to divide a large environment into small pieces, then record motion interacting with each piece separately, and finally combine motion data into a single, large piece of data covering the entire environment. In this way, the character's motion in a large environment can be collected. However, this approach requires a rich amount of motion data at every portion of the environment, and thus the motion capture process can be quite laborious and painful. A significant amount of redundancy exists in the motion set because it includes the same motion performed in different parts of the environment. This redundancy can be avoided by reusing motion data captured at one location to animate characters at other locations.

We present a new technique for allowing our animated characters to navigate through and interact with a large virtual environment in real time. In order to reuse motion data collected from one environment to another, the key idea of our approach is to identify a set of building blocks from the source environment, embed recorded motion data in these blocks, and fit them to the target environment so that the embedded motion data can be transferred to the target environment. These building blocks annotated with the availability of motions are called *motion patches*. The set of motion data embedded in a motion patch informs what actions are available for animated characters within the patch. The overview of our approach is as follows:

- **Data collection and processing.** We first build a physical environment in the motion capture studio and collect motion data viable in the environment. The recorded motion data is preprocessed such that the frames in the motion data sets are sorted into groups. The clustering allows us to construct and stitch motion patches efficiently.

- **Patch construction.** A set of motion patches is identified by analyzing the geometric regularities of the environment and the recorded motion data. The motion data embedded in each patch form a directed graph to achieve flexibility in the characters motion within the patch.

- **Fitting to the target environment.** Once the target environment is created, the set of building blocks can be fitted in the target environment such that the environment is covered by the embedded motion patches. By establishing the connections between motion patches, the target environment can be automatically annotated with a rich, connected set of motion data, which allows characters to navigate through the environment. We implemented two types of motion patches: tilable and non-tilable patches. Non-tilable patches are connected to each other by finding intersections at overlapping regions, while tilable patches can be seamlessly tiled in a regular pattern without much effort.

- **Animation and control.** Our system allows the user to change the environment dynamically at runtime and control animated characters in the environment interactively. The motion patches make it possible to achieve real-time performance in finding collision-free paths through complex virtual environments and animating multiple characters while avoiding collisions between them.

2.2 Background

Animation and control of human figures in synthetic environments have been studied in computer graphics for the last decade [Bandi and Thalmann 1997; Bindiganavale et al. 1994; Jung et al. 1994; Noser et al. 1995; Thorne et al. 2004]. This problem is very difficult because the human motion is high-dimensional, and many degrees of freedom need to be choreographed in a coordinated, collision-free, human-like manner.

Captured motion data have frequently been used in character animation for reproducing the naturalness of human movements. Recently, a number of researchers have explored the method of representing a significant amount of motion data as a directed graph and using it to animate and control human figures [Arikan and Forsyth 2002; Kovar et al. 2002; Lee et al. 2002; Pullen and Bregler 2002]. This method has further been explored for better controllability [Arikan et al. 2003; Hsu et al. 2004; Stone et al. 2004], efficient search [Lee and Lee 2004], parameterizing and blending motions [Kovar and Gleicher 2004; Park et al. 2004], synchronizing with sound [Kim et al. 2003], parameter tuning [Wang and Bodenheimer 2004], classification [Kwon and Shin 2005], simulating group behavior [Lai et al. 2005], responsiveness to external forces [Arikan et al. 2005], and evaluating the effectiveness of a motion graph in a specific environment [Reitsma and Pollard 2004].

Lee and his colleagues [2002] showed the capability of the graphbased motion representation to reuse motion data collected from a poles and holes terrain environment to an extended terrain environment. Their character control algorithm is based on state space search techniques and barely achieves its interactive performance (approximately 5 to 10 frames per second) with a single character. We address the same problem with much flexibility in selecting target environments and aiming to achieve real time performance with multiple characters. To do so, we annotate the target environment with a repertoire of character motions available at each location. This annotation makes path planning and state space search in the environment very efficient and straightforward. Our work is related to animation techniques that annotate environment objects with the availability of motions [Abaci et al. 2005; Shao and Terzopoulos 2005; Sung et al. 2004]

Our problem is also related to the path planning of articulated figures in the presence of obstacles, which is a classical problem in a wide range of disciplines. There is a vast amount of literature on path planning [Latombe 1991]; however, only a few works addressed human motion planning, which yields a high-dimensional (typically, 20 to 100) configuration space. With such a highdimensional configuration space, most optimal path planning algorithms are either computation-intensive for searching through configuration spaces exhaustively or memory-intensive for maintaining discretized configuration spaces. Many researchers used a lowdimensional configuration space (e.g., body and footprint locations) and randomized sampling techniques for producing character animation of locomotion, crawling, and climbing [Choi et al. 2003; Kalisiak and van de Panne 2001; Kuffner et al. 2001; Lau and Kuffner 2005; Pettre et al. 2003; Sung et al. 2005], and grasping and manipulating an object [Koga et al. 1994; Yamane et al. 2004]. Our motion patches can be thought of as a way to create discrete configuration spaces memory-efficient without losing the diversity and subtle details of captured motion data.

Reitsma and Pollard [2004] embedded human motion data in a square tile and allowed a character to navigate a large environment covered with a grid of square tiles. Chenney [2004] also discussed the use of square tiles for animating characters. We extend their work to deal with several challenges, which include embedding motion data into arbitrarily-shaped objects other than square tiles, allowing animated characters to navigate around and interact with these objects in a collision-free manner, and allowing locomotion and the other types of human motion to be handled in a uniform way.

2.3 Data Acquisition and Processing

All of the motion data used in our experiments were captured from a Vicon optical system with sixteen cameras at the rate of 120 frames/second and then down-sampled to 30 frames/second for real-time display. Our motion capture studio allows an effective capture region of 4 by 4 by 2.5 meters. Motion capture data contains trajectories for the position and orientation of the root node (pelvis) as well as relative joint angles for each body part.

We built several physical environments, each of which can be accommodated in our motion capture studio (see Figure 2.1). Each environment was designed to include some geometric features of the target (possibly much larger) environment we intend to create. All of the geometric features distributed in the physical environments can be rearranged and assembled to reconstruct the target environment. We also prepared polygonal models that match the physical environments.

In motion capture sessions, we collected a variety of human motions that are viable in a given environment. Our motion database contains about 70 minutes of data (see Table 2.1). To create the database, our subject walked, climbed, and slid in the playground and walked up and down the stairs. In the office environment, our subject approached the chair, sat down, stood up, and left repeatedly. We also captured our subject walking, stopping, idling, chatting, and making a presentation in an empty environment. Motion data were recorded in long clips so that seamless, natural transitions between motions could be captured. Our subjects were instructed to repeat each action several times to capture variations in each action. We denote the set of recorded motion data in the database as $\{\mathbf{p}_i | i = 1, \cdots, n\}$, where each frame $\mathbf{p}_i$ is the joint angle representation of a specific pose of the character.

Contact. The motion data is automatically preprocessed to annotate body-environment contact information at each frame. A body segment and an environment object are considered to be in contact if any joint adjacent to the segment is sufficiently close to the object and its velocity is below some threshold.

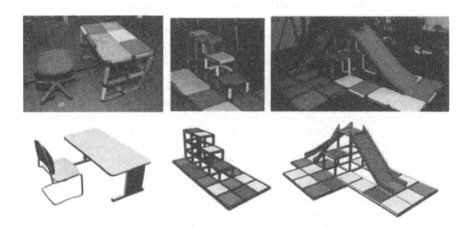

Fig. 2.1 The physical environments we built in our motion capture studio for collecting human motion data and their polyhedral models. The playground construction kit was used for building the desk, the steps, and the playground. We removed the back of the chair in order to avoid the occlusion of reflective markers from motion capture cameras.

Clustering. Clustering. The construction and stitching of motion patches involve searching pairs of similar frames that allow smooth transition from one patch to another. At a preprocessing phase, we sort motion frames into groups to accelerate this similarity search. The agglomerative hierarchical k-means algorithm [Duda et al. 2000] is employed to guarantee that the distance between any frames in a group is below a user-specified threshold. The threshold is determined through experimentation such that transitions within a group can generate smoothly blended motions. Here, in order to measure the distance between motion frames, we consider six features of the frames. All of the features were selected such that the distance became invariant under horizonal translation and rotation about the vertical (up direction) axis. Given two frames $\mathbf{p}_i$ and $\mathbf{p}_j$, the features are:

- *Joint angles:* The differences in all of the joint angles are considered. In our system, joint angles are described with unit quaternions and the difference between two unit quaternions q_i and q_j is measured by their geodesic distance $\min(\| \log(q_j^{-1} q_i)\|, \| \log(q_j^{-1}(-q_i))\|)$.

Motion sets	Environments		# of	Time
	source	target	frames	(sec)
walk/climb/slide	playground(S)	playground(L)	51169	1706
idle	empty	office	3685	123
chat	empty	office	3653	122
dispute	empty	office	3213	107
presentation	empty	office	3179	106
sit down/stand up	desk/chair	office	11778	393
work at the desk	desk/chair	office	5122	171
chat at the desk	desk/chair	office	10171	339
walk up/down	stairs	office	19421	324
walk-stop-walk	empty	office	4385	146
walk	empty	both	23911	797

Table 2.1 The motion sets collected for our experiments. Each data set was captured in the source environment and used for animating characters in the target environment.

- *Root height:* The difference $(y_i - y_j)$ in the height of the root nodes from the reference ground plane is considered. The horizontal coordinates of the root nodes are disregarded.
- *Root orientation:* The orientations of the root nodes are also described with unit quaternions. To effectively ignore the rotation about the vertical axis in the difference between two orientations q_i and q_j, we first rotate q_i about the vertical axis so that it can be brought as close to q_j as possible. The optimal rotation about the vertical axis $\hat{y}$ is denoted as $\exp(\theta\hat{y})$, where θ is the rotation angle about the vertical axis. Then, the geodesic distance between $q_i' = \exp(\theta\hat{y})q_i$ and q_j is invariant under rotation about the vertical axis. θ is computed as the solution of finding the closest point on the geodesic curve $G(\theta) = \exp(\theta\hat{y})$ from the unit quaternion $q = q_j q_i^{-1} = (w,v)$, where $w \in \mathbb{R}$ and $v \in \mathbb{R}^3$.

$$\theta = \begin{cases} -\alpha + \frac{\pi}{2}, & \text{if } q \cdot G(-\alpha + \frac{\pi}{2}) > q \cdot G(-\alpha - \frac{\pi}{2}), \\ -\alpha - \frac{\pi}{2}, & \text{if } q \cdot G(-\alpha + \frac{\pi}{2}) < q \cdot G(-\alpha - \frac{\pi}{2}), \end{cases}$$

where $\tan\alpha = w/(v \cdot \hat{y})$.

- *The velocities of joints, root translation, and root rotation:* The joint velocity at a joint is computed as a difference between angles at the next and the previous frames, that is, $v_i = \log(q_{i-1}^{-1} q_{i+1})/2$. The linear and angular velocities of the root node can also be given by differencing the next and the previous frames. We represent the linear and angular velocities of the root node with respect to a local, moving coordinate system attached to the root node. This allows the velocities to be rotation-invariant.

The above six features are weighted, squared, and summed to compute the squared distance between motion frames. For effective clustering of motion frames, contact with the environments is an important perceptual feature of motion, which is not reflected in the distance between motion frames. Given a motion frame, we consider the contact states at three successive frames including the previous and next frames for evaluating the similarity between motion frames. In the process of agglomerative clustering, motion frames are considered to be dissimilar if their contact states or the contact states of their neighboring frames are different.

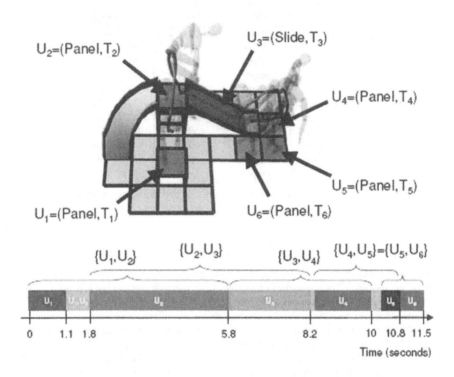

Fig. 2.2 Identifying building blocks from motion data. The environment consists of three unit objects: the ground panels, the straight slide, and the curved slide. A short segment of motion capture data is used for uncluttered illustration. The root trajectory is depicted as a series of small spheres. The motion frames at the bottom of the figure are partitioned depending on to which unit objects the frames belong. The frames colored in lime green belong to two objects simultaneously and correspond to the character's motion transitioning from one object to another. Our algorithm identified four building blocks: $\{U_1,U_2\},\{U_2,U_3\},\{U_3,U_4\},\{U_4,U_5\}$. Note that $\{U_4,U_5\}$ and $\{U_5,U_6\}$ are identical.

2.4 Motion Patch Construction

We intend to create virtual environments that consist of a reasonably small number of *unit objects*. A unit object is defined by its geometric shape, which cannot be modified or changed, and the bounding box. The virtual environment may contain multiple instances of each individual object and the location of each instance in the environment is described by a rigid transform. We denote the environment as $\{(u_1,T_1),(u_2,T_2),\cdots,(u_m,T_m)\}$, where u_i is a unit object and T_i is a rigid transform with respect to the world coordinate system.

A motion patch consists of either one or more unit objects. The single-object patch maintains the characters motions occurred within a single object. The multiple-object patch maintains motions that interact with multiple objects simultaneously and that make transitions from one object to another. A patch $\{(\hat{u}_1,\hat{T}_1),...,(\hat{u}_k,\hat{T}_k)\}$ can be fitted in the environment if there exists a rigid transform T such that every object $(\hat{u}_i,T \circ \hat{T}_i), i=1,...,k$, in the patch can be transformed to match a part of the environment geometrically. A pose in the motion data is included in a unit object if the pose intersects the bounding box of the object. The pose can be included in more than one objects simultaneously. A segment of successive motion frames in the database is included in a motion patch if every frame in the segment is included in one of its objects.

A pose in the motion data is included in a unit object if the pose intersects the bounding box of the object. The pose can be included in more than one objects simultaneously. A segment of successive motion frames in the database is included in a motion patch if every frame in the segment is included in one of its objects.

Given an environment and the set of motion data captured in that environment, the algorithm for identifying a set of motion patches containing k objects is as follows (see Figure 2.2). For example, if $k = 2$, the following algorithm identifies all motion patches consisting of two objects. We begin with an empty set of patches. The motion data set is scanned to find a segment of successive frames that is included in any k objects. If a patch containing the same k objects already exists, we simply register the segment of frames to the existing patch. Otherwise, we create a new patch and register the segment to the new one. When we decide if two patches are geometrically equivalent, the relative locations and rotational symmetry of objects are considered to match the shapes of the patches. However, the absolute locations of objects with respect to a global, fixed coordinate system are disregarded. In this way, motions recorded in different, yet geometrically similar parts of the source environment can be collected and embedded in a motion patch.

The embedding of motion data in each individual patch forms a directed graph. All poses in the database have been sorted into groups at a preprocessing phase. We approximate each patch using a regular grid of cells. Each cell is indexed by two-dimensional location (x, y), yaw orientation θ, and the index p of groups of the character's poses. A frame of the motion data belongs to a cell if the root of the body is located within the cell and the pose belongs to the p-th group. The cells become the nodes of the directed graph. The connecting transitions between cells are created if any motion segment embedded in the patch allows transition from one cell to the other. More specifically, the connecting transitions between cells are formed as follows. For every motion segment in the database, we check all of its $O(n^2)$ sub-sequences by double looping over the frames. For every sub-sequence longer than 20 frames (0.66 second), we insert a connecting transition between the cells where the sub-sequence originates and terminates. The minimum length constraint is required to avoid too frequent transitions in animation. We repeat this procedure for every motion segment embedded in the patch.

Once the graph is constructed, the character can navigate through the patch traversing the graph. Since a path traversing the graph corresponds to a series of motion segments, the animation of characters along the graph path involves the concatenation of motion segments. Transition from one motion segment to another is made smooth by warping both segments at the boundary and enforcing foothold constraints, as done in [Lee et al. 2002].

Patch size. We do not have a simple rule to determine the geometric size of motion patches. Through experiments, we have found several heuristic rules. The size of patches should be determined by the content of capture motion data. Each individual patch should be large enough to accommodate a single recognizable action in the data set. With walking motion data, for example, we select the square ground panel as a unit object, of which width and height are about the same as the distance travelled by two cycles of walking. There exists a trade-off, however, for different patch sizes. Large patches allow rich connections through the embedding, while smaller patches provide flexibility in designing virtual environments.

Practical implementation. The current implementation of our system allows motion patches to contain either one or two objects. Our algorithm can construct patches containing more than two objects. However, we found that those patches were not particularly useful in our experiments because our motion data could be effectively managed in one- and two-object patches. For the convenience in shape matching, the rotation of motion patches has sometimes been limited to 0, 90, 180, and 270 degrees. In the playground example, two-object patches can be stitched only when they share a unit object in common. These limitations make the shape matching procedure (finding a rigid transform $\mathbf{T}$) simple and practical.

2.5 Stitching Motion Patches

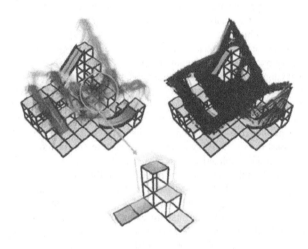

Fig. 2.3 (Top left) The motion patches covering the target environment are depicted as the root trajectories rendered in different colors. (Bottom) Building blocks are fitted into the target environment by shape matching. (Top right) The motion patches are stitched and then pruned to leave a single strongly connected component.

The user is provided with a user interface system that allows the user to design a target environment using a set of unit objects. Our system fits a set of building blocks automatically into the target environment such that the target environment is covered by the building blocks (see Figure 2.3). Transitions between motion patches are established where the patches overlap. Given two overlapping patches, the transition from cell $(x_1, y_1, \theta_1, p_1)$ of one patch to cell $(x_2, y_2, \theta_2, p_2)$ of the other patch is formed if the pose indexes are identical and the distance between the cell centers and the angle between the yaw orientations are below certain thresholds. In our experiments, the thresholds are the same as the size of the cells. The position threshold ranges from 5 to 10cm and the orientation threshold ranges from 5 to 10 degrees.

Once the connections among motion patches are established, we obtain a large, connected graph covering the target environment. Some connecting transitions between cells should be disabled to avoid collision and dead ends. For each motion patch, we first disable transitions that cause the collision between the animated character and the environment. Then, we run a strongly connected component algorithm [Tarjan 1972] on the graph and prune connecting transitions that are not contained in the largest strongly connected component.

Memory efficiency. In the worst case, the memory requirement of motion patches would scale in proportion to the square of the number of frames in the database, because the directed graph in the patches could have $O(n^2)$ connecting transitions for n nodes. In practice, the memory requirement is much less than the worst case for several reasons. At first, the motion database is divided into subsets, and each subset of motion frames constructs a motion patch. Therefore, the memory requirement is asymptotically not proportional to the size of the entire data sets, but related to the size of the largest motion patch. Secondly, since the database contains many unrelated motions, the directed graph is actually sparse in practice. The storage cost of the graph is also mitigated by the clustering of motion frames. The cluster-to-cluster transition graph is significantly smaller than the frame-to-frame transition graph. Finally, the storage cost for creating multiple instances of a motion patch is modest, because each instance does not need to include motion data and their graph structure. In each instance, we maintain only an array of bits that mark cells and transitions disabled by either obstruction or insufficient connections.

2.6 Tilable Patches

We also implemented a special type of patches that can be tiled in a regular pattern, such as square ground panels and stairs. In this section, we will explain the construction of square ground patches that allow the character to enter and leave the patch in any of four directions. The other types of tilable patches can be constructed in a similar way.

Tilable patches differ from non-tilable patches in two aspects: One is the boundary conditions of tilable patches and the other is the method of creating transitions between nodes. Tilable patches have nodes (x, y, θ, p) sampled on the boundary (see Figure 2.4). Each node is either an entry or exit depending on the direction of motion. Any entry on a boundary edge should have its corresponding exit on the opposite edge and vice versa. This boundary condition allows patches to be aligned and tiled without much effort. Entries and exits are connected by motion segments chosen from input motion data. Whereas the location and direction of motion data in nontilable patches are fixed with respect to the coordinate system of the patch, tilable patches allow flexibility in translation and rotation of motion data. A motion segment in the motion database can be used to link an entry-exit pair if the motion segment can be translated, rotated about the vertical axis, and then edited within a user-specified threshold to match the entry-exit pair at both ends. We use a simple linear model of Reitsma and Pollard [2004] to determine the extent to which the motion segment can be edited.

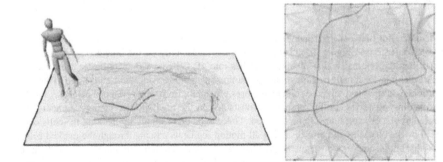

Fig. 2.4 The construction of square ground patches. (Left) We collected the motion of our subject walking around for about ten minutes. The motion data are depicted as the root trajectories that are projected on to the ground. (Right) The square patch has entries and exits sampled evenly on the boundary. The connections between the entries and the exits are formed by selecting appropriate motion segments from the walking motion data.

Pruning. A tilable motion patch is *safe* if two conditions are satisfied. The first condition is that every entry must have at least one out-going motion for each of the four directions. Even with a large collection of motion data, we may not be able to find enough connecting motions for some entries if the entries are heading toward a corner of the patch. We remove those entries and their corresponding exits on the opposite edges to avoid dead ends and ensure flexibility in steering animated characters. The second condition requires that motion patches should produce a strongly connected graph when they are tiled on a surface. This condition ensures that the entire motion sets can be fully utilized in animating characters. We employ the torus idea of Reitsma and Pollard [2004]. A torus is constructed from the square patch by gluing both pairs of opposite edges. On the torus, the embedding of motion data creates a boundary-less directed graph. We run Tarjans algorithm [Tarjan 1972] on the boundary-less graph to identify the largest strongly connected component. To ensure both conditions simultaneously, we enforce two safety conditions repeatedly and alternatingly until no connection is pruned.

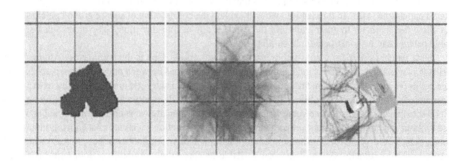

Fig. 2.5 The desk and chair on the tiled surface. (Left) The red motion segments embedded in the ground panel and the blue motion segments embedded in the desk and chair have coincident frames, at which characters are allowed to make a transition between the patches. (Center) The blue cells in the ground panel are concealed by the desk and chair and thus disabled. (Right) The red motion segments are disabled because they are obstructed by the obstacles. The blue motion segments are disabled because they have all following motions disabled.

Connection between patches. Tiled patches can be connected to other patches overlaid on the tiled surface (see Figure 2.5). Though we create nodes only on the boundary, we still need to partition the internal region of tilable patches into 4D cells (x, y, θ, p) in order to accelerate patch stitching. Each cell maintains a list of motion segments passing through the cell. This cell partitioning allows us to find the coincident poses efficiently from the overlapped patches.

Avoiding obstacles. In the presence of obstacles on the tiled surface, motion segments obstructed by the obstacles need to be disabled. This can be done simply by marking the cells concealed by the obstacles and then disabling all motion segments passing through the marked cells. After disabling some motion segments, we have to check if their adjacent motion segments have at least one out-going transition. Otherwise, those adjacent segments would cause dead ends and should be disabled. This procedure is repeated until no more motion segments are disabled. In practice, this procedure can be finished in one or two iterations.

2.7 Animation and Control

We built a simple interactive editing system for designing various virtual environments. Our system allows the user to create, remove, or drag building blocks interactively to change the environment. Accordingly, motion patches are created, connected to each other, or detached from each other in order to dynamically update the connected structure of motion patches in the environment. The user can also control each character by specifying either a goal location to move to or a specific behavior such as idling, chatting, and roaming around.

The environment is annotated with a graph of motions covering the whole area of the environment. The animation and control of characters along the graph is computationally very efficient. At every node of the graph, characters are provided with a set of motions immediately available at that moment and can proceed with any choice among available motions. Assuming that the decision is made based on local information, the computation time for animation and control is often negligible, and the total computation time is dominated by rendering the scenes on the computer screen.

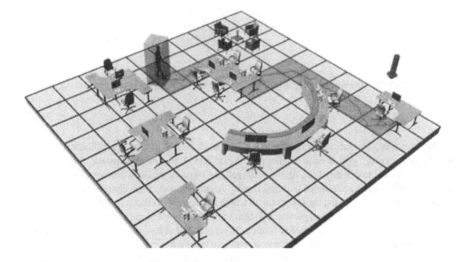

Fig. 2.6 Two-layer path planning.

The capability of global path planning is an important feature of our system for controlling characters in complex environments. Optimal path planning algorithms, such as Dijkstra's shortest path algorithm, require an explicit representation of the entire connected graph, which is often implausible for large environments. The storage efficiency of our approach is largely due to the distributed representation of the motion graph annotated in the environment. We actually do not maintain an explicit representation of the graph, but the graph is implicitly maintained in the connections among motion patches. We address this problem in a hierarchical manner. In our system, the motion data are organized in a two-layer structure. The higher layer is a directed graph of which nodes are motion patches. The higher layer maintains the connectivity among motion patches. The lower layer is a directed graph of motion segments embedded in motion patches. Our two-layer path planning algorithm first finds a path to the goal at the resolution of patches in the higher layer and then refines the path by running a shortest path algorithm through the lower layer (see Figure 2.6). In this way, we can run path planning algorithms time-efficiently within limited storage space.

2.8 Experimental Results

The timing data provided in this section was measured on a 2.8GHz Intel Pentium 4 computer with 2Gbyte main memory and an nVidia Quadro FX1100 graphics accelerator.

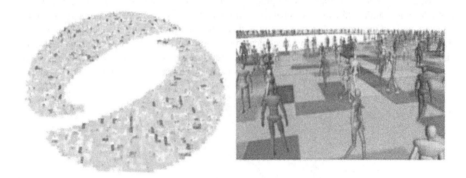

Fig. 2.7 (Left) One thousand of animated characters on the SIGGRAPH logo. (Right) A close-up view.

Performance. To evaluate the performance of our system, we created one thousand of animated characters on a grid of walk patches (see Figure 2.7). A 13-minute sequence of motion was captured and used to construct the tilable walk patch. Collisions between characters are avoided approximately at the resolution of building blocks. At any instance, each character occupies two blocks (the one it belongs and the other one on which it will move to shortly) and avoids the collision with the other characters by preventing them from entering the occupied blocks. Our system required about 66 seconds to create 300 frames (10 seconds) of video images. Actually, rendering dominated the computation time. Our system required only 2.8 seconds to create the same animation with video disabled. It means that the motion of one thousand characters is computed and controlled at a rate of more than 100 frames per second.

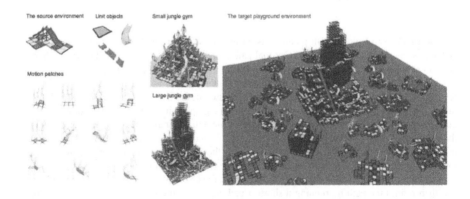

Fig. 2.8 From the source playground environment, we selected five unit objects that include the square ground panel, the curved slide, and the straight slide divided into three pieces. Our algorithm identified eleven building blocks. Motion data collected from the source environment were transferred to the target environments using motion patches.

Playground. We recorded motions of about 28 minutes duration (51169 frames) from the playground environment (see Figure 2.8). In the recorded data, our subject walked, climbed, and slid repeatedly in the playground. The clustering of motion frames produced 4928 pose groups. From the source environment, we selected five unit objects by hand: the ground panel, the curved slide, two outer parts of the straight slide, and its intervening part.Our system identified eleven motion patches (see the figure on the front page). Each patch consists of two unit objects, except for the intervening part of the straight slide, which consists of a single unit. The intervening part can be duplicated and strung together in order to generate arbitrarily long slides. In the small jungle gym, 536 instances of motion patches were fitted through shape matching (the eleven patches were instantiated 132, 181, 21, 75, 62, 3, 3, 36, 5, 13, and 5 times, respectively). These patches produced a strongly connected component with 43,516 nodes and 346,507 transitions. Our system required about 4 minutes and 30 seconds to annotate the small jungle gym. This computation time includes 0.7 second for shape matching, 257.7 seconds for stitching patches, 10 seconds for generating transitions, and 4 seconds for finding a strongly connected component. In the large jungle gym, 2063 instances of motion patches were fitted. Stitching these patches produced a strongly connected component with 227,583 nodes and 1,474,971 transitions. The target playground environment is equipped with 32 jungle gyms, which are connected to a 30 by 30 grid of walk patches. 8775 instances of motion patches were required to cover the whole environment, which is annotated with a motion graph with 16,745,035 nodes and 15,326,250 transitions. This graph encodes about 6847.57 hours of motion.

Office. For the office example, 40 minutes of motion were collected, and the motion data were sorted into 2337 pose groups (see Figure 2.9). We constructed eight motion patches for the office example, except for the tilable walk patch that is used in all of our examples. The desk and the chair are considered as a single unit. Three patches (sit down/stand up, work at the desk, and chat at the desk) are embedded in the desk-and-chair. Five patches (idle, chat, dispute, presentation, and walk-to-stop) describe human behaviors in an empty space and are embedded in the square ground panel. Our system required less than one second to create, remove, or drag a desk-and-chair on the grid of walk patches. The location of a behavior patch is not fixed with respect to a world coordinate system, but determined appropriately when the character makes a transition to the patch such that the transition could be made immediately.

2.9 Discussion

Motion patches are useful for graphics applications in which multiple characters are animated and controlled at interactive rates in a large virtual environment. Motion patches are simple, versatile, and easy to implement. The primary advantage of our approach is that it scales well with the size of motion data and the complexity of virtual environments. Computer games can benefit from the versatility and compactness of motion patches. In many computer games, we see characters that can move only in four or eight axis-aligned directions. Our motion patches provide diversity in choosing motions through rich connections within patches even if the patches are tiled regularly on a grid.

All of the building blocks consist of either one or two unit objects in our experiments. This is because our motion data sets do not include character poses touching more than two units simultaneously. We have had difficulty building bigger and heavier physical environments in our motion capture studio because of its limited space and the occlusion of reflective markers from motion capture cameras. Commercial studios have larger spaces and more cameras to capture more challenging motions, such as climbing in the playground, which use both hands and feet to touch several units simultaneously. We would need blocks consisting of more than two units to accommodate those motions.

In our experiments, it was reasonably easy to select the set of unit objects and design the source environment by hand. However, with an enormously large and complex target environment, inspecting the entire structures and selecting unit objects can be tedious and laborious. Ideally, we wish that our system would be able to take target environment data, such as architectural CAD data,

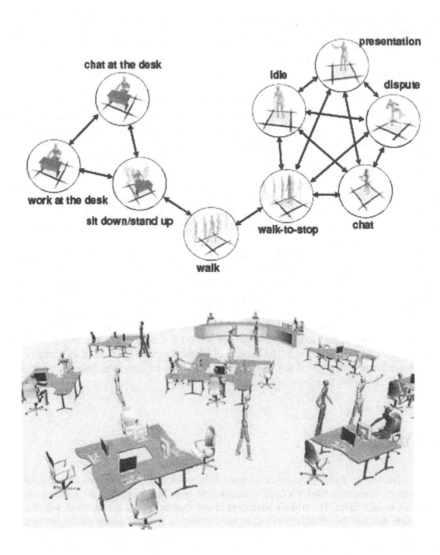

Fig. 2.9 Office. (Top) The connectivity among motion patches. (Bottom) Multiple characters animated and controlled in the office environment.

as input, analyze the environment data automatically to identify a set of unit objects, and suggest several source environments that could be physically realized in the motion capture studio.

Our approach is particularly suitable for artificial environments, such as architectural structures and urban areas, in which regularities in geometric features are abundant. One limitation of our approach is that we need too many building blocks for building natural, irregular environments. This could be alleviated by allowing the free-form deformation of motion patches. We might be able to fit the target environment approximately with a reasonably small number of deformable patches. Motion data embedded in the deformable patches could be edited accordingly using off-the-shelf motion editing techniques [Lee and Shin 1999]. Our system cannot cope with dynamically changing environments as well.

Another limitation of our approach is that physics is simply ignored in our framework. The characters on very long slides do not accelerate properly because the character's motion was created by repeating the ones recorded from a short slide. We arbitrarily accelerated characters on long slides to make them more realistic. Combining data-driven techniques with physically based methods will open up many possible directions for future research.

Motion patches	Unit objects		Size $(cm)^2$	Cell partitioning			Tilable	
	# of units	objects		grids	cells	transitions	entries/exits	connections
playground1	2	two panels	80×40	16×8	9037	235026		
playground2	2	two panels	80×40	16×8	30199	246705		
playground3	2	two panels	80×40	16×8	1978	83291		
playground4	2	two panels	80×80	16×16	2837	23584		
playground5	2	two panels	80×80	16×16	2012	39832		
playground6	2	panel and curved slide	123×83	24×16	1578	66826		
playground7	2	panel and curved slide	121×82	24×16	1008	18013		
playground8	2	two panels	120×40	24×8	876	32065		
playground9	2	panel and slide up	59×42	11×8	1079	27956		
playground10	1	slide middle	83×42	16×8	212		1	17
playground11	2	panel and slide down	58×42	11×8	581	6293		
idle	1	panel	120×120	24×24	73	610		
chat	1	panel	120×120	24×24	74	1054		
dispute	1	panel	120×120	24×24	1453	105571		
presentation	1	panel	120×120	24×24	130	4324		
sit down/stand up	1	panel-desk-chair	160×160	32×32	771	0		
work at the desk	1	panel-desk-chair	120×120	24×24	84	741		
chat at the desk	1	panel-desk-chair	120×120	24×24	1428	53879		
walk-to-stop	1	panel	120×120	24×24	116	0		
walk	1	panel	120×120	24×24	75973		144	7967

Table 2.2 The motion patches constructed in our experiments.

References

ABACI, T., CI GER, J., AND THALMANN, D. 2005. Planning with smart objects. In WSCG (Short Papers), 25C28.

ARIKAN, O., AND FORSYTH, D. A. 2002. Interactive motion generation from examples. ACM Transactions on Graphics (SIG- GRAPH 2002) 21, 3, 483C490.

ARIKAN, O., FORSYTH, D. A., AND OBRIEN, J. F. 2003. Motion synthesis from annotations. ACM Transactions on Graphics (SIGGRAPH 2003) 22, 3, 402C408.

ARIKAN, O., FORSYTH, D., AND OBRIEN, J. 2005. Pushing people around. In SCA 05: Proceedings of the 2005 ACM SIG- GRAPH/Eurographics Symposium on Computer Animation, 59C 66.

BANDI, S., AND THALMANN, D. 1997. A configuration space approach for efficient animation of human figures. In Proc. of IEEE Non Rigid and Articulated Motion Workshop, IEEECS Press. BINDIGANAVALE,

R., GRANIERI, J. P., WEI, S., ZHAO, X., AND BADLER, N. I. 1994. Posture interpolation with collision avoidance. In Proceedings of Computer Animation 94, 13C20.

CHENNEY, S. 2004. Flow tiles. In SCA 04: Proceedings of the 2004 ACM SIGGRAPH/Eurographics Symposium on Computer Animation, 233C242.

CHOI, M. G., LEE, J., AND SHIN, S. Y. 2003. Planning biped locomotion using motion capture data and probabilistic roadmaps. ACM Transactions on Graphics 22, 2, 182C203.

DUDA, R. O., HART, P. E., AND STORK, D. G. 2000. Pattern Classification. Wiley-Interscience.

GROCHOW, K., MARTIN, S. L., HERTZMANN, A., AND POPOVIC , Z. 2004. Style-based inverse kinematics. ACM Trans- actions on Graphics (SIGGRAPH 2004) 23, 3, 522C531.

HSU, E., GENTRY, S., AND POPOVIC, J. 2004. Example-based control of human motion. In SCA 04: Proceedings of the 2004 ACM SIGGRAPH/Eurographics Symposium on Computer Animation, 69C77.

JUNG, M. R., BADLER, N. I., AND NOMA, T. 1994. Animated human agents with motion planning capability for 3d-space postural goals. The Journal of Visualization and Computer Animation 5, 4, 225C246.

KALISIAK, M., AND VAN DE PANNE, M. 2001. A grasp-based motion planning algorithm for character animation. The Journal of Visualization and Computer Animation 12, 3, 117C129.

KIM, T., PARK, S. I., AND SHIN, S. Y. 2003. Rhythmic-motion synthesis based on motion-beat analysis. ACM Transactions on Graphics (SIGGRAPH 2003) 22, 3, 392C401.

KOGA, Y., KONDO, K., KUFFER, J., AND LATOMBE, J. 1994. Planning motions with intensions. Proceedings of SIGGRAPH 94 28 (July), 395C408.

KOVAR, L., AND GLEICHER, M. 2004. Automated extraction and parameterization of motions in large data sets. ACM Transac- tions on Graphics (SIGGRAPH 2004) 23, 3, 559C568.

KOVAR, L., GLEICHER, M., AND PIGHIN, F. 2002. Motion graphs. ACM Transactions on Graphics (SIGGRAPH 2002) 21, 3, 473C482.

KUFFNER, J. J., NISHIWAKI, K., KAGAMI, S., INABA, M., AND INOUE, H. 2001. Footstep planning among obstacles for biped robots. In Proc. IEEE/RSJ Int. Conf. on Intelligent Robots and Systems (IROS01).

KWON, T., AND SHIN, S. Y. 2005. Motion modeling for on-line locomotion synthesis. In SCA 05: Proceedings of the 2005 ACMSIGGRAPH/Eurographics Symposium on Computer Animation, 29C38.

LAI, Y.-C., CHENNEY, S., AND FAN, S. 2005. Group motion graphs. In SCA 05: Proceedings of the 2005 ACM SIGGRAPH/Eurographics Symposium on Computer Animation, 281C290.

LATOMBE, J. C. 1991. Robot Motion Planning. Kluwer Academic Publishers.

LAU, M., AND KUFFNER, J. J. 2005. Behavior planning for character animation. In SCA 05: Proceedings of the 2005 ACM SIGGRAPH/Eurographics Symposium on Computer Animation, 270C280.

LEE, J., AND LEE, K. H. 2004. Precomputing avatar behavior from human motion data. In SCA 04: Proceedings of the 2004 ACM SIGGRAPH/Eurographics Symposium on Computer Animation, 79C87.

LEE, J., AND SHIN, S. Y. 1999. A hierarchical approach to interactive motion editing for human-like figures. In Proceedings of SIGGRAPH 99, 39C48.

LEE, J., CHAI, J., REITSMA, P. S. A., HODGINS, J. K., AND POLLARD, N. S. 2002. Interactive control of avatars animated with human motion data. ACM Transactions on Graphics (SIGGRAPH 2002) 21, 3, 491C500.

NOSER, H., RENAULT, O., THALMANN, D., AND THALMANN, N. M. 1995. Navigation for digital actors based on synthetic vision, memory, and learning. Computer & Graphics 19, 1, 7C19.

PARK, S. I., SHIN, H. J., KIM, T., AND SHIN, S. Y. 2004. On-line motion blending for real-time locomotion generation. Computer Animation and Virtual Worlds 15, 3, 125C138.

PETTRE, J., LAUMOND, J.-P., AND SIMEON, T. 2003. A 2-stages locomotion planner for digital actors. In SCA 03: Proceed- ings of the 2003 ACM SIGGRAPH/Eurographics Symposium on Computer Animation, 258C264.

PULLEN, K., AND BREGLER, C. 2002. Motion capture assisted animation: Texturing and synthesis. ACM Transactions on Graphics (SIGGRAPH 2002) 21, 3, 501C508.

REITSMA, P. S. A., AND POLLARD, N. S. 2004. Evaluating motion graphs for character navigation. In SCA 04: Proceedings of the 2004 ACM SIGGRAPH/Eurographics Symposium on Com- puter Animation, 89C98.

SHAO, W., AND TERZOPOULOS, D. 2005. Autonomous pedestrians. In SCA 05: Proceedings of the 2005 ACM SIG- GRAPH/Eurographics Symposium on Computer Animation, 19C 28.

STONE, M., DECARLO, D., OH, I., RODRIGUEZ, C., STERE, A., LEES, A., AND BRE-GLER, C. 2004. Speaking with hands: Creating animated conversational characters from recordings of human performance. ACM Transactions on Graphics (SIGGRAPH 2004) 23, 3, 506C513.

SUNG, M., GLEICHER, M., AND CHENNEY, S. 2004. Scalable behaviors for crowd simulation. Computer Graphics Forum (Eu- rographics 2004) 23, 3, 519C528.

SUNG, M., KOVAR, L., AND GLEICHER, M. 2005. Fast and accurate goal-directed motion synthesis for crowds. In SCA 05: Proceedings of the 2005 ACM SIGGRAPH/Eurographics Symposium on Computer Animation, 291C300.

TARJAN, R. 1972. Depth first search and linear graph algorithms. SIAM Journal of Computing 1, 146C160.

THORNE, M., BURKE, D., AND VAN DE PANNE, M. 2004. Motion doodles: An interface for sketching character motion. ACM Transactions on Graphics (SIGGRAPH 2004) 23, 3, 424C431.

WANG, J., AND BODENHEIMER, B. 2004. Computing the duration of motion transitions: An empirical approach. In SCA 04: Proceedings of the 2004 ACM SIGGRAPH/Eurographics Symposium on Computer Animation, 337C346.

YAMANE, K., KUFFNER, J. J., AND HODGINS, J. K. 2004. Synthesizing animations of human manipulation tasks. ACM Trans- actions on Graphics (SIGGRAPH 2004) 23, 3, 532C539.

Chapter 3
Video Completion by Motion Field Transfer*

Takaaki Shiratori, Yasuyuki Matsushita, Sing Bing Kang and Xiaoou Tang

Abstract Existing methods for video completion typically rely on periodic color transitions, layer extraction, or temporally local motion. However, periodicity may be imperceptible or absent, layer extraction is difficult, and temporally local motion cannot handle large holes. This paper presents a new approach for video completion using *motion field transfer* to avoid such problems. Unlike prior methods, we fill in missing video parts by sampling spatio-temporal patches of local motion instead of directly sampling color. Once the local motion field has been computed within the missing parts of the video, color can then be propagated to produce a seamless hole-free video. We have validated our method on many videos spanning a variety of scenes. We can also use the same approach to perform frame interpolation using motion fields from *different* videos.[2]

3.1 Introduction

Video completion refers to the process of filling in missing pixels or replacing undesirable pixels in a video. One useful application of video completion is restoration of damaged or vintage videos. This technology can also be applied in other areas: post-production in the movie-making industry (e.g., to remove unwanted objects), and restoration of corrupted internet video streams due to packet drops.

In this paper, we propose a new approach for video completion. Instead of transferring color/intensity information directly, our approach transfers motion field into missing areas or areas targeted for removal. The key idea is to use the local motion field of a video as its intrinsic representation. While previous video completion methods typically rely on color, our method relies on local motion information. We call our approach *motion field transfer*: it warps known local motion vectors to predict motion in the holes. This approach is particularly effective in cases where periodic motion (such as a person walking) is imperceptible or absent.

Takaaki Shiratori
The University of Tokyo, Tokyo, Japan, e-mail: siratori@cvl.iis.u-tokyo.ac.jp

Yasuyuki Matsushita and Xiaoou Tang
Microsoft Research Asia, Beijing , P.R.China, e-mail: {yasumat,xitang}@microsoft.com

Sing Bing Kang
Microsoft Research, WA, U.S.A., e-mail: sbkang@microsoft.com

* Source: Computer Vision and Pattern Recognition, 2006 IEEE Computer Society Conference on, Volume 1, 17-22 June 2006 Pages:411 - 418 Copyright ©2006 IEEE. Reprinted with permission. DOI:10.1109/CVPR.2006.330

[2] This work was done while the first author was visiting Microsoft Research Asia.

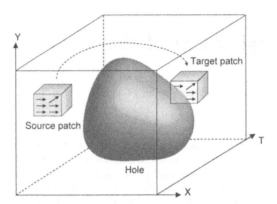

Fig. 3.1 Illustration of motion field transfer. The spatio-temporal video hole is filled in by motion fields sampled from other portions of the video.

3.1.1 Related Work

Video completion can be considered as an extension of 2D image completion to 3D. The problem of filling in 2D holes has been well studied: image completion [10, 9, 15, 7, 22] and inpainting [2, 16]. Inpainting approaches typically handle smaller or thinner holes compared to image completion approaches. The 3D version of the problem, video completion [20, 14, 19, 23], has been getting increasing attention. Unfortunately, video completion is less effective if the video is treated as a set of independent 2D images [20, 18]. While the temporal independence assumption simplifies the problem, temporal consistency in the filled areas cannot be guaranteed.

One approach to ensure temporal consistency is to first separate the input video into foreground and background layers. Jia *etal.* [14] and Patwardhen *etal.*[19] separated the video into a static background and dynamic foreground, and filled the holes separately. Zhang *etal.* [23] used motion segmentation to achieve layer extraction. These methods work well if the layers are correctly estimated; however, it is difficult to obtain accurate layers in general, especially for scenes with complex motion.

Our method is inspired by Wexler *etal.*'s technique [20]. Their technique fills holes by sampling spatio-temporal patches from other portions of the video. In addition, global optimization is performed in order to enforce consistency in the holes. The method worked well in cases where the video contains periodic motion. The approach proposed by Matsushita *etal.* [18] also bears some similarity with our approach in that their method propagates the local motion field towards the missing image areas. However, their method is limited to temporally thin holes because their hole-filling process is done on a per-frame basis. Additionally, their propagation is based on simple diffusion, which cannot handle holes with complex motion fields well.

We borrow the fundamental idea of *motion warping* [21], in which motion parameter curves are warped for human body animation. Gleicher [12] and Cheung [6] adapted this idea to transfer articulated motion parameters to different objects. While these methods have been successful, motion warping has been limited to 3D targets which have the similar degrees of freedom. Instead of using high-level motion parameters, our method instead transfers low-level local motion field which can be estimated from videos. Haro *etal.* [13]'s work on transferring video effects has shown interesting results, including transfer of motion blur. Unlike their technique, however, we do not require input/output training pairs.

3.1.2 Overview of Our Approach

Our method is based on the assumption that motion information is sufficient to fill holes in videos. This assumption is valid if object motion is continuous in the video, which is usually the case. We regard the sequence of local motion field as an intrinsic video representation that is independent of color. By using motion field, we increase the chances of good matches for hole-filling. We need only match based on similarity in motion (regardless of color), which is surprisingly effective, as shown in our results.

Our approach consists of the following steps:

Local motion estimation. The pixelwise local motion vector field in the video is computed except at the holes.

Motion field transfer. The motion vectors in the holes are progressively estimated by sampling spatio-temporal patches of motion field from different portions of the video.

Color propagation. The motion field computed in holes is used to propagate color information from surrounding video pixels to finally complete the video.

The primary contribution of this paper is the motion field transfer step, which warps the local motion field for video completion.

Why motion field instead of color? Fig. 3.2 illustrates the scenario where our motion-based method is effective while a color-based sampling method may fail. Here we have a common scenario where the foreground object is moving in front of a stationary background that has a unique distribution of colors. The color-based sampling technique has a matching problem similar to that of window-based stereo within the vicinity of object boundaries. The motion-based technique mimics motion observed elsewhere, and it works well because it does not rely on the distribution of color (which can be temporally discontinuous).

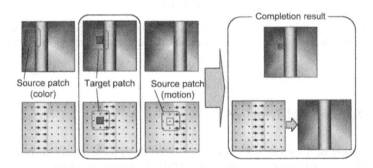

Fig. 3.2 A simple example where motion based method performs better.

3.2 Video Completion Algorithm

This section describes how our proposed algorithm works.

3.2.1 Local motion estimation

The first step of our method is to compute the local motion field. To do this, we use the hierarchical Lucas-Kanade optical flow computation method [17,3]. In a coarse-to-fine manner, the method estimates the motion vector $(u,v)^T$ that minimizes the error function

$$\arg\min_{(u,v)} \sum \left(u\frac{\partial I}{\partial x} + v\frac{\partial I}{\partial y} + \frac{\partial I}{\partial t} \right), \tag{3.1}$$

where $\frac{\partial I}{\partial x}$, $\frac{\partial I}{\partial y}$ and $\frac{\partial I}{\partial t}$ are image derivatives along spatial and temporal axes. We represent the estimated motion vector at point $\mathbf{p} = (x,y,t)^T$ in the video sequence by $(u(\mathbf{p}),v(\mathbf{p}))^T$.

3.2.2 Dissimilarity measure of motion vectors

Before we describe the next step (motion field transfer), we first define our patch dissimilarity measure for the motion data. Our video completion is based on non-parametric sampling of the motion field. Since the 2D optical flow can be viewed as a 3D vector in spatio-temporal domain with the constant temporal element being t, the 3D vector $\mathbf{m}$ is defined as $\mathbf{m} \equiv (ut, vt, t)^T$. We measure the distance between two motion vectors using the angular difference (in 3D space) as was done in Barron *et al.* [1]:

$$d_{\mathrm{m}}(\mathbf{m}_0,\mathbf{m}_1) = 1 - \frac{\mathbf{m}_0 \cdot \mathbf{m}_1}{|\mathbf{m}_0||\mathbf{m}_1|} = 1 - \cos\theta, \tag{3.2}$$

where θ is the angle between two motion vectors $\mathbf{m}_0$ and $\mathbf{m}_1$. This angular error measure accounts for differences in both direction and magnitude, since measurements are in homogeneous coordinates.

3.2.3 Motion Field Transfer

Using the dissimilarity measure defined in Eq. (3.2), the algorithm next seeks the most similar source patch given the target patch in order to assign the motion vectors to the missing pixels in the target patch. The dissimilarity between the source patch P_s and the target patch P_t is calculated by aggregating the dissimilarity measure over the patch (ignoring missing pixels in the target patch). Suppose the set of valid pixels in the target patch is $\mathscr{D}$; the aggregate distance between the source and target patches is then defined as

$$d\big(P_s(\mathbf{x}_s),P_t(\mathbf{x}_t)\big) = \frac{1}{|\mathscr{D}|} \sum_{\mathbf{p}\in\mathscr{D}} d_m\big(\mathbf{m}(\mathbf{p}+\mathbf{x}_s),\mathbf{m}(\mathbf{p}+\mathbf{x}_t)\big), \tag{3.3}$$

where $|\mathscr{D}|$ is the number of defined pixels, $\mathbf{x}_s$ and $\mathbf{x}_t$ represent the position of the source and target patches, and $\mathbf{p}$ is the relative position from the center of each patch. Given the target patch P_t with its location $\mathbf{x}_t$, the optimal source patch $\hat{P}_s$ is obtained by finding the appropriate $\mathbf{x}_s$ which minimizes Eq. (3.3) as

$$\hat{P}_s(\hat{\mathbf{x}}_s) = \arg\min_{P_s(\mathbf{x}_s)} d(P_s(\mathbf{x}_s),P_t(\mathbf{x}_t)). \tag{3.4}$$

Once the optimal source patch $\hat{P}_s$ is found, the missing pixels in the target patch are filled by copying the motion vectors from the corresponding positions of the source patch.

The computation of the motion field transfer starts from the boundary of the holes, progressively advancing towards the inner holes. The holes are gradually filled with the new motion vectors which are copied from the source patches. Once the missing pixel is assigned a motion vector, the pixel is treated as a defined video pixel in the following computation. The order of fill-in, i.e., the order selection of the target patch, is determined by the number of non-hole pixels in the target patch, and the target patch with the highest number of non-hole pixels is first used for completion.

For efficiency, matching is done hierarchically through a Gaussian pyramid [5] of the video volume. Let l_m be the number of levels in the pyramid. Starting from the finest level $l = 1$, the coarser levels of the video volume are successively generated by convolving with a Gaussian kernel and sub-sampling. The patch size for matching in pyramid level l is set to $2^\beta \times 2^\beta \times 2^\beta$, where $\beta = l_m - l + 1$. The Gaussian kernel sigma used to blur one level to the next coarser level is set to one-fourth the patch size for matching [?], i.e., in our case, $2^{\beta-2}$.

3.2.4 Color Propagation

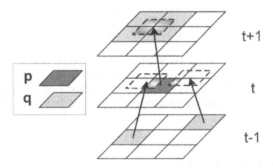

Fig. 3.3 Illustration of color propagation. Color values of missing video pixels are computed by propagating the color information from the defined image pixels using the transferred motion vector field.

Once the motion vectors have been found in the holes, color information is then propagated to generate the output video. The transferred motion vectors in the holes indicate the missing pixels' relationship with their neighbors; the motion vectors form a graph as shown in Fig. 3.3. Our color propagation method uses this graph to assign color values in the holes. We treat the motion vectors as undirected edges which represent pixel correspondences among frames.

Suppose we are to assign a color value to a pixel $\mathbf{p}$ using the connected pixels $\mathbf{q} \in \mathcal{N}$. Note that the edge originating from $\mathbf{p}$ may point to a fractional location in the neighboring frame as shown in Fig. 3.3. Similarly, a point $\mathbf{q}$ in the previous frame may be connected to a fractional location of pixel $\mathbf{p}$. We use the sizes of overlapped areas $s(\mathbf{p}, \mathbf{q})$ as weight factors to determine the contribution of neighboring pixels $\mathbf{q}$ to pixel $\mathbf{p}$. We also use the reliability of the edge $r(\mathbf{p}, \mathbf{q})$, which is measured by the inverse of dissimilarity measure defined in Eq. (3.3). The contribution from the neighboring pixel $\mathbf{q}$ to the pixel $\mathbf{p}$ is given by the product of r and s as

$$w(\mathbf{p}, \mathbf{q}) = r(\mathbf{p}, \mathbf{q})s(\mathbf{p}, \mathbf{q}). \tag{3.5}$$

Thus, the color $\mathbf{c}(\mathbf{p})$ at pixel $\mathbf{p}$ is a weighted average of colors at the neighboring pixels $\mathbf{q}$:

$$c(\mathbf{p}) = \frac{\sum_{\mathbf{q} \in \mathcal{N}} w(\mathbf{p}, \mathbf{q}) c(\mathbf{q})}{\sum_{\mathbf{q} \in \mathcal{N}} w(\mathbf{p}, \mathbf{q})}. \tag{3.6}$$

Given n hole pixels, for each pixel $\{\mathbf{p}_i; i = 1, \ldots, n\}$ an equation is obtained from Eq. (3.6). Assuming there are m boundary pixels $\{\mathbf{p}_j^b; j = 1, \ldots, m\}$ with known colors, the n equations form the following linear system of equations:

$$\mathbf{C} = [\mathbf{W}|\mathbf{W}_b] \begin{bmatrix} \mathbf{C} \\ \mathbf{C}_b \end{bmatrix}, \tag{3.7}$$

where $\mathbf{C}$ is a $3 \times n$ matrix $\mathbf{C} = [c(\mathbf{p}_1), \ldots, c(\mathbf{p}_n)]^T$, $\mathbf{C}_b$ is a $3 \times m$ matrix $\mathbf{C}_b = [c(\mathbf{p}_{b_1}), \ldots, c(\mathbf{p}_{b_m})]^T$, and the $n \times n$ matrix $\mathbf{W}$ and $m \times n$ matrix $\mathbf{W}_b$ are given by

$$\mathbf{W} = \begin{bmatrix} 0 & w_{12} & \cdots & w_{1n} \\ w_{21} & 0 & \cdots & w_{2n} \\ \vdots & \vdots & \ddots & \vdots \\ w_{n1} & w_{n2} & \cdots & 0 \end{bmatrix}, \mathbf{W}_b = \begin{bmatrix} w_{11}^b & \cdots & w_{1m}^b \\ \vdots & \ddots & \vdots \\ w_{n1}^b & \cdots & w_{nm}^b \end{bmatrix}.$$

Here w_{ij} represents the weight factor $w(\mathbf{p}_i, \mathbf{p}_j)$ after normalization, such that each row of $[\mathbf{W}|\mathbf{W_b}]$ sums to one. Therefore, w_{ij} falls in the range $[0, 1]$. The diagonal elements of $\mathbf{W}$ are all zero, since the motion vector never points the source pixel to itself. In order to obtain $\mathbf{C}$, Eq. (3.7) can be written as

$$\mathbf{C} = (\mathbf{I} - \mathbf{W})^{-1} \mathbf{W}_b \mathbf{C}_b, \tag{3.8}$$

where $\mathbf{I}$ is the $n \times n$ identity matrix. The matrix $(\mathbf{I} - \mathbf{W})$ is usually invertible, and the solution can be efficiently obtained by LU decomposition since the matrix is structurally symmetric and sparse. If the determinant of $(\mathbf{I} - \mathbf{W})$ is very small (indicating closeness to singularity), we compute its pseudo-inverse through singular value decomposition to obtain the least-squares solution.

3.3 Experimental Results

To validate our proposed method, we used it on a variety of videos. For all our experiments, a three-level Gaussian pyramid was used ($l_m = 3$).

3.3.1 Results of Video Completion

We have tested our method on 15 different videos, each containing a variety of motion and color.

Walking scene We first show the result for a video involving a walking person. The top row of Fig. 3.4 shows five frames of the original 80-frame input video of resolution 240×180. In the second row, the spatio-temporal hole created in the middle of the scene can be seen together with computed local motion field (overlaid). The volume of the spatio-temporal hole is about $12,000$ pixels, spanning five frames. Using motion field transfer, the hole is filled with the estimated local motion field as shown in the third row. Video completion is achieved by propagating color as shown in the bottom row. Our method was able to produce results that are visually identical to the ground truth.

Performer scene Fig. 3.5 shows the video completion result for the video '*performer*' captured with a moving camera. The resolution of the 60-frame input video is 352×240. The top row shows

Fig. 3.4 *Walking* scene result (five frames shown). Top row: original frames, second row: spatio-temporal hole and computed local motion field, third row: result of motion field transfer. bottom row: result of video completion. Notice the frames in the first and last rows are virtually identical.

the original image sequence, and the corresponding image sequence with a spatio-temporal hole is shown in the middle row. The hole size is 72×120, spanning three frames. With our video completion method, the spatio-temporal hole is seamlessly filled as shown in the bottom row in Fig. 3.5. Fig. 3.6 is a close-up view of the result in the vicinity of the hole. From left to right, the figure shows (a) the ground truth, (b) the result of our method, (c) the intensity difference of the two images (b) and (a) in l^2 norm, (d) the result of the color-based method and (e) the intensity difference of (d) and (a) in l^2 norm. Although the result (b) looks slightly blurry due to the bilinear interpolation in the color propagation step, the structure of the moving object and background were well preserved. On the other hand, the color based method produces a significant amount of artifacts, especially around the leg, because the motion of the leg is not well observed in the image sequence. As we can see in the difference images (c) and (e) of Fig. 3.6, our method did significantly better than the color-based sampling method.

Fig. 3.5 *Performer* video result (five frames shown). Top row: original image sequence, middle row: corresponding image sequence with a hole, and bottom row: result of video completion using our method.

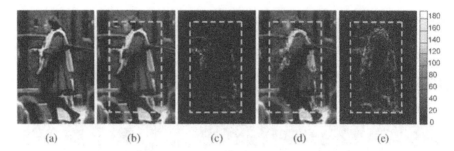

Fig. 3.6 Close-up views. (a) Ground truth, (b) result of video completion using our method, (c) intensity difference between (b) and (a), (d) result of video completion using color-based sampling, and (e) intensity difference between (d) and (a). The dashed boxes indicate the location of the spatio-temporal hole.

Object Removal Fig. 3.7 shows a useful application of video completion: object removal. Here, we manually removed the foreground person and automatically filled the hole using our motion-based technique. The size of the spatio-temporal hole is about 700,000 pixels spanning about 60 frames. Even though there is complex motion in the background, the fill-in was accomplished well. There were noticeable blur effects, which was not surprising, since the hole is large. We briefly discuss the blur effect in Sec. 3.4.

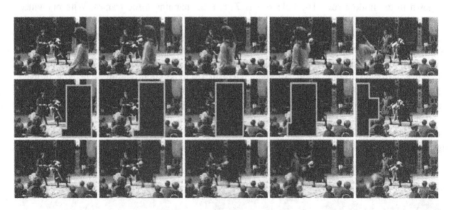

Fig. 3.7 Object removal example (five representative frames shown). Top row: input video, where the two performers are occluded by a foreground person walking across the view. Middle row: after manually removing the foreground person. Bottom row: result of fill-in using our method.

Quantitative evaluation To further validate our proposed method, we performed a quantitative comparison between our method and the color-based non-parametric sampling method. For this evaluation, we used short video clips whose lengths range from 35 to 100 frames. We believe these videos are reasonably good representatives of videos captured by the average consumer. Fig. 3.8 shows the deviation from the ground truth for the two methods. The deviation is represented by the root-mean-squared (RMS) error in intensity. For all these 10 video samples, our method performed better than the color-based sampling method.

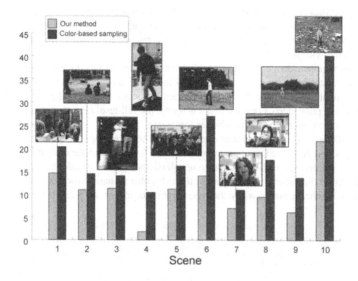

Fig. 3.8 Reconstruction errors for our method and the color-based sampling method for 10 different videos.

3.3.2 Another Application: Frame Interpolation

Fig. 3.9 shows another result of video completion for a *breakdance* scene. Unlike previous examples, here we recover *entire* frames (within dashed boxes). The video contains rather complex motions that are not periodic. Despite this, our method was able to interpolate frames by treating the new intermediate frames as holes.

Fig. 3.9 *Breakdance* scene result. The frames within dashed boxes were recovered by applying our video completion method to the entire set of missing frames.

Since the motion field is low-level information that is independent of color, we can extend our video completion method to fill holes in one video using motion fields from *another video*. This should work in principle if the two video sequences have similar motions (such as a person walking). This property suggests it is plausible to accumulate a video library of all types of motions for the purpose of general video completion.

The idea of using a precomputed set of motion fields as priors for video completion is particularly germane to internet video applications, where frames do get dropped occasionally due to heavy traffic. To prevent the video on the client side from appearing choppy, one can fill in the dropped frames using our video completion technique.

More specifically, we concentrated on the video chat scenario. This seems tractable because the motions in such a video are those of the human head, and they are rather limited. In our experiment, we pre-store the full-rate video as shown in the top row of Fig. 3.10. We use this video to help complete other videos.

To use the prior video, the local motion field of the prior video is pre-computed. Given a low-frame rate input video, we recompute the local motion in the prior video with the same frame rate as the input video. Motion field transfer is then performed to find out the most similar motion patch from the prior video. Once the patch is found, the full-resolution motion field is warped to the low-frame rate video to achieve a higher frame rate.

Fig. 3.10 shows the result of frame rate recovery. The prior video is captured at 30 frames per second (fps), and the frame rate of the input video is 15 fps. Although the color distributions in two videos are different, our method was able to seamlessly generate intermediate frames using motion field transfer. In this example, we only show the video chat scenario; however, the same technique can be used in other scenarios where the types of possible motion are predictable.

Prior video

Output video

Fig. 3.10 Result of frame rate recovery using the motion field prior. By transferring the motion field from the prior video, intermediate frames (within dashed boxes) that appear seamless can be synthesized. Note that here we are *doubling* the frame rate.

3.4 Discussion

While our motion field transfer approach to video completion has been shown to be effective for a variety of videos, it has limitations. For one, we are computing and comparing first-order derivatives of video data, and such measures tend to be more sensitive to noise than directly using color. However, we can alleviate the problem by prefiltering (if the extent of noise is somewhat known) and/or using more robust motion estimation algorithms (such as [11, 4]). As with any motion estimation techniques, large motions cannot be reliably extracted. Such an example is the running animal video in the rightmost column of Fig. 3.8; notice the large prediction error. Color-based methods would likely work better for videos with large motions that are periodic (the running animal video is not periodic).

Our method also tends to produce slightly blurry results due to bilinear resampling in the color propagation step. While better resampling techniques may be used (e.g., cubic interpolation), blur artifacts would still persist.

To overcome this problem, one can apply a color-based sampling pass to replace the estimated colors from the motion-based approach, since the color-based method produces directly copies the patches and thus avoids the blurring problem. This is the main idea behind the deblurring method of Matsushita *etal*. [18], which transfers sharper pixels from neighboring frames.

Directly copying pixels from one location to another ignores the effect of mixed pixels. The proper approach would be to separate colors (together with the blending factor or matting infor-

Fig. 3.11 Effect of temporal size of hole on resulting blur. (a) Ground truth, (b-e), top row: results of our motion-based sampling with the hole set to 50×50 (within dashed boxes) spanning 2, 5, 7, and 10 frames respectively, (b-e), bottom row: results of color-based method under the same conditions.

mation) and move the colors independently, very much in the spirit of Zitnick *etal.*'s approach [24]. They simultaneously estimate motion vectors and matting information for frame interpolation specifically to handle the mixed pixel problem.

The color-based sampling method is expected to work better for videos with clear-cut periodic color variations and large motions. Both color-based and motion-based techniques have complementary strengths and weaknesses. This is illustrated in Fig. 3.11, which compares results for the video of walking people. As described earlier, our method produced blurry effects (depending on the temporal extent of the hole). On the other hand, the color-based method produced some missing parts, especially around the head, but parts that do show up look sharp. It seems logical to combine these two techniques. As future work, it would be interesting to investigate the effectiveness of this hybrid approach.

Computational Cost The most time-consuming part of our method is searching the source patches. Given a video of resolution $w \times h$ and length L frames, the number of matches performed for each target patch is roughly $w/4 \times h/4 \times L/4$ when $l_m = 3$. It took about 40 minutes to process the *performer* video ($w = 352$, $h = 240$, $L = 60$) using a P4 3GHz PC.

3.5 Conclusion

In this paper, we proposed the idea of *motion field transfer* for video completion, which involves sampling similar motion patches from different portions of the video. Motion field is an intrinsic information embedded in a video that is independent of color. Motion field transfer works better than conventional color-based non-parametric sampling techniques in cases where periodic motion is either imperceptible or absent. Our method has been tested on a number of videos spanning a variety of motion and color distributions, and has been shown to have significantly better performance over the color-based non-parametric sampling method.

In addition to hole-filling, we have shown results of seamless frame interpolation, using motion information within the same video and from another video.

References

[1] J. L. Barron, D. J. Fleet, and S. S. Beauchemin. Performance of optical flow techniques. Intl Journal of Computer Vision, 12(1):43C77, 1994.

[2] M. Bertalmio, G. Sapiro, V. Caselles, and C. Ballester. Image inpainting. In SIGGRAPH 2000, pages 417C424, 2000.

[3] J.-Y. Bouguet. Pyramidal implementation of the Lucas Kanade feature tracker: Description of the algorithm. In Intel Research Laboratory, Technical Report., 1999.

[4] T. Brox, A. Bruhn, N. Papenberg, and J. Weickert. High accuracy optical flow estimation based on a theory for warping. In Proc. Europ. Conf. on Computer Vision (4), pages 25C36, 2004.

[5] P. J. Burt and E. H. Adelson. The Laplacian pyramid as a compact image code. IEEE Trans. on Communications, COM-31,4:532C540, 1983.

[6] G. K. M. Cheung, S. Baker, J. K. Hodgins, and T. Kanade. Markerless human motion transfer. In Intl Symp. on 3D Data Processing, Visualization and Transmission, pages 373C378, 2004.

[7] A. Criminisi, P. Perez, and K. Toyama. Object removal by exemplarCbased inpainting. In Proc. Computer Vision and Pattern Recognition, volume 2, 2003.

[8] R. Deriche. Fast algorithms for low-level vision. IEEE Trans. on Pattern Analysis and Machine Intelligence, 12(1):78C87, 1990.

[9] A. A. Efros and W. T. Freeman. Image quilting for texture synthesis and transfer. In SIGGRAPH 2001, pages 341C346, 2001.

[10] A. A. Efros and T. Leung. Texture synthesis by nonC parametric sampling. In Proc. Intl Conf. on Computer Vision, pages 1033C1038, 1999.

[11] G. Farneback. Very high accuracy velocity estimation using orientation tensors parametric motion and simultaneous segmentation of the motion field. In Proc. Intl Conf. on Computer Vision, pages 171C177, 2001.

[12] M. Gleicher. Retargetting motion to new characters. In SIGGRAPH 98, pages 33C42, 1998.

[13] A. Haro and I. Essa. Learning video processing by example. In Proc. Intl Conf. on Pattern Recognition (1), pages 487C 491, 2002.

[14] J. Jia, T.-P. Wu, Y.-W. Tai, and C.-K. Tang. Video repairing: Inference of foreground and background under severe occlusion. In Proc. Computer Vision and Pattern Recognition, volume 1, pages 364C371, 2004.

[15] V. Kwatra, A. Schodl, I. Essa, G. Turk, and A. Bobick. Graphcut textures: Image and video synthesis using graph cuts. ACM Trans. on Graphics (SIGGRAPH), 22(3), 2003.

[16] A. Levin, A. Zomet, and Y. Weiss. Learning how to inpaint from global image statistics. In Proc. Intl Conf. on Computer Vision, pages 305C312, 2003.

[17] B. D. Lucas and T. Kanade. An iterative image registration technique with an application to stereo vision. In Proc. 7th Intl Joint Conf. on Artificial Intelligence, pages 674C679, 1981.

[18] Y.Matsushita, E. Ofek, X. Tang, and H.-Y. Shum. Full-frame video stabilization. In Proc. Computer Vision and Pattern Recognition, volume 1, pages 50C57, 2005.

[19] K. A. Patwardhan, G. Sapiro, and M. Bertalmio. Video inpainting of occluding and occluded objects. In Proc. Intl Conf. on Image Processing, 2005.

[20] Y. Wexler, E. Shechtman, and M. Irani. SpaceCtime video completion. In Proc. Computer Vision and Pattern Recognition, volume 1, pages 120C127, 2004. 1,

[21] A. Witkin and Z. Popovic. Motion warping. In SIGGRAPH 95, pages 105C108, 1995.

[22] Q. Wu and Y. Yu. Feature matching and deformation for texture synthesis. ACM Trans. on Graphics (SIGGRAPH), 23(3):364C367, 2004.

[23] Y. Zhang, J. Xiao, and M. Shah. Motion layer based object removal in videos. In Proc. IEEE Workshop on Applications of Computer Vision, pages 516C521, 2005.

[24] L. Zitnick, N. Jojic, and S. Kang. Consistent segmentation for optical flow estimation. In Proc. Intl Conf. on Computer Vision, pages 1308C1315, 2005. 7

Chapter 4
Correlative Multi-Label Video Annotation[*]

Guo-Jun Qi, Xian-Sheng Hua, Yong Rui, Jinhui Tang, Tao Mei and Hong-Jiang Zhang

Abstract Automatically annotating concepts for video is a key to semantic-level video brows-
ing, search and navigation. The research on this topic evolved through two paradigms. The first
paradigm used binary classification to detect each individual concept in a concept set. It achieved
only limited success, as it did not model the inherent correlation between concepts, e.g., urban and
building. The second paradigm added a second step on top of the individual-concept detectors to
fuse multiple concepts. However, its performance varies because the errors incurred in the first detection step can propagate to the second fusion step and therefore degrade the overall performance.
To address the above issues, we propose a third paradigm which simultaneously classifies concepts
and models correlations between them in a single step by using a novel *Correlative Multi-Label*
(CML) framework. We compare the performance between our proposed approach and the state-of-
the-art approaches in the first and second paradigms on the widely used TRECVID data set. We
report superior performance from the proposed approach.[2]

Key words: Video Annotation, Multi-Labeling, Concept Correlation

4.1 Introduction

Automatically annotating video at the semantic concept level has emerged as an important topic
in the multimedia research community [11][16]. The concepts of interest include a wide range
of categories such as scenes (e.g., urban, sky, mountain, etc.), objects (e.g., airplane, car, face,
etc.), events (e.g., explosion-fire, people-marching, etc.) and certain named entities (e.g. person,
place, etc.) [16][12]. Before we discuss the details of this topic, we would like to first define a few
terminologies. The annotation problem of interest to this paper, as well as to other research efforts
[16][12], is a *multi-labeling* process where a video clip can be annotated with multiple labels.

Guo-Jun Qi and Jinhui Tang
University of Science and Technology of China, Hefei, Anhui, 230027 China
e-mail: {qgj,jhtang}@mail.ustc.edu.cn

Xian-Sheng Hua and Tao Mei
Microsoft Research Asia, 49 Zhichun Road, Beijing 100190 China
e-mail: {xshua,tmei}@microsoft.com

Yong Rui and Hong-Jiang Zhang
Microsoft Advanced Technology Center, 49 Zhichun Road, Beijing, 100190 China
e-mail: {yongrui,hjzhang}@microsoft.com

 * Source: Multimedia 2007, in proceedings of the 15th international conference on Multimedia,
Pages: 17 - 26, 2007 Copyright ©2007 Association for Computing Machinery, Inc. Reprinted by
permission. DOI Bookmark: http://doi.acm.org/10.1145/1291233.1291245

[2] This work was performed when G.-J. Qi and J. Tang were visiting Microsoft Research Asia as
research interns.

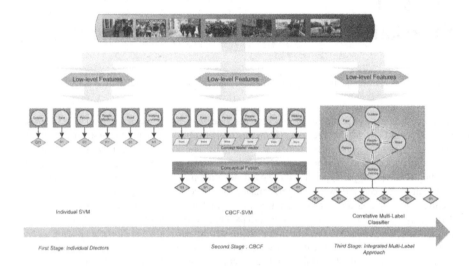

Fig. 4.1 The multi-label video annotation methods in three paradigms. From leftmost to the rightmost, they are the individual SVM, CBCF and our proposed CML.

For example, a video clip can be classified as "*urban*", "*building*" and "*road*" simultaneously. In contrast, *multi-class* annotation process labels only one concept to each video clip. Most of the real-world problems, e.g., the ones being addressed in TRECVID [17], are multi-label annotation, not multi-class annotation. In addition, multi-label is more complex and challenging than multi-class, as it involves non-exclusive detection and classification. This paper focuses on multi-label annotation.

Research on multi-label video annotation evolved through two paradigms: individual concept detection and annotation, and *Context Based Conceptual Fusion* (CBCF) [8] annotation. In this paper, we propose the third paradigm: integrated multi-label annotation. We next review these three paradigms.

4.1.1 First Paradigm: Individual Concept Annotation

In this paradigm, multiple video concepts are detected *individually* and *independently* without considering correlations between them. That is, the multi-label video annotation is translated into a set of binary detectors with presence/absence of the label for each concept. A typical approach is to independently train a concept model using *Support Vector Machine*(SVM) [4] or *Maximum Entropy Model* (MEM) [13] etc. The leftmost flowchart of Figure 1 illustrates the first paradigm – a set of individual SVMs for video concept detection and annotations. A mathematical alternative is to stack this set of detectors into a single discriminative classifier [14]. However, both the individual detectors and the stacked classifier at their core are independent binary classification formulations.

The first-paradigm approaches only achieved limited success. In real world, video concepts do not exist in isolation. Instead, they appear correlatively and naturally interact with each other at the semantic level. For example, the presence of "crowd" often occurs together with the presence of "people" while "boat ship" and "truck" commonly do not co-occur. Furthermore, while simple concepts can be modeled directly from low level features, it is quite difficult to individually learn the models of complex concepts, e.g., "people marching", from the low-level features. Instead, the complex concepts can be better inferred based on the correlations with the other concepts. For instance, the presence of "people marching" can be boosted if both "crowd" and "walking running" occurs in a video clip.

4.1.2 Second Paradigm: Context Based Conceptual Fusion Annotation

One of the most well-known approaches in this paradigm is to refine the detection results of the individual detectors with a *Context Based Concept Fusion* (CBCF) strategy. For instance, Naphade et al. [10] proposed a probabilistic Bayesian Multinet approach to explicitly model the relationship between the multiple concepts through a factor graph which is built upon the underlying video ontology semantics. Wu et al. [20] used an ontology-based multi-classification learning for video concept detection. Each concept is first independently modeled by a classifier, and then a predefined ontology hierarchy is investigated to improve the detection accuracy of the individual classifiers. Smith et al. [15] presented a two-step Discriminative Model Fusion (DMF) approach to mine the unknown or indirect relationship to specific concepts by constructing model vectors based on detection scores of individual classifiers. A SVM is then trained to refine the detection results of the individual classifiers. The center flowchart of Figure 1 shows such a second-paradigm approach. Alternative fusion strategy can also be used, e.g. Hauptmann et al. [6] proposed to use Logistic Regression (LR) to fuse the individual detections. Jiang et al. [8] used a CBCF-based active learning method. Users were involved in their approach to annotate a few concepts for extra video clips, and these manual annotations were then utilized to help infer and improve detections of other concepts.

Although it is intuitively correct that contextual relationship can help improve detection accuracy of individual detectors, experiments of the above CBCF approaches have shown that such improvement is not always stable, and the overall performance can even be worse than individual detectors alone. For example, in [6] at least 3 out of 8 concepts do not gain better performance by using the conceptual fusion with a LR classifier atop the uni-concept detectors. The unstable performance gain is due to the following reasons:

1. CBCF methods are built on top of the independent binary detectors with a second step to fuse them. However, the output of the individual independent detectors can be unreliable and therefore their detection errors can propagate to the second fusion step. As a result, the final annotations can be corrupted by these incorrect predictions. From a philosophical point of view, the CBCF approaches do not follow the *principle of Least-Commitment* espoused by D. Marr [9], because they are prematurely committed to irreversible individual predictions in the first step which can or cannot be corrected in the second fusion step.
2. A secondary reason comes from the insufficient data for the conceptual fusion. In CBCF methods, the samples needs to be split into two parts for each step and the samples for the conceptual fusion step is usually insufficient compared to the samples used in the first training step. Unfortunately, the correlations between the concepts are usually complex, and insufficient data can lead to "over fitting" in the fusion step, thus the obtained prediction lacks the generalization ability.

4.1.3 Third Paradigm: Integrated Multi-label Annotation

To address the difficulties faced in the first and second paradigms, in this paper, we will propose a third paradigm. The key of this paradigm is to simultaneously model both the individual concepts and their interactions in a single formulation. The rightmost flowchart of Figure 1 illustrates our proposed *Correlative Multi-Label* (CML) method. This approach has the following advantages compared with the second paradigm, e.g., CBCF methods:

1. The approach follows the *Principle of Least-Commitment* [9]. Because the learning and optimization is done in a single step for all the concepts simultaneously, it does not have the error propagation problem as in CBCF.
2. The entire samples are efficiently used simultaneously in modeling the individual concepts as well as their correlations. The risk of overfitting due to the insufficient samples used for modeling the conceptual correlations is therefore significantly reduced.

To summarize, the first paradigm does not address concept correlation. The second paradigm attempts to address it by introducing a separate second correlation step. The third paradigm, on the other hand, addresses the correlation issue at the root in a single step. The rest of the paper is organized as follows. In Section 4.2, we give a detailed description of the proposed *Correlative Multi-Label* (CML) approach, including the classification model, and the learning strategy. In Section 4.3, we will explore the connection between the proposed approach and *Gibbs Random Fields* (GRFs) [19], based on which we can show an intuitive interpretation on how the proposed approach captures the individual concepts as well as the conceptual correlations. Section 4.4 details the implementation issues, including concept label vector prediction and concept scoring. Finally, in Section 4.5, we will report experiments on the benchmark TRECVID data and show that the proposed approach has superior performance over state-of-the-art algorithms in both first and second paradigms.

4.2 Our Approach-CML

In this section, we will introduce our proposed correlative multi-labeling (CML) model for video semantic annotation. In Section 4.2.1, we will present the mathematical formulation of the multi-labeling classification function, and show that this function captures the correlations between the individual concepts and low-level features, as well as the correlations between the different concepts. Then in Section 4.2.2, we will describe the learning procedure of the proposed CML model.

4.2.1 A Multi-Label Classification Model

Let $x = (x_1, x_2, \cdots, x_D)^T \in \mathcal{X}$ denote the input pattern representing feature vectors extracted from video clips; Let $y \in \mathcal{Y} = \{+1, -1\}^K$ denote the K dimensional concept label vector of an example, where each entry $y_i \in \{+1, -1\}$ of y indicates the membership of this example in the *ith* concept. $\mathcal{X}$ and $\mathcal{Y}$ represent the input feature space and label space of the data set, respectively. The proposed algorithm aims at learning a linear discriminative function

$$F(x, y; w) = \langle w, \theta(x, y) \rangle \tag{4.1}$$

where $\theta(x, y)$ is a vector function mapping from $\mathcal{X} \times \mathcal{Y}$ to a new feature vector which encodes the models of individual concepts as well as their correlations together (to be detailed later); w is the linear combination weight vector. With such a discriminative function, for an input pattern x, the label vector y^* can be predicted by maximizing over the argument y as

$$y^* = \max_{y \in \mathcal{Y}} F(x, y; w) \tag{4.2}$$

As to be presented in the next section, such a discriminative function can be intuitively interpreted in the Gibbs random fields (GRFs) [19] framework when considering the defined feature vector $\theta(x,y)$. The constructed feature $\theta(x,y)$ is a high-dimensional feature vector, whose elements can be partitioned into two types as follows. And as to be shown later these two types of elements actually account for modeling of individual concepts and their interactions, respectively.

Type I   The elements for *individual* concept modeling:

$$\theta_{d,p}^{l}(x,y) = x_d \cdot \delta \llbracket y_p = l \rrbracket ,$$
$$l \in \{+1, -1\}, 1 \le d \le D, 1 \le p \le K \tag{4.3}$$

where $\delta \llbracket y_p = l \rrbracket$ is an indicator function that takes on value 1 if the predict is true and 0 otherwise; D and K are the dimensions of low level feature vector space $\mathscr{X}$ and the number of the concepts respectively. These entries of $\theta(x,y)$ serve to model the connection between the low level feature x and the labels $y_k (1 \le k \le K)$ of the concepts. They have the similar functionality as in the traditional SVM which models the relations between the low-level features and high-level concepts.

However, as we have discussed, it is not enough for a multi-labeling algorithm to only account for modeling the connections between the labels and low-level features without considering the semantic correlations of different concepts. Therefore, another element type of $\theta(x,y)$ is required to investigate the correlations between the different concepts.

Type II   The elements for concept correlations:

$$\theta_{p,q}^{m,n}(x,y) = \delta \llbracket y_p = m \rrbracket \cdot \delta \llbracket y_q = n \rrbracket$$
$$m, n \in \{+1, -1\}, 1 \le p < q \le K \tag{4.4}$$

where the superscripts m and n are the binary labels (positive and negative label), and subscripts p and q are the concept indices. These elements serve to capture all the possible pairs of concepts and labels. Note that, both positive and negative relations are captured with these elements. For example, the concept "building" and "urban" is a positive concept pair that often co-occurs while "explosion fire" and "waterscape waterfront" is negative concept pair that usually does not occur at the same time.

Note that we can model high-order correlations among these concepts as well, but it will require more training samples. As to be shown in Section 4.5, such an order-2 model successfully trades off between the model complexity and concept correlation complexity, and achieves significant improvement in the concept detection performance.

We concatenate the above two types of elements to form the feature vector $\theta(x,y)$. It is not difficult to see that the dimension of vector $\theta(x,y)$ is $2KD + 4C_K^2 = 2K(D+K-1)$. When K and D are large, the dimension of $\theta(x,y)$ will be extraordinary high. For example, if $K = 39$ and $D = 200$, $\theta(x,y)$ will have $18,564$ dimensions. However, this vector is *sparse* thanks to the indicator function $\delta \llbracket \cdot \rrbracket$ in Eqns. (7.3) and (7.4). This is a key step in the mathematical formulation. As a result, the kernel function (i.e. the dot product) between the two vectors, $\theta(x,y)$ and $\theta(\tilde{x},\tilde{y})$, can be represented in a very compact form as

$$\langle \theta(x,y), \theta(\tilde{x},\tilde{y}) \rangle = \langle x,\tilde{x} \rangle \sum_{1 \le k \le K} \delta \llbracket y_k = \tilde{y}_k \rrbracket$$
$$+ \sum_{1 \le p < q \le K} \delta \llbracket y_p = \tilde{y}_p \rrbracket \delta \llbracket y_q = \tilde{y}_q \rrbracket \tag{4.5}$$

where $\langle x,\tilde{x} \rangle$ is the dot product over the low-level feature vector x and $\tilde{x}$. Of course, a Mercer kernel function $K(x,\tilde{x})$ (such as Gaussian Kernel, Polynomial Kernel) can be substituted for $\langle x,\tilde{x} \rangle$ as in the conventional SVMs, and *nonlinear* discriminative functions can then be introduced with the use of these kernels. In the next subsection, we will present the learning procedure of this model. As to be described, the above compact kernel representation will be used explicitly in the learning procedure instead of the original feature vector $\theta(x,y)$.

4.2.2 Learning the Classifier

Using the feature vector we constructed above and its kernel representation in (7.5), the learning procedure trains a classification model as delineated in (7.1). The procedure follows a similar derivation as in the conventional SVM (details about SVM can be found in [4]) and in particular one of its variants for the structural output spaces [18]. Given an example x_i and its label vector y_i from the training set $\{x_i, y_i\}_{i=1}^n$, according to Eqn. (7.1) and (7.2), a misclassification occurs when we have

$$\Delta F_i(y) \stackrel{\Delta}{=} F(x_i, y_i) - F(x_i, y) \\ = \langle w, \Delta \theta_i(y) \rangle \leq 0, \forall y \neq y_i, y \in \mathcal{Y} \tag{4.6}$$

where $\Delta \theta_i(y) = \theta(x_i, y_i) - \theta(x_i, y)$. Therefore, the empirical prediction risk on training set wrt the parameter w can be expressed as

$$\hat{R}(\{x_i, y_i\}_{i=1}^n; w) = \frac{1}{n} \sum_{i=1}^n \sum_{y \neq y_i, y \in \mathcal{Y}} \ell(x_i, y; w) \tag{4.7}$$

where $\ell(x_i, y; w)$ is a loss function counting the errors as

$$\ell(x_i, y; w) = \begin{cases} 1 \text{ if } \langle w, \Delta \theta_i(y) \rangle \leq 0, \forall y \neq y_i, y \in \mathcal{Y}; \\ 0 \text{ if } \langle w, \Delta \theta_i(y) \rangle > 0, \forall y \neq y_i, y \in \mathcal{Y}. \end{cases} \tag{4.8}$$

Our goal is to find a parameter w that minimizes the empirical error $\hat{R}(\{x_i, y_i\}_{i=1}^n; w)$. Considering the computational efficiency, in practice, we use the following convex loss which upper bounds $\ell(x_i, y; w)$ to avoid directly minimize the step-function loss:

$$\ell_h(x_i, y; w) = (1 - \langle w, \Delta \theta_i(y) \rangle)_+ \tag{4.9}$$

where $(\cdot)_+$ is a hinge loss in classification. Correspondingly, we can now define the following empirical hinge risk which upper bounds $\hat{R}(\{x_i, y_i\}_{i=1}^n; w)$:

$$\hat{R}_h(\{x_i, y_i\}_{i=1}^n; w) = \frac{1}{n} \sum_{i=1}^n \sum_{y \neq y_i, y \in \mathcal{Y}} \ell_h(x_i, y; w) \tag{4.10}$$

Accordingly, we can formulate a regularized version of $\hat{R}_h(\{x_i, y_i\}_{i=1}^n; w)$ that minimizes an appropriate combination of the empirical error and a regularization term $\Omega(||w||^2)$ to avoid over-fitting of the learned model. That is

$$\min_w \{ \hat{R}_h(\{x_i, y_i\}_{i=1}^n; w) + \lambda \cdot \Omega(||w||^2) \} \tag{4.11}$$

where Ω is a strictly monotonically increasing function, and λ is a parameter trading off between the empirical risk and the regularizer. As indicated in [4], such a regularization term can give some smoothness to the obtained function so that the nearby mapped $\theta(x, y), \theta(\bar{x}, \bar{y})$ have the similar function value $F(\theta(x, y); w), F(\theta(\bar{x}, \bar{y}); w)$. Such a local smoothness assumption is intuitive and can relieve the negative influence of the noise training data.

In practice, the above optimization problem can be solved by reducing it to a convex quadratic problem. Similar to what is done in SVMs [4], by introducing a slack variable $\xi_i(y)$ for each pair (x_i, y), the optimization formulation in (7.11) can be rewritten as

$$\min_w \frac{1}{2} ||w||^2 + \frac{\lambda}{n} \cdot \sum_{i=1}^n \sum_{y \neq y_i, y \in \mathcal{Y}} \xi_i(y) \\ s.t. \langle w, \Delta \theta_i(y) \rangle \geq 1 - \xi_i(y), \xi_i(y) \geq 0 \, y \neq y_i, y \in \mathcal{Y} \tag{4.12}$$

On introducing Lagrange multipliers $\alpha_i(y)$ into the above inequalities and formulating the Lagrangian dual according to Karush-Kuhn-Tucker (KKT) theorem [1], the above problem further reduces to the following convex quadratic problem (QP):

$$\max_\alpha \sum_{i, y \neq y_i} \alpha_i(y) - \frac{1}{2} \sum_{i, y \neq y_i} \sum_{j, \tilde{y} \neq y_j} \alpha_i(y) \alpha_j(\tilde{y}) \langle \Delta \theta_i(y), \Delta \theta_j(\tilde{y}) \rangle$$

$$s.t. 0 \leq \sum_{y \neq y_i, y \in \mathscr{Y}} \alpha_i(y) \leq \frac{\lambda}{n}, y \neq y_i, y \in \mathscr{Y}, 1 \leq i \leq n \tag{4.13}$$

and the equality

$$w = \sum_{1 \leq i \leq n, y \in \mathscr{Y}} \alpha_i(y) \Delta \theta_i(y) \tag{4.14}$$

Different from those dual variables in the conventional SVMs which only depend on the training data of observation and the associated label pairs $(x_i, y_i), 1 \leq i \leq n$, the Lagrangian duals in (7.13) depend on all assignment of labels y, which are not limited to the true label of y_i. We can iteratively find the active constraints and the associated label variable y^* which most violates the constraints in (7.9) as $y^* = \arg\max_{y \neq y_i} F(x_i, y; w)$ and $\Delta F_i(y^*) < 1$. An active set is maintained for these corresponding active dual variables $\alpha_i(y^*)$, and w is optimized over this set during each iteration using commonly available QP solvers (e.g. SMO [4]).

4.3 Connection with Gibbs Random Fields for Multi-Label Representation

In this section we give an intuitive interpretation of our multi-labeling model through Gibbs Random Fields (GRFs). Detailed mathematical introduction about GRFs can be found in [19]. We can rewrite Eqn. (7.1) as

$$\begin{aligned} F(x, y; w) &= \langle w, \theta(x, y) \rangle \\ &= \sum_{p \in \wp} D_p(y_p; x) + \sum_{(p,q) \in \mathscr{N}} V_{p,q}(y_p, y_q; x) \end{aligned} \tag{4.15}$$

and

$$\begin{aligned} D_p(y_p; x) &= \sum_{1 \leq d \leq D, l \in \{+1, -1\}} w_{d,p}^l \theta_{d,p}^l(x, y) \\ V_{p,q}(y_p, y_q; x) &= \sum_{m, n \in \{+1, -1\}} w_{p,q}^{m,n} \theta_{p,q}^{m,n}(x, y) \end{aligned} \tag{4.16}$$

where $\wp = \{i | 1 \leq i \leq K\}$ is a finite index set of the concepts with every $p \in \wp$ representing a video concept, and $\mathscr{N} = \{(p,q) | 1 \leq p < q \leq K\}$ is the set of interacting concept pairs. From the GRFs point of view, $\wp$ is the set of sites of a random field and $\mathscr{N}$ consists of adjacent sites of the concepts. For example, in Figure 2, the corresponding GRF has 6 sites representing "outdoor", "face", "person", "people marching", "road" and "walking running", and these sites are interconnected by the concept interactions, such as (outdoor, people marching), (face, person), (people marching, walking running) etc, which are included in the neighborhood set $\mathscr{N}$ of GRF. In the CML framework, the corresponding $\mathscr{N}$ consists of all pairs of the concepts, i.e., this GRF has a fully connected structure.

Now we can define the energy function for GRF given an example x as

$$\begin{aligned} H(y | x, w) &= -F(x, y; w) \\ &= -\left\{ \sum_{p \in \wp} D_p(y_p; x) + \sum_{(p,q) \in \mathscr{N}} V_{p,q}(y_p, y_q; x) \right\} \end{aligned} \tag{4.17}$$

and thus we have the probability measure for a particular concept label vector y given x in the form

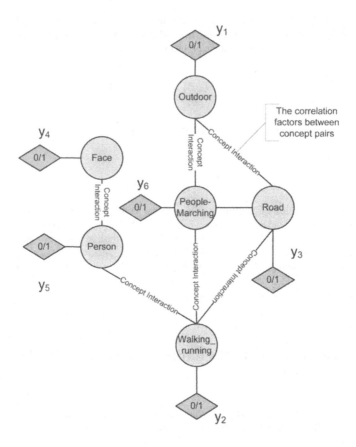

Fig. 4.2 Gibbs Random Fields for a correlative multi-label representation. The edges between concepts indicate the correlation factors $P_{p,q}(y_p, y_q|x)$ between concept pairs.

$$P(y|x,w) = \frac{1}{Z(x,w)} \exp\{-H(y|x,w)\} \qquad (4.18)$$

where $Z(x,w) = \sum_{y \in \mathscr{Y}} \exp\{-H(y|x,w)\}$ is the partition function. Such a probability function with an exponential form can express a wide range of probabilities that are strictly positive over the set $\mathscr{Y}$ [19]. It can be easily seen that when inferring the best label vector y, maximizing $P(y|x,w)$ according to the *Maximum A Posteriori Probability* (MAP) criterion is equal to minimizing the energy function $H(y|x,w)$ or equivalently maximizing $F(x,y;w)$, which accords with Eqn. (7.2). Therefore, our CML model is essentially equivalent to the above defined GRF.

Based on this GRF representation for multi-labeling video concepts, the CML model now has a natural probability interpretation. Substitute Eqn. (7.17) into (7.18), we have

$$P(y|x,w) = \frac{1}{Z(x,w)} \prod_{p \in \wp} P(y_p|x) \cdot \prod_{(p,q) \in \mathscr{N}} P_{p,q}(y_p, y_q|x) \qquad (4.19)$$

where

$$P(y_p|x) = \exp\{D_p(y_p;x)\}$$
$$P_{p,q}(y_p, y_q|x) = \exp\{V_{p,q}(y_p, y_q;x)\}$$

Here $P(y|x,w)$ has been factored into two types of multipliers. The first type, i.e., $P(y_p|x)$, accounts for the probability of a label y_p for the concept p given x. These factors indeed model the relations between the concept label and the low-level feature x. Note that $P(y_p|x)$ only consists of the first type of our constructed features in Eqn. (7.3), and thus it confirms our claim that the first type of the elements in $\theta(x,y)$ serves to capture the connections between x and the individual concept labels. The same discussion can be applied to the second type of the multipliers $P_{p,q}(y_p,y_q|x)$. These factors serve to model the correlations between the different concepts, and therefore our constructed features in Eqn. (7.4) account for the correlations of the concept labels.

The above discussion justifies the proposed model and the corresponding constructed feature vector $\theta(x,y)$ for the multi-labeling problem on video semantic annotation. In the next section, we will give further discussion based on this GRF representation.

4.4 Implementation Issues

In this section, we will discuss implementation considerations about CML.

4.4.1 Interacting concepts

In Section 4.3, we have revealed the connection between the proposed algorithm and GRFs. As has been discussed, the neighborhood set $\mathcal{N}$ is a collection of the interacting concept pairs, and as for CML, this set contains all possible pairs.

However, in practice, some concept pairs may have rather weak interactions, including both positive and negative ones. For example, the concept pairs (airplane, walking running), (people marching, corporate leader) indeed do not have too many correlations, that is to say, the presence/absence of one concept will not contribute to the presence/absence of another concept (i.e., they occur nearly independently). Based on this observation, we can only involve the strongly interacted concept pairs into the set $\mathcal{N}$, and accordingly the kernel function (7.5) used in CML becomes

$$\begin{aligned}\langle \theta(x,y),\theta(\tilde{x},\tilde{y})\rangle &= \langle x,\tilde{x}\rangle \sum_{1\leq k\leq K}\delta[\![y_k=\tilde{y}_k]\!]\\ &+\sum_{(p,q)\in\mathcal{N}}\delta[\![y_p=\tilde{y}_p]\!]\delta[\![y_q=\tilde{y}_q]\!]\end{aligned} \tag{4.20}$$

The selection of concept pairs can be manually determined by experts or automatically selected by data-driven approaches. In our algorithm, we adopt an automatic selection process in which the expensive expert labors are not required. First, we use the normalized mutual information [21] to measure the correlations of each concept pair (p, q) as

$$NormMI(p,q) = \frac{MI(p,q)}{\min\{H(p),H(q)\}} \tag{4.21}$$

where $MI(p,q)$ is the mutual information of the concept p and q, defined by

$$MI(p,q) = \sum_{y_p,y_q} P(y_p,y_q)\log\frac{P(y_p,y_q)}{P(y_p)P(y_q)} \tag{4.22}$$

and $H(p)$ is the marginal entropy of concept p defined by

$$H(p) = -\sum_{y_p\in\{+1,-1\}} P(y_p)\log P(y_p) \tag{4.23}$$

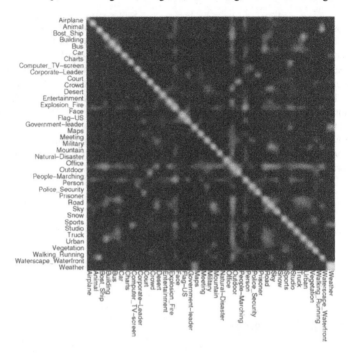

Fig. 4.3 The normalized mutual information between each pair of the 39 concepts in the LSCOM-Lite annotations data set. These are computed based on the annotations of the development data set in the experiments (see Section 4.5).

Here the label prior probabilities $P(y_p)$ and $P(y_q)$ can be estimated from the labeled ground-truth of the training dataset. According to the information theory [21], the larger the $NormMI(p,q)$ is, the stronger the interaction between concept pair p and q is. Such a normalized measure of concept interrelation has the following advantages:

- It is normalized into the interval [0, 1]: $0 \leq NormMI(p, q) \leq 1$;
- $NormMI(p,q) = 0$ when the concept p and q are statistically independent;
- $NormMI(p,p) = 1$

The above properties are accordant with our intuition about concept correlations, and can be easily proven based on the above definitions. From the above properties, we can find that the normalized mutual information is scaled into the interval [0, 1] by the minimum concept entropy. With such a scale, the normalized mutual information only considers the concept correlations, which is irrelevant to the distributions of positive and negative examples of the individual concepts. From the normalized mutual information, the concept pairs whose correlations are larger than a threshold are selected. Figure 3 illustrates the normalized mutual information between the 39 concepts in LSCOM-Lite annotation data set. The brighter the grid is, the larger the corresponding normalized mutual information is, and hence the correlation of the concept pair. For example, ("boat ship", "waterscape waterfront"), ("weather", "maps") etc. have larger normalized mutual information. The white dots in Figure 4 represent the selected concept pairs.

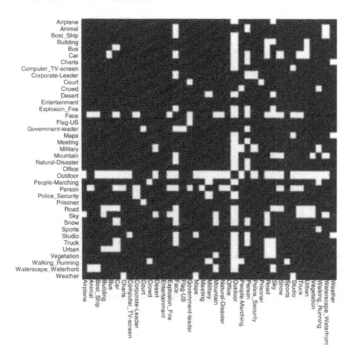

Fig. 4.4 The selected concept pairs according to the computed normalized mutual information. The white blocks indicate the selected concept pairs with significant correlations.

4.4.2 Concept Label Vector Prediction

Once the classification function is obtained, the best predicted concept vector y^* can be obtained from Eqn. (7.2). The most direct approach is to enumerate all possible label vectors in $\mathcal{Y}$ to find the best one. However, the size of the set $\mathcal{Y}$ will become exponentially large with the increment of the concept number K, and thus the enumeration of all possible concept vectors is practically impossible. For example, when $K = 39$, the size is $2^{39} \approx 5.5 \times 10^{11}$.

Fortunately, from the revealed connection between CML and GRF in Section 4.4, the prediction of the best concept vector y^* can be performed on the corresponding GRF form. Therefore, many popular approximate inference techniques on GRF can be adopted to predict y^*, such as *Annealing Simulation*, *Gibbs Sampling*, etc. Specifically, these approximation techniques will be based on the output optimal dual variables $\alpha_i(y)$ in (7.14). Following the discussion in Section 4.3, we can give the dual form of the GRF energy function accordingly. Such a dual energy function comes from Eqn. (7.14). Substituting (7.14) into (7.1) and considering the kernel representation (7.5), we can obtain the following equations:

$$F(\bar{x},\bar{y};w) = \langle \sum_{1 \le i \le n, y \in \mathcal{Y}} \alpha_i(y) \Delta \theta_i(y), \theta(\bar{x},\bar{y}) \rangle \\ = \sum_{p \in \wp} \tilde{D}_p(y_p;x) + \sum_{(p,q) \in \mathcal{N}} \tilde{V}_{p,q}(y_p, y_q;\bar{x})$$

(4.24)

where

$$\tilde{D}_p(\bar{y}_p;\bar{x}) = \Sigma_{1 \le i \le n, y \in \mathscr{Y}}\, \alpha_i(y)k(x_i,\bar{x})\{ \begin{smallmatrix} \delta\,[\![y_{ip}=\bar{y}_p]\!]\,- \\ \delta\,[\![y_p=\bar{y}_p]\!] \end{smallmatrix}\}$$

$$\tilde{V}_{p,q}(\bar{y}_p,\bar{y}_q;\bar{x}) =$$
$$\Sigma_{1 \le i \le n, y \in \mathscr{Y}}\, \alpha_i(y)\{ \begin{smallmatrix} \delta\,[\![y_i=\bar{y}_p]\!]\,\delta\,[\![y_{iq}=\bar{y}_q]\!]\,- \\ \delta\,[\![y_p=\bar{y}_p]\!]\,\delta\,[\![y_q=\bar{y}_q]\!] \end{smallmatrix}\}$$

$$(4.25)$$

And hence the dual energy function is

$$\tilde{H}(\bar{y}|\bar{x},w) = -\left\{ \begin{matrix} \Sigma_{p \in \wp}\tilde{D}_p(\bar{y}_p;\bar{x})+ \\ \Sigma_{(p,q) \in \mathscr{N}}\tilde{V}_{p,q}(\bar{y}_p,\bar{y}_q;\bar{x}) \end{matrix} \right\} \qquad (4.26)$$

and the corresponding probability form of GRF can be written as

$$P(\bar{y}|\bar{x},w) = \frac{1}{\tilde{Z}(\bar{x},w)}\exp\left\{-\tilde{H}(\bar{y}|\bar{x},w)\right\} \qquad (4.27)$$

where $\tilde{Z}(\bar{x},w) = \Sigma_{y \in \mathscr{Y}}\exp\left\{-\tilde{H}(y|\bar{x},w)\right\}$ is the partition function of the dual energy function. With the above dual probabilistic GRF formulation, we use *Iterated Conditional Modes* (ICM) [19] for inference of y^* considering its effectiveness and easy implementation. Other efficient approximation inference techniques (e.g., A*nnealing Simulation*, etc.) can also be directly adopted given the above dual forms.

4.4.3 Concept Scoring

The output of our algorithm given a sample x is the predicted binary concept label vector. However, for the video retrieval applications, we would like to give each concept of each sample a ranking score for indexing. With these scores, the retrieved video clips can be ranked according to the presence possibility of detecting the concept. Here we give a ranking scoring scheme based on the probability form (Eqn. 4.27). Given the predicted concept vector y^*, the conditional expectation of y_p for the concept p can be computed as

$$E(y_p|x,y^*_{\wp \backslash p}) = P(y_p = +1|x,y^*_{\wp \backslash p})$$
$$-P(y_p = -1|x,y^*_{\wp \backslash p}) \qquad (4.28)$$

where

$$P(y_p|x,y^*_{\wp \backslash p}) = \frac{\exp\{-H(y_p \circ y^*_{\wp \backslash p}|x,w)\}}{Z_p}$$
$$= \frac{\exp\{F(x,y_p \circ y^*_{\wp \backslash p};w)\}}{Z_p} \qquad (4.29)$$

and

$$Z_p(x,y^*_{\wp \backslash p}) = \Sigma_{y_p \in \{+1,-1\}}\exp\{-H(y_p \circ y^*_{\wp \backslash p}|x,w)\} \qquad (4.30)$$

is the partition function on the site p. Then we can use this label expectation to rank the video clips for a certain concept.

4.5 Experiments

In this section, we evaluate our algorithm on a widely used benchmark video data set and compare it with other state-of-the-art approaches.

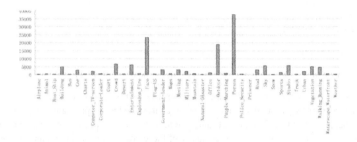

Fig. 4.5 The numbers of labels for the video clips in LSCOM-Lite Annotation data set.

4.5.1 Data Set Description

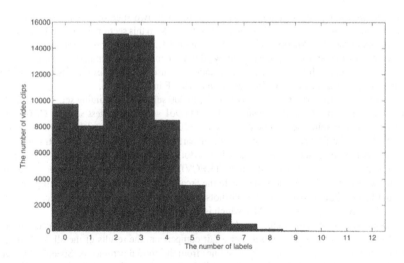

Fig. 4.6 Video Concepts and their distribution in LSCOM-Lite data set

To evaluate the proposed video annotation algorithm, we conduct the experiments on the benchmark TRECVID 2005 data set [17]. This is one of the most widely used data sets by many groups in the area of multimedia concept modeling[2][3][7]. This data set contains about 170 hours international broadcast news in Arabic, English and Chinese. These news videos are first automatically segmented into 61,901 subshots. All subshots are then processed to extract several kinds of low-level features, including

1   Block-wise Color Moment in Lab color space;
2   Co-occurrence Texture;
3   Wavelet Texture;
4   Edge Distribution Layout;

and some mid-level features

5   Face - consisting of the face number, face area ratio, the position of the largest face.

For each subshot, 39 concepts are multi-labeled according to LSCOM-Lite annotations [12]. These annotated concepts consist of a wide range of genres, including program category, setting/scene/site, people, object, activity, event, and graphics. Figure 4.6 illustrates these concepts and their distribution in the data set. Intuitively, many of these concepts have significant semantic correlations between each other. Moreover, these correlations are also proven statistically significant by the normalized mutual information (See Figure 4.3).

Figure 4.5 illustrates the multi-labeling nature of the TRECVID data set. As shown, many subshots (71.32%) have more than one label, and some subshots are even labeled with 11 concepts. Such rich multi-labeled subshots in the video data set as well as the significant correlative information between the concepts validate the necessity of exploiting the relationship between the video concepts.

4.5.2 Experiment Setup

For performance evaluation, we compare our algorithm with two state-of-the-art approaches in first and second paradigms. The first approach, called IndSVM in this section, is the combination of multiple binary encoded SVMs (see the left part of Figure 4.1.) which are trained independently on each concept; the other approach is developed by adding a contextual fusion level on the detection output of the first approach [5]. In our implementation, we use the SVM for this fusion level. We denote this context-based concept fusion approach as CBCF in this section.

The video data is divided into 3 parts with 65% (40,000 subshots) as training set, 16% (10,000 subshots) as validation set and the remaining 19% (11,901 subshots) as test set. For CBCF, the training set is further split into two parts: one part (32000 subshots) is used for training the individual SVMs in the first detection step, the other part (8000 subshots) is used for training the contextual classifier in the second fusion step. For performance evaluation, we use the official performance metric *Average Precision* (AP) in the TRECVID tasks to evaluate and compare the algorithms on each concept. The AP corresponds to the area under a non-interpolated recall/precision curve and it favors highly ranked relevant subshots. We average the AP over all the 39 concepts to create the mean average precision (MAP), which is the overall evaluation result.

The parameters of the algorithms are determined through a validation process according to their performances on the validation set. For a fair comparison, the results of the all 3 paradigm algorithms reported in this section are the best ones from the chosen parameters. Specifically, two parameters need to be estimated in the proposed CML: the trading-off parameter λ and the Gaussian kernel bandwidth σ of the Gaussian kernel function $\langle x, \tilde{x} \rangle$ in Eqns. (7.5) and (4.24). They are respectively selected from sets $\{0.5, 1.0, 10, 100\}$ and $\{0.65, 1.0, 1.5, 2.0\}$ via the validation process. Similarly, the trading-off parameter λ and the Gaussian kernel bandwidth σ in the IndSVM and CBCF are also respectively selected from $\{0.5, 1.0, 10, 100\}$ and $\{0.65, 1.0, 1.5, 2.0\}$, and the best one on the validation set is chosen.

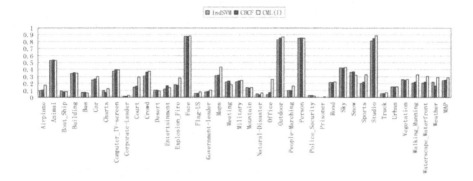

Fig. 4.7 The performance comparison of IndSVM, CBCF and CML(I).

4.5.3 Experiment Results

In this section, we report experiment results on TRECVID data set. Two different modeling strategies are adopted in the experiments. In the first experiment, all concept pairs are taken into consideration in the model and the kernel function in Eqn. (7.5) is adopted. We denote this method by CML(I) in our experiment. In the second one, we adopt the strategy described in Section 4.4.1 and a subset of the concept pairs is applied based on their interacting significance. Accordingly, the kernel function in Eqn. (4.24) is used, and this approach is denoted by CML(II).

4.5.3.1 Experiment I

Figure 4.7 illustrates the performance of CML(I) compared to that of IndSVM (first paradigm) and CBCF (second paradigm). The following observations can be obtained:

- CML(I) obtains about 15.4% and 12.2% relative improvements on MAP compared to IndSVM and CBCF. Compared to the improvement of CBCF (2%) relative to the baseline IndSVM, Such an improvement is significant.
- CML(I) performs the best on 28 of the all 39 concepts. Some of the improvements are significant, such as "office" (477% better than InidSVM and 260% better than CBCF), "people-marching" (68% better than IndSVM and 160% better than CBCF), "walking running" (55% better than IndSVM and 48% better than CBCF).
- CML(I) deteriorates on some concepts compared to IndSVM and CBCF. For example, it has 12% and 14% deterioration on "snow" respectively and 11% and 17% deterioration on "bus" respectively. As discussed in Section 4.4.1, the performance deterioration is due to insignificant concept relations. Next subsection will present CML(II), which solves this deterioration problem and obtains a more consistent and robust performance improvement.

4.5.3.2 Experiment II

Following the proposed approach in Section 4.4.1, the deterioration problem can be solved by removing concept pairs with insignificant correlations.

Figure 4.3 illustrates the normalized mutual entropy between all concepts. They are computed on the development set which includes training set and validation set, but does NOT include the test

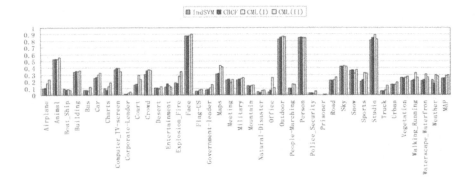

Fig. 4.8 The performance comparison of IndSVM, CBCF and CML(II).

set. The average normalized mutual information entropy is $Avg_{EN} = 0.02$. An important aspect of a good algorithm is if its parameters can be determined automatically. Following such a principle, the threshold Th_{EN} is automatically determined to be $Th_{EN} = 2Avg_{EN}$ such that any concept pairs whose normalized mutual entropy less than Th_{EN} are removed. Figure 4.4 shows these selected concept pairs. As we can see, these preserved concept pairs either have intuitive semantic correlations e.g. "waterscape waterfront" and "boat ship" or statistically tend to co-occur in the news broadcast videos, e.g. "maps" and "weather" in weather forecast video subshots.

Figure 4.8 illustrates the performance of CML(II) with these selected concept pairs compared to IndSVM, CBCF and CML(I). We can find

- CML(II) has the best overall performance compared to the other algorithms. It outperforms IndSVM, CBCF and CML(I) by 17%, 14% and 2%, respectively.
- Furthermore, CML(II) has a more consistent and robust performance improvement over all 39 concepts compared to IndSVM and CBCF. For example, on "bus" and "snow", CML(I) gave worse performance than IndSVM and CBCF. In the contrary, CML(II) gains about 71% and 3% improvement compared to IndSVM and 58% and 1% improvement compared to CBCF with no deterioration.

In summary, CML(II) is the best approach because its best overall MAP improvement as well as its consistent and robust performance on the diverse 39 concepts.

Finally, we give an empirical comparison of computational cost between the proposed CML and the other two state-of-the-art algorithms (IndSVM and CBCF). In fact, under the different parameter settings, the computational cost is different largely. But in general, as for IndSVM and CBCF, the models of each concept are independent without coupled with each other, so they can be trained in parallel. Therefore the computing time needed is much less than CML in which the modeling of the whole concept set is conducted in a coupled manner and is unable to be operated in parallel. In our experiment, the speed of CML is about 25 times slower than IndSVM and CBCF. Thus how to accelerate the computation speed of CML will be the focus of our future work.

4.6 Conclusions and Future Works

In this paper, we proposed a correlative multi-labeling (CML) approach to exploit how the concept correlations help infer the video semantic concepts. Different from the first and second paradigms, where they suffer from insufficient modeling of concept correlations, the proposed approach is able to simultaneously model both the individual concept and the conceptual correlations in an integrated framework. In addition, CML is highly efficient in utilizing the data set. Experiments on the widely used benchmark TRECVID data set demonstrated that CML is superior to state-of-the-art approaches in the first and second paradigms, in both overall performance and the consistency of performance on diverse concepts.

We will continue our future works in two directions. First, we will study how the performance changes with the increment of video concept number, and if the algorithm can get more improvement gain by exploiting a large number of concepts. Second, we will also apply the proposed algorithm to other applications, such image annotation, text categorization in which there exists a large number of correlative concepts.

References

1. S. Boyd and L. Vandenberghe.*Convex Optimization*.CambridgeUniversity Press, 2004.
2. M. Campbell and et al.Ibm research trecvid-2006 video retrieval system. In *TREC Video Retrieval Evaluation (TRECVID) Proceedings*, 2006.
3. S.-F. Chang and et al.Columbia university trecvid-2006 video search and high-level feature extraction. In *TREC Video Retrieval Evaluation (TRECVID) Proceedings*, 2006.
4. N. Cristianini and J. Shawe-Taylor. *An introduction to support vector machines and other kernel-based learning methods*. Cambridge University, 2000.
5. S. Godbole and S. Sarawagi. Discriminative methods for multi-labeled classification. In *PAKDD*, 2004.
6. A. Hauptmann, M.-Y. Chen, and M. Christel. Confounded expectations: Informedia at TRECVID 2004.In *TREC Video Retrieval Evaluation Online Proceedings*, 2004.
7. A. G. Hauptmann and et al. Multi-lingual broadcast news retrieval. In *TREC Video Retrieval Evaluation (TRECVID) Proceedings*, 2006.
8. W. Jiang, S.-F. Chang, and A. Loui. Active concept-based concept fusion with partial user labels. In *Proceedings of IEEE International Conference on Image Processing*, 2006.
9. D. Marr. *Vision*. W.H.Freeman and Company, 1982.
10. M. Naphade, I. Kozintsev, and T. Huang. Factor graph framework for semantic video indexing. *IEEE Trans. on CSVT*, 12(1), Jan. 2002.
11. M. R. Naphade. Statistical techniques in video data management. In *IEEE Workshop on Multimedia Signal Processing*, 2002.
12. M. R. Naphade, L. Kennedy, J. R. Kender, S.-F. Chang, J. R. Smith,P. Over, and A. Hauptmann. A light scale concept ontology for multimedia understanding for TRECVID 2005.In *IBM Research Report RC23612 (W0505-104)*, 2005.
13. K. Nigam, J. Lafferty, and A. McCallum. Using maximum entropy for text classification. In *IJCAI-99 Workshop on Machine Learning for Information Filtering*, pages 61–67, 1999.
14. X. Shen, M. Boutell, J. Luo, and C. Brown. Multi-label machine learning and its application to semantic scene classification.In *International Symposium on Electronic Imaging*, 2004.
15. J. R. Smith and M. Naphade. Multimedia semantic indexing using model vectors. In *Proceeding of IEEE International Conferences on Multimedia and Expo*, 2003.
16. C. Snoek and et al.The challenge problem for automated detection of 101 semantic concepts in multimedia. In *Proceedings of the ACM International Conference on Multimedia*, pages 421–430, Santa Barbara, USA, October 2006.
17. TRECVID.http://www-nlpir.nist.gov/projects/trecvid/.
18. I. Tsochantaridis, T. Hofmann, T. Joachims, and Y. Altun. Support vector machine learning for intedependent and structured output spaces. In *Proc. of Internatial Conference on ICML*, 2004.
19. G. Winkler.*Image analysis, random fields and dynamic Monte Carlo methods: A mathematical introduction*.Springer-Verlag, Berlin, Heidelberg, 1995.

20. Y. Wu, B. L. Tseng, and J. R. Smith. Ontology-based multi-classification learning for video concept detection. In *Proceeding of IEEE International Conferences on Multimedia and Expo*, 2004.
21. Y. Y. Yao.*Entropy measures, maximum entropy principle, and emerging applications*, chapter Information-theoretic measures for knowledge discovery and data mining, pages 115–136. Springer, 2003.

Chapter 5
Stereoscopic Video Synthesis from a Monocular Video[*]

Guofeng Zhang, Wei Hua, Xueying Qin, Tien-Tsin Wong and Hujun Bao

Abstract This paper presents an automatic and robust approach to synthesize stereoscopic videos from ordinary monocular videos acquired by commodity video cameras. Instead of recovering the depth map, the proposed method synthesizes the binocular parallax in stereoscopic video directly from the motion parallax in monocular video. The synthesis is formulated as an optimization problem via introducing a cost function of the stereoscopic effects, the similarity, and the smoothness constraints. The optimization selects the most suitable frames in the input video for generating the stereoscopic video frames. With the optimized selection, convincing and smooth stereoscopic video can be synthesized even by simple constant-depth warping. No user interaction is required. We demonstrate the visually plausible results obtained given the input clips acquired by ordinary hand-held video camera.

Key words: Stereoscopic video synthesis, parallax, optimization.

5.1 Introduction

Stereo visualization provides users the important depth cue experienced in our daily life. Since the introduction of the parallax principle of stereo [1], various stereoscopic systems for displaying stereoscopic images and videos have been developed. Examples include the recently developed 3DTV system [2].

However, stereoscopic videos are normally inaccessible by general public due to the difficulty in generating stereoscopic videos. Acquiring stereoscopic videos from real world usually requires specialized devices. In addition, processing the captured videos requires specialized software or hardware and specialized skills. On the other hand, low-cost ordinary monocular video cameras are widely available. In this paper, we propose an automatic and efficient video-based rendering method to synthesize stereoscopic videos from the monocular videos. Although not all kinds of monocular videos can be used to synthesize stereoscopic videos, many are feasible, e.g. aerophotographic video.

A monocular video can be regarded as a set of plenoptic samples of the scene [3]. The synthesis of stereoscopic videos is basically a process of determining the proper samples and compositing

Guofeng Zhang, Wei Hua, Xueying Qin and Hujun Bao
State Key Lab of CAD&CG, Zhejiang University, Hangzhou, 310058 P.R. China
e-mail: {zhangguofeng, huawei, xyqin, bao}@cad.zju.edu.cn

Tien-Tsin Wong
The Chinese University of Hong Kong, Shatin, Hong Kong
e-mail: ttwong@cse.cuhk.edu.hk

 * Source: IEEE TRANSACTIONS ON VISUALIZATION AND COMPUTER GRAPHICS, VOL. 13, NO. 4, JULY/AUGUST 2007 Pages:686 - 696 Copyright ©2007 IEEE. Reprinted with permission. DOI: 10.1109/TVCG.2007.1032

them to give the left- and right- view sequences. Our method assumes the camera motion contains translational movement and the scene is fixed.

To synthesize stereoscopic videos, one may recover the depth values of samples, and reproject the samples to synthesize both views for each frame. This approach strongly relies on the accuracy of recovered depth values which in turn strongly depends on the availability of textures in the scene. Moreover, when the scene exhibits mirror reflection or highlight, the accuracy of depth recovery is even lowered. Our major contribution is to make use of the *motion parallax* in the monocular video and convert it to *binocular parallax* in a robust way, instead of explicitly recovering the dense depth maps. The whole process is done automatically. To synthesize realistic stereoscopic video, we formulate it as an optimization problem with an objective function that measures the loss of stereoscopic effects, similarity, and smoothness constraints. With the optimally selected frames, convincing stereoscopic video can be synthesized by simple view warping (Figure 5.1).

There are 3 major steps in our method. Firstly, we track the camera motion in the monocular video by a robust camera-tracking algorithm. Secondly, an iterative optimization algorithm is performed to determine the most suitable mono-frames for stereoscopic video synthesis. It selects two sequences of frames from the monocular video. The i-th frames in the two sequences are then warped into the binocular views corresponding to the i-th desired eyes (left and right) in the final step. Our major contribution is the optimization in the second step. It minimizes a cost function with the following objectives:

- The selected frames exhibit the most realistic stereoscopic effects after warping.
- The warped views are similar to the original ones.
- The synthesized stereo frames are smooth temporally.

5.2 Related Works

Early work in stereoscopic video generation employs 3D geometry [4]. However, 3D models are usually difficult to obtain for real-world scene. Generating stereo views from monocular video sequences can be achieved by first recovering the depth map [5, 6]. There have been many work in recovering depth in the area of computer vision. Stereo reconstruction [7], two-view or multi-view reconstruction [8, 9] have been proposed. However, fully automatic, context-independent, and accurate dense 3D reconstruction is still an open problem.

Image-based rendering [10, 11] aims at synthesizing novel views from images. Methods like light field [12, 13] and lumigraph [14] densely sample the scene in order to synthesize reasonable novel views even no geometry information is given. Other methods try to reduce the sampling rate by incorporating depth information or coarse 3D models. They include 3D warping [15], view interpolation [16], view morphing [17], image tours [18], and layered-depth images [19]. Sawhney et al. [20] synthesized high-resolution stereoscopic video given one high-resolution and one low-resolution views. Recent work in video-based rendering [21] utilizes multiple synchronized video cameras to generate the 3D video [22], or free viewpoint video [23]. Their goals are to synthesize arbitrary novel views. However, specialized hardware and/or reconstruction of 3D models are usually required. Techniques for stereo panoramic images [24, 25] have been proposed. They stitch images obtained from a single rotating camera mounted on a special rig or equipped with a specialized optical lens.

Homography can be used for rectifying a pair of still images to a stereo pair in stereo vision [26]. However, it may not suit for the video sequence since the change of orientations of rectified stereo pairs may not be smooth, which causes the resultant video looks shaky. Moreover, the baselines (the lines joining the stereo image pairs) of rectified stereo pairs may also not be the same throughout the video. This violates the property of the stereoscopic video. Rotem et al. [27] calculated a planar transformation between images in the sequence and aligned one input frame to another in order to synthesize the stereoscopic video sequence. This relies on the human capability to sense the residual parallax. Since it only uses a simple homograhy without the accurate camera

Π^L, Π^R	the index subsequences in which the i-th elements $\Pi^L[i]$ and $\Pi^R[i]$ are the indices of the base frames to be warped to the i-th left-eye and right-eye frame in stereoscopic video sequence.
$\mathbf{s}$	a stereo-camera.
$\mathbf{S}$	the ordered set (sequence) of stereo-camera. $\mathbf{S}[i]$ is the i-th stereo-camera, equivalent to $\mathbf{s}_i$.
$\mathbf{b}$	a base camera.
$\mathbf{B}$	the ordered set (sequence) of base camera. $\mathbf{B}[i]$ is the i-th base camera, equivalent to $\mathbf{b}_i$.
$\mathbf{L}(\mathbf{s}), \mathbf{R}(\mathbf{s})$	the left and right cameras of stereo-camera $\mathbf{s}$.
$\mathbf{v}(\mathbf{b})$	the viewpoint of camera $\mathbf{b}$.
$\mathbf{v}(\mathbf{L}(\mathbf{s})), \mathbf{v}(\mathbf{R}(\mathbf{s}))$	the left and right viewpoint of stereo-camera $\mathbf{s}$.
$\mathbf{q}(\mathbf{b}), \mathbf{q}(\mathbf{s})$	the orientation of base camera $\mathbf{b}$ or stereo-camera $\mathbf{s}$ respectively, expressed by Euler angles.
$\mathbf{f}(\mathbf{m})$	the frame corresponding to camera $\mathbf{m}$
$\mathbf{f}_k$	the k-th base frame, equivalent to $\mathbf{f}(\mathbf{b}_k)$.
$\mathbf{f}(\mathbf{m}_1) \rightarrow \mathbf{f}(\mathbf{m}_2)$	the warped view $\mathbf{f}$ from camera $\mathbf{m}_1$ to that of camera $\mathbf{m}_2$.

Table 5.1 Notations.

motion recovery, the baseline of a stereo pair may not be calculated accurately, resulting in the length of baseline changes vigorously in the generated stereoscopic video sequence. In addition, there is no attempt to control the parallax errors along vertical direction. Hence there will be shaky motion in the generated stereoscopic video as evidenced by their results.

The proposed work synthesizes stereoscopic video from a monocular video sequence by *utilizing the motion parallax alone. No depth map recovery* is required. We make an in-depth analysis based on precise camera motion recovery, and formulate it as an optimization problem of the stereoscopic effects, the similarity, and the smoothness constraints.

5.3 Overview

Before presenting our algorithm, we first define the terminologies. We call the input monocular video sequence the *base frame sequence*, in which each frame is a *base frame*. The camera corresponding to a base frame is a *base camera*, and its viewpoint and viewing direction are called by *base viewpoint* and *base viewing direction* respectively. The ordered sequence of base viewpoints form a *base trajectory*. A *stereo-camera* consists of two monocular cameras, *left camera* and *right camera*. Both of them are in the same orientation and orthogonal to the line joining them. The center of projections of left and right cameras are called the left and right viewpoints respectively. The center of the *stereo-camera* lies at the midpoint of two cameras. These notations are listed in Table 5.1.

We assume the interocular distance, the distance between the left and right viewpoints, is constant and denoted by d_{eye}. Thus, the extrinsic parameters of the stereo-camera can also be described by its center and the orientation of its viewing coordinate frame. We also assume that the intrinsic parameters of both left and right cameras are the same and unchanged throughout the whole sequence.

Our method exploits the temporal coherence of the monocular video sequence. The novel binocular views are synthesized by warping two properly selected base frames. The warping error between the warped and the true views is small when the difference (in terms of viewing parameters) between the original and target views is small. Thus, we need to carefully determine the center and the orientation of the desired stereo-camera, as well as the selection of two base frames, so that the following three objectives are achieved: (a) the binocular views obtained by warping exhibit the stereoscopic effects as realistic as possible; (b) the binocular views are close to the selected base frames; and (c) the change in viewpoint position and orientation of consecutive stereo-cameras are minimized. Otherwise, the generated stereoscopic video will be shaky. We begin the description with the input base frame sequence $\mathbf{F} = \{\mathbf{f}_k | k = 1, ..., K\}$. Here are the three major steps to perform:

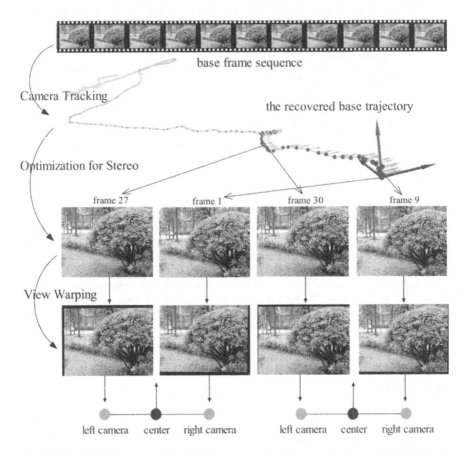

Fig. 5.1 Synthesizing stereoscopic video from monocular frames. At the bottom of this example, $\Pi^L = 27,30$ and $\Pi^R = 1,9$. The first frame in the stereoscopic video is warped from the base frame pair $(\mathbf{f}_{27}, \mathbf{f}_1)$, while the second one is warped from base frame pair $(\mathbf{f}_{30}, \mathbf{f}_9)$. The actual base frames for warping are selected by optimizing the cost function.

Step 1   For each base frame $\mathbf{f}_k$, we recover the extrinsic parameters of the corresponding base camera $\mathbf{b}_k$ in the set $\mathbf{B} = \{\mathbf{b}_k | k = 1,...,K\}$.

Step 2   Determine the stereo-camera sequence $\mathbf{S} = \{\mathbf{s}_i | i = 1,...,N\}$ and the two index subsequences, Π^L and Π^R, satisfying criteria (a), (b) and (c) (explained in Section 5.4).

Step 3   For $i = 1,...,N$, performing view warping operations:

$$
\begin{aligned}
\mathbf{f}(\mathbf{b}_l) &\rightarrow \mathbf{f}(\mathbf{L}(\mathbf{s}_i)), l = \Pi^L[i] \\
\mathbf{f}(\mathbf{b}_r) &\rightarrow \mathbf{f}(\mathbf{R}(\mathbf{s}_i)), r = \Pi^R[i].
\end{aligned}
\tag{5.1}
$$

The output frames $\{\mathbf{f}(\mathbf{L}(\mathbf{s}_i)), \mathbf{f}(\mathbf{R}(\mathbf{s}_i)) | i = 1,...,N\}$ form the resultant stereoscopic video sequence. This procedure is illustrated in Figure 5.1.

Step 1 involves the structure and motion recovery which is a classical problem in computer vision. Several methods [28, 8, 29, 30] have been proposed to recover the camera extrinsic parameters given a video sequence. In our implementation, we adopt the method proposed in [30] to automatically extract the camera motion parameters and the 3D positions of sparse feature points for each frame.

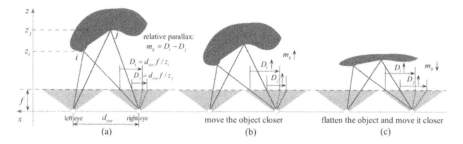

Fig. 5.2 Absolute parallax and relative parallax. (a) illustrates the absolute and relative parallax. (b) Moving the scene nearer, the absolute parallaxes become larger. (c) Extruding the scene toward the nearer distance, the relative parallaxes become smaller while the absolute parallaxes become larger.

Step 2 is the most challenging and difficult part. We adopt an optimization process to determine $(\mathbf{S}, \Pi^L, \Pi^R)$ by minimizing the cost function $E(\mathbf{S}, \Pi^L, \Pi^R)$. This cost function consists of the stereo cost, the similarity cost, and the continuity cost, corresponding to the 3 objectives mentioned above. Section 5.4 describes them in details.

Finally, in Step 3, we can warp the pair of chosen base frames (from Step 2) to obtain the left and right frames. There are several possible ways to achieve this view warping. A classical way for view warping is to produce 3D meshes by triangulating the sparse point cloud, and render each mesh with texture map to synthesize the desired view. However, the 3D points recovered in the first step are too sparse and unevenly distributed. Missing geometry and outlying points can sometimes cause distracting artifacts. Another approach is planar-homography that restricts the warping on a plane (planar impostor). It computes a planar transformation (or homography) by minimizing the average warping/disparity error of the recovered sparse 3D feature points. However, in our application to generate stereo frames, apparent visual artifact will be resulted if the warping plane is allowed to be arbitrarily oriented. Figure 5.9(a) shows one such example. The building and streetlamps are not parallel to each other in the synthetic left and right views, as the warping planes for generating the left and right views are not parallel. Note that human vision is more sensitive to such misalignment than the disparity errors. To avoid the artifact, we restrict the warping planes to be perpendicular to the viewing direction and aligned to the up vector of the stereo-camera. In other words, all pixels in the warped frame have the same depth z_c. Due to the uneven distribution of the recovered sparse 3D points, we use $z_c = 2(z_{min}^{-1} + z_{max}^{-1})^{-1}$ instead of a mean value. Here, $[z_{min}, z_{max}]$ is the depth range of the scene with respect to viewpoint of the associated base camera, which can be estimated automatically with the recovered sparse 3D points. This restriction is also adopted in the plentopic sampling analysis [13]. Even with such crude *constant-depth* assumption, convincing stereo frames can be synthesized (Figure 5.9(b)).

5.4 The Cost Function

The cost function $E(\mathbf{S}, \Pi^L, \Pi^R)$ consists of three terms, the stereo cost E_S, the similarity cost E_Q, and the continuity costs of camera orientation E_{CQ} and location E_{CV}. Mathematically, $E(\mathbf{S}, \Pi^L, \Pi^R)$ is defined as:

$$E(\mathbf{S}, \Pi^L, \Pi^R) = w_S E_S + w_Q E_Q + (w_{CQ} E_{CQ} + w_{CV} E_{CV}), \qquad (5.2)$$

where w_S, w_Q, w_{CQ} and w_{CV} are weights of the cost terms.

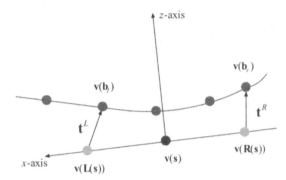

Fig. 5.3 The relationship between two base cameras and stereo-camera $\mathbf{s}$. $\mathbf{v}(\mathbf{L}(\mathbf{s}))$ and $\mathbf{v}(\mathbf{R}(\mathbf{s}))$ are the left and right viewpoints of stereo-camera $\mathbf{s}$ respectively. $\mathbf{v}(\mathbf{s})$ is the center of stereo-camera $\mathbf{s}$. $\mathbf{b}_l$ and $\mathbf{b}_r$ are the two base cameras, and their corresponding base frames will be warped to generate a pair of stereoscopic frames. $\mathbf{v}(\mathbf{b}_l)$ and $\mathbf{v}(\mathbf{b}_r)$ are their viewpoints respectively.

5.4.1 Stereo Cost

5.4.1.1 Relative Parallax

The sense of stereo is due to the fact that our left and right eyes see differently. The same scene/object is spatially shifted in our left and right views. Such apparent position difference is called *binocular parallax*. In the 2D illustration of Figure 5.2(a), the viewing rays corresponding to the points i and j in the left view are overlaid onto the right view as indicated by the dotted red and blue lines. The displacements D_i and D_j are the parallaxes (binocular parallaxes). They are related to the interocular distance (d_{eye}), focal length (f), and depth (z_i). Obviously closer object results in larger parallax.

In this article, we argue that the sense of stereo relies *not* on the *absolute parallax*, but on the *relative parallax*. Relative parallax is the difference in parallax of two objects. The notion of relative parallax has long been used in the area of astronomy [31]. In this paper, the relative parallax is formally defined as follow. Consider Figure 5.2, a pixel $\mathbf{p}_i^L$ in the left view and its corresponding pixel $\mathbf{p}_i^R$ in the right view. The parallax of this pixel $\mathbf{p}_i$ is $D_i = \mathbf{p}_i^L - \mathbf{p}_i^R$. The relative parallax with reference to another pixel $\mathbf{p}_j^L$ is defined as $\mathbf{m}_{ij} = D_i - D_j$. The parallax depends on their depths, focal length, and the interocular distance, $\mathbf{m}_{ij} = d_{eye} f(z_i^{-1} - z_j^{-1})$. Thus, for a pair of binocular images, we can define the *relative parallax matrix* $\mathbf{M}$ in which its element $\mathbf{m}_{ij}$ being the relative parallax of every pair of pixels $\mathbf{p}_i$ and $\mathbf{p}_j$.

Figure 5.2 explains why the relative parallax is more sensible than the absolute parallax in expressing the stereoscopic effect. The object in Figure 5.2(b) is moved closer to the viewer. The values of both the relative ($\mathbf{m}_{ij}$) and absolute (D_i, D_j) parallaxes are increased. In Figure 5.2(c), the object is not just moved closer but also flattened. Although the absolute parallax is increased, its relative parallax decreases.

To account for the relative parallax, we estimate the error in relative parallax between the synthetic (view-warped) and ideal stereo image pairs. Given the stereo-camera in the current iteration (it may change in the next iteration), the synthetic stereo frame is the one warped with the constant-depth assumption. It is the one that we can compute. The ideal stereo frame is the one that we can obtain if the true depth map is known. Obviously, the true depth map is *not* available. But we can still estimate the upper bound of this relative parallax error.

Each stereoscopic frame pair is synthesized by warping two chosen base frames. Let's denote the two base frames being considered for view warping in the current round of optimization as $\mathbf{f}_l$

(left candidate) and $\mathbf{f}_r$ (right candidate). If we have the true depth maps, we can correctly synthesize stereo pair $\mathbf{f}'_l$ and $\mathbf{f}'_r$ by a per-pixel warping. Let's denote the relative parallax matrix of this ideal stereo pair $(\mathbf{f}'_l, \mathbf{f}'_r)$ by $\mathbf{M}_G$. It is the ideal relative parallax matrix. Since the true depth map is not available, we can only warp the images with the constant-depth assumption. The relative parallax matrix of this synthetic stereo pair is denoted as $\mathbf{M}_W$. The matrix $\mathbf{M}_W - \mathbf{M}_G$ measures the error in relative parallax. Although we do not know $\mathbf{M}_G$, we can estimate a upper bound ε for the norm of the elements in $\mathbf{M}_W - \mathbf{M}_G$ (see Appendix for the derivation).

$$\varepsilon(\mathbf{s}, \mathbf{f}_l, \mathbf{f}_r) = fh_d \sqrt{(d_x + \frac{w}{2f} \cdot d_z)^2 + \mu(d_y + \frac{h}{2f} \cdot d_z)^2}, \qquad (5.3)$$

where f is the focal length; $h_d = z_{min}^{-1} - z_{max}^{-1}$; w and h are the width and height of the base frames; μ is a constant greater than 1; and

$$d_x = |\mathbf{t}_x^L - \mathbf{t}_x^R|, \quad d_y = |\mathbf{t}_y^L - \mathbf{t}_y^R|, \quad d_z = |\mathbf{t}_z^L| + |\mathbf{t}_z^R|. \qquad (5.4)$$

where $\mathbf{t}^L = \mathbf{v}(\mathbf{b}_l) - \mathbf{v}(\mathbf{L}(\mathbf{s}))$ and $\mathbf{t}^R = \mathbf{v}(\mathbf{b}_r) - \mathbf{v}(\mathbf{R}(\mathbf{s}))$ are the displacement vectors as illustrated in Figure 5.3. The intuition is that the deviation of the two displacement vectors, $\mathbf{t}^L$ (displacement between the candidate and ideal left viewpoints) and $\mathbf{t}^R$ (displacement between the candidate and ideal right viewpoints) should be close, especially in y axis.

Constant μ is the weight on y component. In our formulation, the x-axis is aligned with the line connecting the left and right viewpoints of the stereo-camera, the positive direction of z-axis is the viewing direction, and the positive direction of y-axis is the upward vector of the camera. The y component of relative parallax should be zero according to the stereovision theory, and any nonzero value will damage the stereoscopic effect. Therefore, we use $\mu(> 1)$ to penalize any change in y direction caused by our view warping.

5.4.1.2 Warping Error

Besides the relative parallax error, the error due to warping should also be controlled to minimize visual artifact. We estimate the warping error as the maximum deviation between the pixel positions warped with constant-depth assumption and the ideal pixel positions if the true depths are known. If the deviation is too large, it will be easily aware by audiences. Note that minimizing the relative parallax error not necessarily minimizes the warping error. It is easy to demonstrate that the error due to warping the base frame pair $(\mathbf{f}_l, \mathbf{f}_r)$ is bounded by δ (see Appendix for the derivation),

$$\delta(\mathbf{s}, \mathbf{f}_l, \mathbf{f}_r) = \frac{\sqrt{2}}{2} fh_d \max(1, \frac{\sqrt{w^2 + h^2}}{2f}) \sqrt{\|\mathbf{t}^L\|^2 + \|\mathbf{t}^R\|^2}, \qquad (5.5)$$

The goal of Equation 5.5 is to minimize the pixel position deviation via minimizing the displacement of viewpoints ($\mathbf{t}^L$ and $\mathbf{t}^R$). One assumption of Equation 5.5 is that the target and original views have the same viewing orientation. If the camera orientation of the target and original views are different, we can rectify the original views. The error due to the difference of camera orientation is accounted by the similarity cost (explained in Section 5.4.2).

Finally, we use both ε and δ to estimate the overall loss of stereoscopic effects due to the view warping. As the maximum relative parallax is $fh_d d_{eye}$, we use this maximum value to normalize ε and δ. Hence, the stereo cost of the entire stereoscopic sequence is defined as:

$$E_S(\mathbf{S}, \Pi^L, \Pi^R) = \frac{1}{(fh_d d_{eye})^2} \sum_{i=1}^{N} (\varepsilon^2(\mathbf{S}[i], \Pi^L[i], \Pi^R[i])$$

$$+ \delta^2(\mathbf{S}[i], \Pi^L[i], \Pi^R[i])). \qquad (5.6)$$

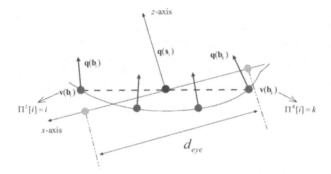

Fig. 5.4 Determination of the initial value of $(S[i], \Pi^L[i], \Pi^R[i])$. $q(s_i)$, $q(b_i)$ and $q(b_k)$ are the orientations of camera s_i, b_i, and b_k respectively. The blue arrows indicate the viewing direction of these cameras.

5.4.2 Similarity Cost

The orientation of the two chosen base cameras b_l and b_r should be as close to that of the stereo-camera s as possible. This guarantees that the binocular views generated by viewing warping look similar to the original ones and they share the large common scene region. Therefore, we define the similarity cost for one stereo frame by:

$$\gamma(s, f_l, f_r) = \|q(s) - q(b_l)\|^2 + \|q(s) - q(b_r)\|^2, \tag{5.7}$$

where, $q(s)$, $q(b_l)$ and $q(b_r)$ are the orientations of the stereo-camera s, the left and right base cameras b_l and b_r respectively. Each is represented by a triplet of Euler angles. The similarity cost of the entire video sequence is defined by:

$$E_Q(S, \Pi^L, \Pi^R) = \sum_{i=1}^{N} \gamma(S[i], \Pi^L[i], \Pi^R[i]). \tag{5.8}$$

5.4.3 Continuity Cost

The discontinuity of a video sequence is mainly caused by the unsteady rotational and translational speed of the camera. Therefore, to ensure the visual smoothness of the synthesized stereoscopic video, the rotational and translational acceleration should be minimized. Besides, since our stereo-scopic video sequence is obtained by view warping, the change of the loss of stereoscopic effect should also be minimized to achieve visual smoothness. From Equations 5.5 and 5.3, the stereo-scopic effect loss is dependent on the viewpoints of stereo-camera and the two candidate cameras. Thus, to ensure the stereo-camera moves steadily, the corresponding candidate cameras also have to move steadily. Hence, we define the continuity costs of the camera orientations, E_{CQ} and the location, E_{CV} as:

$$E_{CQ}(\mathbf{S}, \Pi^L, \Pi^R) = \sum_{i=2}^{N-1} \|2\mathbf{q}(\mathbf{s}_i) - \mathbf{q}(\mathbf{s}_{i+1}) - \mathbf{q}(\mathbf{s}_{i-1})\|^2$$

$$E_{CV}(\mathbf{S}, \Pi^L, \Pi^R) = \frac{1}{d_{eye}^2} \left(\sum_{i=2}^{N-1} \|2\mathbf{v}(\mathbf{s}_i) - \mathbf{v}(\mathbf{s}_{i+1}) - \mathbf{v}(\mathbf{s}_{i-1})\|^2 \right.$$
$$+ \sum_{i=2}^{N-1} \|2\mathbf{v}(\mathbf{b}_{\Pi^L[i]}) - \mathbf{v}(\mathbf{b}_{\Pi^L[i+1]}) - \mathbf{v}(\mathbf{b}_{\Pi^L[i-1]})\|^2 \qquad (5.9)$$
$$\left. + \sum_{i=2}^{N-1} \|2\mathbf{v}(\mathbf{b}_{\Pi^R[i]}) - \mathbf{v}(\mathbf{b}_{\Pi^R[i+1]}) - \mathbf{v}(\mathbf{b}_{\Pi^R[i-1]})\|^2 \right).$$

Here, we minimize the second derivative of the camera orientations and locations in order to reduce the discontinuity. It has been pointed out [32] that human are more sensitive to rotational vibrations, therefore E_{CQ} should be given larger weight. Generally, the weights of E_S and E_{CV} should be close to ensure the tradeoff between the warping errors and translational smoothness.

5.5 Optimization

Computing the optimal solution is challenging, as it involves both the combinatorial and continuous optimizations. We design an iterative algorithm to accomplish this task. Table 5.2 shows the pseudocode.

---

1. Find an initial solution of $\mathbf{S}$, Π^L, and Π^R.
2. Fix Π^L, Π^R, and find the optimal viewpoints of the stereo-cameras $\mathbf{V} = \{\mathbf{v}(\mathbf{s}_i) | \mathbf{s}_i = \mathbf{S}[i], i = 1, ..., N\}$, and viewing orientations $\mathbf{Q} = \{\mathbf{q}(\mathbf{s}_i) | \mathbf{s}_i = \mathbf{S}[i], i = 1, ..., N\}$ by minimizing E.
3. If E is small enough or doesn't improve from last iteration, terminate the iteration; otherwise, continue.
4. for $(i = 1, ..., N)$
   fix $\mathbf{v}(\mathbf{s}_i)$ and $\mathbf{q}(\mathbf{s}_i)$, and find the optimal $\Pi^L[i], \Pi^R[i]$ to minimize $w_S E_S + w_Q E_Q$.
5. Fix $\mathbf{Q}$, Π^L & Π^R, and refine $\mathbf{V}$ to minimize E.
6. Fix $\mathbf{Q}$ and $\mathbf{V}$, and refine Π^L and Π^R *locally* to minimize E.
7. Goto step 2.

Table 5.2 Algorithm of optimization.

Solving Π^L and Π^R involves a combinatorial optimization, which is too complicated to search globally for the best solution. However, if Π^L and Π^R are fixed, it becomes a nonlinear continuous optimization and can be optimized by Levenberg-Marquardt method (LM) efficiently. Therefore, we employ an optimization strategy which alternates between the continuous optimization and the discrete search. That is, instead of letting all parameters to change simultaneously, we temporarily fix discrete parameters to allow continuous optimization. Then we temporarily fix certain continuous parameters to allow discrete search. Such alternation continues in the next iteration.

We first initialize $\mathbf{S}$ (i.e. $\mathbf{V}$ and $\mathbf{Q}$), Π^L and Π^R (Section 5.5.1). The initial $\mathbf{V}, \Pi^L$ and Π^R are usually already close to optimal ones. Then in step 2, we fix Π^L and Π^R, and optimize the $\mathbf{V}$ and $\mathbf{Q}$ using standard continuous optimization method like Levenberg-Marquardt. If E is not sufficiently small, it means that Π^L and Π^R are not good enough and need to be adjusted in the following steps.

Steps 4-6 are mainly designed for adjusting the discrete parameters Π^L and Π^R. However, adjusting Π^L and Π^R is computationally expensive. In order to efficiently adjust Π^L and Π^R, we temporarily freeze E_{CQ} and E_{CV} (contain complex combinatorial optimization if Π^L and Π^R are not fixed) to their current values (step 4). Instead of optimizing the whole E, we only minimize for $w_S E_S + w_Q E_Q$. This is an implementation trick. Then in the following steps 5 and 6, we patch on this partial optimization. In step 5, we allow $\mathbf{V}$ to adjust in order to reflect the effect due to the previous change of Π^L and Π^R. This time we minimize for the whole E, (not just $w_S E_S + w_Q E_Q$). Once $\mathbf{V}$ adjusts, it affects Π^L and Π^R immediately. Finally in step 6, we *locally* adjust Π^L and Π^R to minimize for the whole E. With the partial optimization and the local adjustment, the adjustment on Π^L and Π^R becomes efficient.

5.5.1 Initialization

Firstly, we construct the initial selection. Let $\Pi^L[i] = i$ for $i = 1, ..., N$, *i.e.*, the base frame $\mathbf{f}_i$ will be the current candidate to be warped into the left view corresponding to the i-th left camera. Then, the remaining task is to search the proper base frame as the current candidate for the corresponding right view. Consider the i-th left camera, base camera $\mathbf{b}_k$ is the desired one if the distance between $\mathbf{b}_k$ and $\mathbf{b}_i$ is the closest one to the interocular distance d_{eye}. Its index is assigned to $\Pi^R[i]$, or $\Pi^R[i] = k$ such that $k > i$. It is natural to let the center and orientation of the i-th stereo-camera be the average of those of $\mathbf{b}_i$ and $\mathbf{b}_k$, i.e., $\mathbf{v}(\mathbf{s}_i) = (\mathbf{v}(\mathbf{b}_i) + \mathbf{v}(\mathbf{b}_k))/2$ and $\mathbf{q}(\mathbf{s}_i) = (\mathbf{q}(\mathbf{b}_i) + \mathbf{q}(\mathbf{b}_k))/2$. Next, according to the local coordinate system of the stereo-camera, if $\mathbf{b}_k$ is not on the right hand side of $\mathbf{b}_i$ when looking at the positive direction of the z-axis, the values in $\Pi^L[i]$ and $\Pi^R[i]$ are swapped. $\mathbf{v}(\mathbf{R}(\mathbf{s}_i))$ and $\mathbf{v}(\mathbf{L}(\mathbf{s}_i))$ are the left and right viewpoints of $\mathbf{s}_i$ and are equal to $\mathbf{v}(\mathbf{s}_i) \pm 0.5 d_{eye} \mathbf{e}_x$ respectively, where $\mathbf{e}_x$ is the x-axis direction vector. Figure 5.4 illustrates the initialization graphically.

5.5.2 Speed-up

During the adjustment of $\Pi^L[i]$ and $\Pi^R[i]$, the terms E_{CQ} and E_{CV} involve the complex combinatorial optimization in which its complexity grows exponentially with the number of frames. Therefore, we employ a practical trick. It firstly ignores the continuity cost in step 4. Then the continuity consideration is brought back in steps 5 and 6 for improving visual smoothness. In step 4, for each stereo frame i, its best candidate pair $(\Pi^L[i], \Pi^R[i])$ is determined by fixing the stereo-camera $\mathbf{s}_i$ (both viewpoint and orientation) and minimizing the *part of objective function* $w_S E_S + w_Q E_Q$, i.e. $\sigma_i = w_S(\delta^2 + \varepsilon^2) + w_Q \gamma$. Energy terms E_{CQ} and E_{CV} are temporarily fixed and ignored. As $(\Pi^L[i], \Pi^R[i])$ affects the center of stereo-camera $\mathbf{v}_i$, we then optimize $\mathbf{v}_i$ according to the selected pair using LM method in step 5.

The key is to efficiently select the best candidate pair in step 4. For stereo-camera $\mathbf{s}_i$, $\sigma_i = w_S(\delta^2 + \varepsilon^2) + w_Q \gamma$. From Equation 5.5, we know $\delta^2 = A(\|\mathbf{t}^L\|^2 + \|\mathbf{t}^R\|^2)$, where A is an invariant if w, h, h_d, and f are fixed. So, for either $\|\mathbf{t}^L\| > \sqrt{\sigma/(Aw_S)}$ or $\|\mathbf{t}^R\| > \sqrt{\sigma/(Aw_S)}$, $w_S \delta^2 > \sigma$ is true. Hence, in the k-th iteration of the entire algorithm, we only select base camera pair candidates from those inside the spheres centered at left and right viewpoints with the radius equal to $\sqrt{\sigma_i^{[k-1]}/(Aw_S)}$, where $\sigma_i^{[k-1]}$ is the cost evaluated by using the values of $\Pi^L[i]$ and $\Pi^R[i]$ determined from the last iteration (or the $(k-1)$-th iteration), as shown in Figure 5.5. This scheme discards the inappropriate pairs, whose relevant cost $\sigma_i^{[k]}$ have:

$$\sigma_i^{[k]} \geq w_S(\delta^{[k]})^2 \geq \sigma_i^{[k-1]}, \qquad (5.10)$$

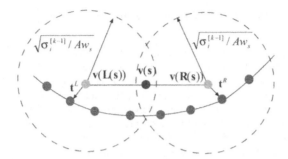

Fig. 5.5 The illustration of the determination of the appropriate base frames inside the spheres.

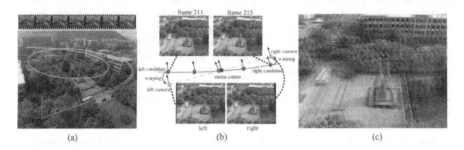

Fig. 5.6 An example of stereoscopic video generation. The input monocular video sequence is taken in the air. (a) shows the recovered base trajectory and a few frames from the base sequence. (b) illustrates the generation of a stereoscopic view pair. The blue dot coupled with 2 green dots indicate the virtual stereo-camera, where the green dots are the left and right cameras. (c) shows the composed stereo frame.

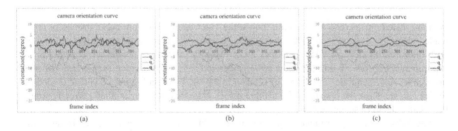

Fig. 5.7 Plots of Euler angles of the computed orientation. (a) is the recovered camera orientation of the base sequence (monocular video). (b) and (c) show the camera orientations of the corresponding stereo-camera computed with different w_{CQ} settings. In (b) $w_S = 1, w_Q = 100, w_{CQ} = 100, w_{CV} = 1$ while in (c) $w_S = 1, w_Q = 100, w_{CQ} = 10000, w_{CV} = 1$.

where $\sigma_i^{[k]}$ is the current cost. Therefore, for each candidate pair inside the spheres, its cost $\sigma_i^{[k]}$ is calculated. The candidate pair, whose cost is the minimum and less than $\sigma_i^{[k-1]}$, is the desired one. Their indices are assigned to $\Pi^L[i]$ and $\Pi^R[i]$ accordingly. If there is no pair satisfying Equation 5.10, the current $\Pi^L[i]$ and $\Pi^R[i]$ are retained.

5.5.3 Optimization for Visual Smoothness

To maintain the visual smoothness, we control the accelerations of both left and right eyes. The accelerations are computed by the second-order difference of the eye positions. This smoothness is determined by E_{CQ} and E_{CV}. While E_{CQ} can be optimized easily by LM method in step 2, the optimization of E_S and E_{CV} are highly dependent on $\mathbf{V}$, Π^L and Π^R, and has a high combinatorial complexity. In step 6 of the pseudocode, when the viewpoints of stereo-cameras are fixed, E_{CV} merely relies on the sum of the norm of the acceleration of the left and right eyes. Due to the symmetry, we only explain the left eye in the following discussion.

The shaky candidate cameras are those whose accelerations exceed a tolerance a_{max}. Whenever shaky candidate exists, we should modify our choice of candidate frames. In general, such change of choice should involve the whole candidate index sequence. In practice, we only perform a local adjustment by modifying a candidate index *subsequence* centered at the detected shaky candidate. To simplify the discussion, we only describe the adjustment on the left-view frame index sequence Π^L. The right-view frame Π^R is adjusted similarly. Consider the n-element subsequence $\{\Pi^L[k_o], \Pi^L[k_o + 1], ..., \Pi^L[k_o + n - 1]\}$ where $k_o + \lceil n/2 \rceil$ is the detected shaky element, for every element $\Pi^L[k_o + i] = l_i$, its new value after adjustment can be any value in the range of $[l_i - m, l_i + m]$. In most of our experiments, m is 3 and n is 10. For each possible replacement, $w_S E_S + w_Q E_Q + w_{CV} E_{CV}$ is recomputed and the one with the minimal $w_S E_S + w_Q E_Q + w_{CV} E_{CV}$ is selected for replacement in order to improve smoothness. Then we return to step 2, the viewpoints and orientations of stereo-camera are further optimized according to the updated Π^L and Π^R by means of the LM method.

Since in each iteration the overall cost E is guaranteed to be decreased, the iteration converges at a minimal point. Although it may not be a global optimal solution, convincing solutions are obtained in all of our experiments.

5.6 Results and Discussions

We have tested our method with several monocular video sequences from either movies or home-made video clips acquired via a hand-held video camera. All experiments are carried out on a PC with Intel Pentium IV 2.4 GHz CPU and 1 GB memory. Appealing results are obtained in our experiments. Figures 5.6 and 5.8 show two synthesized stereoscopic video sequences. The input monocular video sequence in Figure 5.6 is taken in the air. Video in Figure 5.8 is taken indoor. In Figure 5.8, we show the disparity of 5 sample pixels. Note that how our method correctly reflects the relative depth of scene objects.

The statistics of the four video sequences are listed in Table 9.4. In the table, d_{eye} is interocular distance, and μ is the penalty factor for parallax in y direction (see Equation 5.3). From the table, the optimization time is small. Camera tracking consumes most of the time. From our experiments, the number of iterations for the optimization is around 1 to 3. Such small number of iterations means that the initial solution is close to the optimal ones.

The weights in the cost function are user-specified. Table 9.4 lists their values. In our experiments, we set $w_S = w_{CV} = 1$, and $w_Q = 100$. The choice of w_{CQ} is highly dependent on the smoothness of the input video sequence. For the sequences extracted from professional movies (normally with smooth motion), w_{CQ} can be set to about 100. For the video captured by hand-held camera (like Figure 5.1), w_{CQ} should be greater than 100. Figure 5.7 shows the camera orientations (in Euler angles) of the base sequence and those of stereo sequence with different w_{CQ} settings. It shows that larger value of w_{CQ} leads to a smoother change of computed orientation, hence the result is less shaky. As the search window m of local adjustment for shaky camera (Section 5.5.3) increases, the smoothness of result also increases, but with the trade-off of higher computational cost. In our experiments, we found $m = 3$ is a good choice to balance the trade-off between the per-

Sequence in	Fig. 5.1	Fig. 5.6	Fig. 5.8	Fig. 5.10
Number of frame	431	861	441	370
Time for camera tracking	26 min.	80 min.	30 min.	22 min.
Iteration number of optimization	2	1	2	3
Time for optimization	27 sec.	20 sec.	35 sec.	21 sec.
Time for view warping and video output	10 min.	20 min.	10 min.	8 min.
d_{eye}	10	4	12	10
μ penalty factor for y dir.	4	4	4	4
w_S	1	1	1	1
w_Q	100	100	100	100
w_{CQ}	10,000	100	100	10,000
w_{CV}	1	1	1	1

Table 5.3 The performance statistics.

formance and quality. In general, adjusting the weights trades among the smoothness, stereoscopic effect and/or visual similarity.

Recall that in Section 5.3, we have justified why the simple but restrictive constant-depth view warping, instead of the more general planar-homography, is adopted. Figure 5.9(a) shows a stereo-frame from view warping with the planar-homography. Note that the building and streetlamps in the left and right synthetic views are not parallel. This artifact can be easily recognized by human vision. Even worse, some farther objects have much larger disparities than those closer objects. In contrast, the result from the constant-depth view warping (Figure 5.9(b)) does not cause similar objectionable artifacts.

Since no depth map is used, our approach has some limitations.

1. The scene should be static, otherwise the moving objects will be warped incorrectly. Because the left-eye and right-eye views are the warping results of the input frames at different time instances, warping them results in inconsistent object motion. Nevertheless, human vision may accept small inconsistent movements.
2. As our method relies on the motion parallax to synthesize the stereo parallax, it fails when there is no horizontal parallax in the input video. Examples include the case when the video is captured from a fixed viewpoint, the case when the viewing and motion directions coincide (Figure 5.10), and when the input video contains only vertical motion.
3. Our method tries to minimize the relative parallax error and warping error, and keep them consistent. However, since it is based on a crude *constant-depth* assumption, a large relative parallax/warping error may still occur and not be quite consistent in some cases. For example, when a originally panning camera suddenly changes its trajectory and moves forward, it is very difficult to keep all the parallaxes consistent. In this case, the objects whose depths are close to the optimal depth value (i.e. $z_c = 2(z_{min}^{-1} + z_{max}^{-1})^{-1}$) have more consistent parallaxes. On the other hand, the parallaxes of the objects whose depths are far away from the optimal depth value may be jittered. In practice, the regions with inconsistent parallaxes are usually not the visual focus and human vision have a higher tolerance.
4. If the focal length of input video varies, the output video may contain error. The simplest way to work around the problem is to preprocess the input video. A more sophisticated approach is to incorporate focal-length variation in the cost function. This is one of our future directions.

Fig. 5.8 Another example of stereoscopic video generation. (a) shows the recovered base trajectory. The two images in the (c) and (d) are the warping result of the base frames, and form a stereoscopic view pair in the result. The arrows in the images show the degree of binocular parallax of five points in the scene. It can be found that the remote points have the small parallax, whereas the near points have the large ones. (b) is the composition image of (c) and (d).

Fig. 5.9 Comparison of planar-homography and constant-depth view warping. In (a), the building and the streetlamps in the left and right views are not parallel. Moreover, some farther objects even have much larger disparities than those nearer ones. Not similar objectionable artifact are found in the result from constant-depth warping (b).

5.7 Conclusions

In this paper, we present a novel automatic synthesis of stereoscopic video sequence from the monocular one. Instead of recovering the depth map, we exploit the motion parallax. This allows us to avoid the objectionable visual artifact due to the inaccurately recovered 3D information. We formulate the video synthesis problem as an optimization problem. The introduced cost function considers the stereoscopic effects, the similarity, and the smoothness objectives. Users can adjust the weights to trade among these three objectives. Convincing results evidence the robustness and the efficiency of our approach. Despite of limitations, the proposed method is useful in many scenarios in which the video contains the panning motion.

(a)   (b)

Fig. 5.10 A poor example of stereoscopic video generation. The input monocular sequence is taken by a hand-held camera moving in the direction of the camera viewing direction. (a) shows the recovered base trajectory. Since the angle between the moving direction and the viewing direction is very small, the binocular parallax is hard to be converted from the motion parallax. As the result, all binocular parallax of the sample points in the scene are almost identical, and the generated stereoscopic video does not properly show the depth cue.

Acknowledgments

We would like to thank all reviewers for their valuable suggestions to improve the paper. Thanks to Xiaohuang Huang and Yuanlong Shao for their help during video production. This work is supported by 973 Program of China (No. 2002CB312104) and NSF of China (No. 60633070), and partially affiliated with the CUHK Virtual Reality, Visualization and Imaging Research Centre as well as the Microsoft-CUHK Joint Laboratory for Human-Centric Computing and Interface Technologies.

Appendix

Assume the coordinate system is set to align with the left camera (right camera), and the camera views along z-axis. Refer to Table 5.4 for the meaning of the notations used in this appendix. Then the position of the candidate camera is $\mathbf{t} = (\mathbf{t}_x, \mathbf{t}_y, \mathbf{t}_z)$. For simplicity, we assume the candidate camera and left (right) camera have the same orientation. If their orientations are different, we can rectify them beforehand. Without loss of generality, we choose a pixel p which 3D homogeneous coordinate is $(x, y, 1, 1/z)$ in the coordinate system of the candidate camera. From the candidate camera to the left (right) camera, its coordinate becomes $\left(\frac{xz+\mathbf{t}_x}{z+\mathbf{t}_z}, \frac{yz+\mathbf{t}_y}{z+\mathbf{t}_z}, 1, 1/(z+\mathbf{t}_z)\right)$. Then the offset in the image is $d = \left(f\frac{\mathbf{t}_x - x\mathbf{t}_z}{z+\mathbf{t}_z}, f\frac{\mathbf{t}_y - y\mathbf{t}_z}{z+\mathbf{t}_z}\right)^{\top}$. For convenience, we replace $z + \mathbf{t}_z$ with z by simply offset the coordinate, hence $d = \left(f\frac{\mathbf{t}_x - x\mathbf{t}_z}{z}, f\frac{\mathbf{t}_y - y\mathbf{t}_z}{z}\right)^{\top}$. We assume the depths of scene are in the range of $[z_{min}, z_{max}]$. During the view warping, we assume the depth is constant and equal to $z_c = 2(z_{min}^{-1} + z_{max}^{-1})^{-1}$ over the whole image. This results in $d^W = \left(f\frac{\mathbf{t}_x - x\mathbf{t}_z}{z_c}, f\frac{\mathbf{t}_y - y\mathbf{t}_z}{z_c}\right)^{\top}$. Here, we define Δd as the offset error due to the uncertainty of depth.

$$\Delta d = \left(f(\mathbf{t}_x - x\mathbf{t}_z)(\tfrac{1}{z_c} - \tfrac{1}{z}), f(\mathbf{t}_y - y\mathbf{t}_z)(\tfrac{1}{z_c} - \tfrac{1}{z})\right)^{\top}$$
$$\leq \tfrac{fh_d}{2}(|\mathbf{t}_x - x\mathbf{t}_z|, |\mathbf{t}_y - y\mathbf{t}_z|)^{\top}$$

Since $|x_i| \leq \frac{w}{2f}, |y_i| \leq \frac{h}{2f}$, we have

$p_i(x_i, y_i, 1, 1/z_i)$	the homogeneous 3D coordinate of pixel i.
z_i	the depth of pixel i.
w, h	the width and height of the image.
f	the focal length.
$t^L(t^R)$	the relative translation between left (right) and the candidate cameras.
D_i	the parallax of pixel i.
D_i^W	the parallax of pixel i warping with constant depth z_c.
$d_i^L(d_i^R)$	the image offset of pixel i between left (right) and candidate cameras.
$d_i^{LW}(d_i^{RW})$	the image offset of pixel i between left (right) and candidate cameras warping with constant depth z_c.
e_{ij}	the relative parallax error between pixels i and j.

Table 5.4 Notations used in the Appendix.

$$\|\Delta d\| \le \tfrac{1}{2}fh_d\sqrt{(t_x - xt_z)^2 + (t_y - yt_z)^2}$$
$$\le \tfrac{1}{2}fh_d\sqrt{(|t_x| + \tfrac{w}{2f}|t_z|)^2 + (|t_y| + \tfrac{h}{2f}|t_z|)^2}$$
$$\le \tfrac{\sqrt{2}}{2}fh_d \max\left(1, \tfrac{\sqrt{w^2+h^2}}{2f}\right)\|t\|$$

Therefore, considering the parallax errors of both left and right cameras, we obtain Equation 5.5.

Next, we derive Equation 5.3. For any pixel $p_i(x_i, y_i, 1, 1/z_i)$ in the coordinate system of the candidate camera, having the following:

$$d_i^L = \begin{pmatrix} \frac{t_x^L - x_i^L t_z^L}{z_i}f \\ \frac{t_y^L - y_i^L t_z^L}{z_i}f \end{pmatrix}, d_i^{LW} = \begin{pmatrix} \frac{t_x^L - x_i^L t_z^L}{z_c}f \\ \frac{t_y^L - y_i^L t_z^L}{z_c}f \end{pmatrix}$$

$$d_i^R = \begin{pmatrix} \frac{t_x^R - x_i^R t_z^R}{z_i}f \\ \frac{t_y^R - y_i^R t_z^R}{z_i}f \end{pmatrix}, d_i^{RW} = \begin{pmatrix} \frac{t_x^R - x_i^R t_z^R}{z_c}f \\ \frac{t_y^R - y_i^R t_z^R}{z_c}f \end{pmatrix}$$

$$D_i^W = D_i + (d_i^{LW} - d_i^{RW}) - (d_i^L - d_i^R)$$

Then the relative parallax error between pixels i and j:

$$e_{ij} = (D_i^W - D_j^W) - (D_i - D_j)$$
$$= (d_i^{LW} - d_i^{RW}) - (d_i^L - d_i^R) - ((d_j^{LW} - d_j^{RW}) - (d_j^L - d_j^R))$$
$$= f\begin{pmatrix} -(t_x^L - t_x^R)(\frac{1}{z_i} - \frac{1}{z_j}) + P_x^L t_z^L - P_x^R t_z^R \\ -(t_y^L - t_y^R)(\frac{1}{z_i} - \frac{1}{z_j}) + P_y^L t_z^L - P_y^R t_z^R \end{pmatrix}$$
$$\le fh_d\begin{pmatrix} |t_x^L - t_x^R| + (|t_z^L| + |t_z^R|)\frac{w}{2f} \\ |t_y^L - t_y^R| + (|t_z^L| + |t_z^R|)\frac{h}{2f} \end{pmatrix}$$

Here,

$$P_x^L = x_i^L(\tfrac{1}{z_i} - \tfrac{1}{z_c}) - x_j^L(\tfrac{1}{z_j} - \tfrac{1}{z_c}), P_x^R = x_i^R(\tfrac{1}{z_i} - \tfrac{1}{z_c}) - x_j^R(\tfrac{1}{z_j} - \tfrac{1}{z_c})$$
$$P_y^L = y_i^L(\tfrac{1}{z_i} - \tfrac{1}{z_c}) - y_j^L(\tfrac{1}{z_j} - \tfrac{1}{z_c}), P_y^R = y_i^R(\tfrac{1}{z_i} - \tfrac{1}{z_c}) - y_j^R(\tfrac{1}{z_j} - \tfrac{1}{z_c})$$

Hence, we obtain Equation 5.3.

References

1. T. Okoshi, *Three-Dimensional Imaging Techniques*, Academic Press, 1976.

2. W. Matusik and H. Pfister, "3D TV: a scalable system for real-time acquisition, transmission, and autostereoscopic display of dynamic scenes," *ACM Trans. Graph.*, vol. 23, no. 3, pp. 814–824, 2004.
3. E. H. Adelson and J. R. Bergen, "The plenoptic function and the elements of early vision," in *Computational Models of Visual Processing*, M. S. Landy and J. A. Movshon, Eds. MIT Press, 1991, ch. 1, pp. 3–20.
4. D. V. Morland, "Computer-generated stereograms: a new dimension for the graphic arts," in *SIGGRAPH '76: Proceedings of the 3rd annual conference on Computer graphics and interactive techniques.* New York, NY, USA: ACM Press, 1976, pp. 19–24.
5. Y. Matsumoto, H. Terasaki, K. Sugimoto, and T. Arakawa, "Conversion system of monocular image sequence to stereo using motion parallax," in *Proc. of SPIE Stereo. Disp. and VR Sys*, vol. 3012, May 1997, pp. 108–115.
6. P. Harman, "Home based 3D entertainment - an overview." in *IEEE Intl. Conf. on Image Processing*, 2000, pp. 1–4.
7. D. Scharstein and R. Szeliski, "A taxonomy and evaluation of dence two-frame stereo correspondence algorithms," *International Journal of Computer Vision*, vol. 47, no. 1/2/3, pp. 7–42, April – June 2002.
8. R. Hartley and A. Zisserman, *Multiple View Geometry in Computer Vision.* Cambridge University Press, 2000.
9. Y. Lu, J. Z. Zhang, Q. M. J. Wu, and Z.-N. Li, "A survey of motion-parallax-based 3D reconstruction algorithms," *IEEE Transaction on SMC-C*, vol. 34, no. 4, pp. 532–548, December 2004.
10. H.-Y. Shum and S. B. Kang, "A review of image-based rendering techniques," in *Proc. of IEEE/SPIE Visual Communications and Image Processing (VCIP)*, 2000, pp. 2–13.
11. C. Bregler, M. F. Cohen, P. Debevec, L. McMillan, F. X. Sillion, and R. Szeliski, "Image-based modeling, rendering, and lighting," in *SIGGRAPH 1999 Course #39*, 1999.
12. M. Levoy and P. Hanrahan, "Light field rendering," in *SIGGRAPH '96: Proceedings of the 23rd annual conference on Computer graphics and interactive techniques.* New York, NY, USA: ACM Press, 1996, pp. 31–42.
13. J.-X. Chai, X. Tong, S.-C. Chan, and H.-Y. Shum, "Plenoptic sampling," in *SIGGRAPH '00: Proceedings of the 27th annual conference on Computer graphics and interactive techniques.* New York, NY, USA: ACM Press/Addison-Wesley Publishing Co., 2000, pp. 307–318.
14. S. J. Gortler, R. Grzeszczuk, R. Szeliski, and M. F. Cohen, "The lumigraph," in *SIGGRAPH '96: Proceedings of the 23rd annual conference on Computer graphics and interactive techniques.* New York, NY, USA: ACM Press, 1996, pp. 43–54.
15. W. R. Mark, L. McMillan, and G. Bishop, "Post-rendering 3D warping," in *SI3D '97: Proceedings of the 1997 symposium on Interactive 3D graphics.* New York, NY, USA: ACM Press, 1997, pp. 7–ff.
16. S. E. Chen and L. Williams, "View interpolation for image synthesis," in *SIGGRAPH '93: Proceedings of the 20th annual conference on Computer graphics and interactive techniques.* New York, NY, USA: ACM Press, 1993, pp. 279–288.
17. S. M. Seitz and C. R. Dyer, "View morphing," in *SIGGRAPH '96: Proceedings of the 23rd annual conference on Computer graphics and interactive techniques*, NY, USA: ACM Press, 1996, pp. 21–30.
18. Y. Horry, K. Anjyo, and K. Arai, "Tour into the picture: Using a spidery mesh interface to make animation from a single image," in *SIGGRAPH '97: Proceedings of the 24th annual conference on Computer graphics and interactive techniques*, Los Angeles, 1997, pp. 225–232.
19. J. Shade, S. Gortler, L. wei He, and R. Szeliski, "Layered depth images," in *SIGGRAPH '98: Proceedings of the 25th annual conference on Computer graphics and interactive techniques.* New York, NY, USA: ACM Press, 1998, pp. 231–242.
20. H. S. Sawhney, Y. Guo, K. Hanna, R. Kumar, S. Adkins, and S. Zhou, "Hybrid stereo camera: an IBR approach for synthesis of very high resolution stereoscopic image sequences,"

in *SIGGRAPH '01: Proceedings of the 28th annual conference on Computer graphics and interactive techniques*. New York, NY, USA: ACM Press, 2001, pp. 451–460.

21. M. Magnor, M. Pollefeys, G. Cheung, W. Matusik, and C. Theobalt,"Video-based rendering," in *SIGGRAPH 2005 Course #16*, 2005.

22. C. L. Zitnick, S. B. Kang, M. Uyttendaele, S. Winder, and R. Szeliski, "High-quality video view interpolation using a layered representation," *ACM Trans. Graph.*, vol. 23, no. 3, pp. 600–608, 2004.

23. J. Carranza, C. Theobalt, M. A. Magnor, and H.-P. Seidel, "Free-viewpoint video of human actors," *ACM Trans. Graph.*, vol. 22, no. 3, pp. 569–577, 2003.

24. H. Huang and Y. Hung, "Panoramic stereo imaging system with automatic disparity warping and seaming," in *Proceedings of International Conference on Image Processing and Character Recognition (ICS'96)*, December 1996, pp. 48–55.

25. S. Peleg, M. Ben-Ezra, and Y. Pritch, "Omnistereo: Panoramic stereo imaging," *IEEE Transaction on Pattern Ananlysis and Machine Intellegence*, vol. 23, no. 3, pp. 279–290, 2001.

26. C. T. Loop and Z. Zhang, "Computing rectifying homographies for stereo vision." in *CVPR*, 1999, pp. 1125–1131.

27. E. Rotem, K. Wolowelsky, and D. Pelz,"Automatic video to stereoscopic video conversion," A. J. Woods, M. T. Bolas, J. O. Merritt, and I. E. McDowall, Eds., vol. 5664, no. 1.SPIE, 2005, pp. 198–206. [Online]. Available: http://link.aip.org/link/?PSI/5664/198/1

28. A. Fitzgibbon and A. Zisserman, "Automatic camera tracking," in *Video Registration*, M. Shah and R. Kumar, Eds. Kluwer, 2003, ch. 2, pp. 18–35.

29. M. Pollefeys, L. J. V. Gool, M. Vergauwen, F. Verbiest, K. Cornelis, J. Tops, and R. Koch, "Visual modeling with a hand-held camera." *International Journal of Computer Vision*, vol. 59, no. 3, pp. 207–232, 2004.

30. G. Zhang, X. Qin, X. An, W. Chen, and H. Bao, "As-consistent-as-possible compositing of virtual objects and video sequences." *Computer Animation and Virtual Worlds*, vol. 17, no. 3-4, pp. 305–314, 2006.

31. T. W. Backhouse, "Absolute and relative parallax," *The Observatory*, vol. 11, pp. 343–343, Sept. 1888.

32. Z. Duric and A. Rosenfeld, "Stabilization of image sequences," University of Maryland, Tech. Rep. CAR-TR-778, July 1995.

Chapter 6
ShapePalettes: Interactive Normal Transfer via Sketching[*]

Tai-Pang Wu, Chi-Keung Tang, Michael S. Brown and Heung-Yeung Shum

Fig. 6.1 An example of 3D markup using *Shape Palettes*. The 'question mug' is created by linking 2D primitives drawn in the freehand view to their corresponding 3D shape on the "shape palette" (the sphere). For example, the 3D orientation of the top and bottom curves of the mug correspond to the 3D orientation of the green curve on the shape palette. Specifying this relationship will generate a cylinder-like structure. Adding only a few more strokes for extra details and the 'question mug' is created.

Abstract We present a simple interactive approach to specify 3D shape in a single view using "shape palettes". The interaction is as follows: draw a simple 2D primitive in the 2D view and then specify its 3D orientation by drawing a corresponding primitive on a *shape palette*. The shape palette is presented as an image of some familiar shape whose local 3D orientation is readily understood and can be easily marked over. The 3D orientation from the shape palette is transferred to the 2D primitive based on the markup. As we will demonstrate, only sparse markup is needed to generate expressive and detailed 3D surfaces. This markup approach can be used to model freehand 3D surfaces drawn in a single view, or combined with image-snapping tools to quickly extract surfaces from images and photographs.

Key words: Human-computer interaction, interactive modeling, image-based modeling.

Tai-Pang Wu and Chi-Keung Tang
The Hong Kong University of Science and Technology

Michael S. Brown
Nanyang Technological University

Heung-Yeung Shum
Microsoft Research Asia

* Source: Proceedings of ACM SIGGRAPH2007 Article No.44, 2007 Copyright ©2007 Association for Computing Machinery, Inc. Reprinted by permission. DOI Bookmark: http://doi.acm.org/10.1145/1275808.1276432

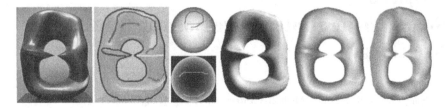

Fig. 6.2 Markup over a photograph using shape palettes. Sparse 2D strokes are drawn over a photograph of Henry Moore's *Working Model for Oval with Points*. The shape palette provides the user a straightforward metaphor to link 3D orientation to the 2D strokes. Dense surface normals are derived from the sparse markup (middle image). A 3D surface is generated from the dense normal image as shown in the last two images. Note the overall similarity to the photograph with details preserved in the reconstruction, including the two silhouetted points which just fail to touch each other at the center of the object.

6.1 Motivation

Humans have a remarkable ability to infer 3D structure from 2D images. This ability is applicable to items ranging from photographs and paintings to simple sketches and line art. Often only a few 2D strokes are necessary to express the 3D shape of an object – the observer instantly makes the analogy of each 2D stroke to its corresponding 3D shape and can infer the overall 3D surface. While this inference is done mentally without effort, it remains difficult to convey this information easily via a 2D interface. The problem lies not in *what* to specify, but in *how* to specify the 3D information.

To address this issue of *how* to specify 3D information, we introduce an approach based on what we term *shape palettes*. In our approach, the user draws a simple 2D primitive in the single view. To assign 3D information to this primitive, the user then draws a corresponding primitive on a shape palette. The shape palette is an image of some familiar object that provides salient 3D orientation information that can be easily understood and marked. For example, a single sphere serves as an excellent shape palette as its shape is universally understood and it provides all possible 3D orientations (in a half-plane).

Similar in fashion to how color palettes are used for color selection, the shape palette provides a familiar metaphor for linking 3D information to the 2D input. As we will demonstrate, this simple interaction approach can be used to create expressive 3D surfaces. Moreover, only sparse markup is necessary to derive dense 3D structure. This interaction style has a variety of uses, from single-view surface modeling, to image-based markup for 3D pop-up or image-relighting.

Figure 6.1 shows an example of a 'mug' that was quickly prototyped using only a few freehand strokes marked up using a shape palette. The first image is the sketched strokes with corresponding markup on the shape palette (second image). The third image is the dense 3D information derived from the sparse markup. The last two images are views of the 3D model that was generated by stitching together a reflected copy of the derived 3D surface. Figure 6.2 shows another example targeting modeling from a photograph. In this example, 2D features in the photograph are related to their corresponding 3D shape using the shape palette. The examples in Figure 6.1 and Figure 6.2 were generated in a matter of minutes with little effort.

6.2 Contributions and Related Work

Our first contribution is the *shape palette* metaphor, which is an intuitive and straightforward way to address the problem of how to specify 3D markup in a single view. A shape palette is simply a 2D image that corresponds to some 3D geometric information easily inferred by the user. One very good example used throughout this paper is a Lambertian shaded sphere. Using a 2D drawing interface, 3D information from the shape palette is transferred to a single 2D view by direct 2D interaction. This allows 3D markup to be specified using the familiar palette metaphor, similar to how color is specified by most drawing tools.

Our second contribution is *one* practical way to implement shape palette markup using surface normals. In our implementation, shape palettes are in fact normal maps. The transfer of 3D shape is a transfer of 3D normal information, copied from the shape palette source to its corresponding 2D primitive. Reasonably complex and expressive 3D structure can be generated using this normals transfer together with some simple transfer "tricks" to provide local detail. Integrating this approach with image-snapping tools, sketches and photographs of 3D surfaces can be quickly "popped up" and used for a variety of purposes.

In terms of information transfer, our method is related to [Sloan et al. 2001] that used a user-generated reference sphere to specify NPR shading for a 3D object. A similar idea on normal transfer was presented in [Hertzmann and Seitz 2005], where multiple images are required and surface normals are transferred based on orientation-consistency. Our ShapePalette idea is also inspired by Pictorial Relief [Koenderink 1998] which suggests that humans are good at assigning local surface normals for specifying local shape. Such local shapes can be, as noted in [DeCarlo et al. 2003; Ohtake et al. 2004], expressed as 3D crease curves, such as valleys and ridges, which provide adequate geometric cues for describing the overall appearance of a detailed 3D surface. These 3D crease curves correspond to salient normal directions on the 3D surface [Nalwa 1993]. Thus, specifying normals is a powerful way to encode up 3D shape. Moreover, only sparse normal information is needed from which a dense normal map can be derived that is capable of generating quality 3D surfaces that satisfy the given normal constraints. An algorithm to derive dense-from-spare normal maps is described in Appendix 6.6. Our approach is related to [van Overveld 1996], which creates shapes by painting a dense gradient map with brushes and operators. Our method, however, is sparse in nature and could be used as a good initializer for further dense refinement using the technique presented by [van Overveld 1996].

Our work is also motivated by single-view and interactive modeling techniques. Successful techniques such as [Criminisi et al. 2000; Hoiem et al. 2005] create rectilinear scenes out of a single photo or picture. The "SmoothSketch"[Karpenko and Hughes 2006] is a successful experimental system for inferring 3D shapes from visible-contour sketches. Many sketch-based modeling techniques (e.g. SKETCH [Zeleznik et al. 1996] and TEDDY [Igarashi et al. 1999]) provide an intuitive interface for creating organic shapes. Interactive modeling techniques such as [Funkhouser et al. 2004; Nealen et al. 2005] edit existing meshes or assemble complex meshes from mesh parts. Our work is distinguished from previous approach in terms of *how* we markup the 3D shape, in our case using the shape palette.

In terms of implementation,[Zhang et al. 2001] also used normal specification to perform 3D modeling. This method considers both height and surface normals and minimizes a thin plate energy to produce a 3D surface. While only sparse normal information is required, this approach performs normal markup in a pointwise fashion. Such pointwise normal markup is time consuming and is not particularly easy to markup for an evolving surface (as shown in our accompanying video). Moreover, a significant number of these constraints are needed to produce a quality 3D surface.

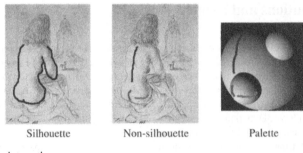

Silhouette   Non-silhouette   Palette

Fig. 6.3 User interaction.

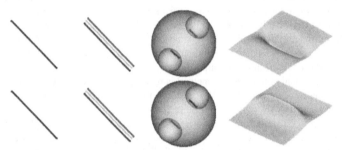

Fig. 6.4 Creating valley (top) and ridge lines (bottom) with two strokes drawn along the black contour and two corresponding strokes on the shape palette.

6.3 Interacting with Shape Palettes

Creating shape palettes. A shape palette can be easily generated using orthographic projection of available 3D models, where the palette stores the inner product of a synthetic light and the 3D normal at that point (i.e. Lambertian shading). There are no restrictions on a shape palette as long as it is a familiar shape with salient 3D structure. To represent all possible normal orientations, an image containing both a concave and convex sphere is sufficient, however, the shape palette can be anything the user feels comfortable using. We find that spheres are quite intuitive. Spheres of different scales can also make marking scale a little easier, but is not necessary.

In the accompanying video, we demonstrate that the markup for creating a particular shape need not be that exact. Users can experiment with different ways to draw and combine strokes to quickly materialize 3D shapes.

User Interface. A typical 2D drawing interface allows the user to draw on top of a blank canvas, or a canvas with a photograph/sketch for the background. For a blank canvas, 2D primitives are drawn freehand on the canvas as well as on the shape palette. For drawing over a photograph or sketch, image-snapping tools (intelligent scissor [Mortensen and Barrett 1995] for instance) can be used to help guide 2D markup on the image, while freehand drawing is used for marking on the shape palettes.

As shown in Figure 6.3, there are two types of 2D contours drawn on the canvas, those that form silhouette curves and those that form non-silhouettes. *Silhouettes* do not require 3D markup as their corresponding normals are considered to lie in the canvas plane and are oriented perpendicular to the 2D drawn curves. *Non-silhouettes* curves have corresponding markup on the shape palettes. In our implementation, non-silhouette curves are typically drawn in a tit for tat fashion with the shape palette, where the user draws a 2D stroke on the canvas and then draws a corresponding 2D stroke on the shape palette.

Markup via Palettes. For a non-silhouette curve, the user draws a corresponding primitive on a shape palette. Normals from the shape palette are transferred to the 2D primitive. This markup can be casually applied to specify orientation information throughout the 2D view. The following

Fig. 6.5 3D modeling of a statuette: (left to right) user supplied strokes; two views of the derived dense normal maps shown using Lambertian shading; four views of the 3D shape.

Fig. 6.6 Parthenon frieze (modeling relief texture conveying human shapes): (left to right) Input image with input strokes; derived dense normal map shown using Lambertian shading; four views of the texture-mapped surface

Logo   Strokes on logo Strokes on palette Dense normals   View 1   View 2

Fig. 6.7 3D markup of the SIGGRAPH logo.

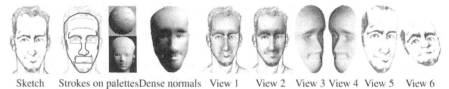

Sketch   Strokes on palettes Dense normals View 1   View 2   View 3 View 4 View 5   View 6

Fig. 6.8 Face modeling. 3D markup of more complex shapes, such as eyes and mouth, can be easily done using the "face shape palette". The face model is used for image-based relighting (views 1 and 2). Other views (without and with texture-mapped) are shown.

simple "tricks" can be quickly learned to add fine surface details in the form of ridge and valley lines. As shown in Figure 6.4, two contours (red and blue) bound the input contour where a ridge or valley is desired. Generating such bounding contours pairs can be controlled via a hot-key. Corresponding strokes on the shape palette are drawn for the contour pair. If the corresponding strokes are of normals pointing away from one another, a ridge will be generated; normals pointing towards one another will form a valley. As shown in the accompanying video, a user can experiment with different locations of strokes drawn on the palettes and can visualize the corresponding 3D effect almost instantly.

Given these sparse normal constraints, we can derive a dense normal field. Our implementation of the dense-from-sparse-normals algorithm is outlined in the appendix. A 3D surface is generated by integrating the dense surface gradients, or by other surface-from-dense-normals algorithms such as [Kovesi 2005; Frankot and Chellappa 1988; Goldman et al. 2005; Wu et al. 2006].

6.4 Shape Palettes in Use

When specifying markup between the 2D view and a shape palette, the length of the corresponding strokes and the relative scale between the 2D view and shape palette are not important. Transfer is applied as simple 1D copying along the corresponding strokes. This is done by parameterizing the two strokes as normalized splines (with length $[0-1]$) and transferring data between these splines. In addition, our dense-from-sparse normal algorithm does not require accurate normal specification to capture coarse shape and degrades gracefully in the face of bad input. The accompany video shows examples where the same overall surface is obtained with similar, but not exact, markup.

We demonstrate the ability of our 3D markup approach in the following examples. Unless otherwise stated, all results are generated using the sphere shape palette. Figure 6.5 shows an example where strokes are drawn on two matchable views of a statuette. Figure 6.6 shows an example of modeling relief texture using a photo input. This relief texture is complicated as both overlapping curved surfaces and flat surfaces are present. Note that all underlying surface orientation discontinuities are preserved in the reconstruction. The appearance of the reconstructed relief is faithful to the original relief. As shown in Figure 6.7, our shape palettes approach is ideal for quick 3D prototyping. The user draws a short stroke on the palette to transfer normals of nearly constant orientations to model the flat part of the SIGGRAPH logo.

Figure 6.8 shows a natural extension of the shape palette idea where patches of normals are transferred to the 2D view. In this example, a "face shape palette" was created by orthographic projection of an existing 3D face model. The eyes and mouth shape are transferred to the single view by specifying matching points between the 2D view and shape palette. Normals from the shape palette are warped to their corresponding regions using Thin Plate Spline (TPS) [Bookstein 1989].]. The derived dense normal image are used to shade and relight the sketch. Related works such as [jJohnston 2002; Okabe et al. 2006] which relight cartoons and real scenes using dense normals can benefit from our markup approach. Other views of the recovered surface (with and without texture) are also shown. Shown in Figure 6.9 is a result where a hair-structure shape palette is used for normal transfer.

The output dense normal maps produced by our method are suitable for generating special effects that require geometric information. Figure 6.10 shows an example which simulates the effect of environment matting for an opaque-turned-to-transparent object, where a few sketch strokes are all it takes to produce the surface normals needed for ray tracing.

6.5 Discussion and Limitations

To examine the usability of our approach, we compare our system with a related work by [Zhang et al. 2001] in terms of the number of primitives drawn and the interaction time used, given that surfaces of comparable visual quality are produced.

The comparison is performed by a user who is reasonably familiar with both ShapePalettes and [Zhang et al. 2001]. Table 6.1 shows the interaction details and the time required for the examples. The corresponding surface results produced by using [Zhang et al. 2001] are shown in Figure 6.11. Better surfaces are produced with shorter interaction time using the ShapePalette markup approach. Note that there is no way to incorporate normal patches to assign surface details (e.g., Figure 6.8) in [Zhang et al. 2001]. Matter of fact, the interface in [Zhang et al. 2001] could benefit from our shape palette approach for specifying normals.

Our method is not without limitations and has room for improvement. Our system can currently only model single surfaces that exhibit little self-occlusion. An example is shown in Figure 6.12. Distortion is observed in the output surface because of the enforcement of the integrability constraint in the applied surface-from-normals method. We also assume the input sketch or photo does not have severe perspective distortion. Even with these limitations, however, the shape palette

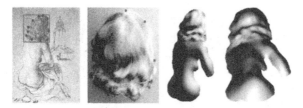

Fig. 6.9 Normals from a "hair shape palette" are transferred to the corresponding region in the 2D view. Additional markup is shown in Figure 3. The output dense normals and one view of the 3D surface are shown.

Fig. 6.10 With the locations and normals of *Oval*, we render the geometry using ray tracing with the Phong illumination model to make the object transparent.

markup approach still provides an attractive method of 3D markup given its ease and straightforward use.

| Input | Image size | ShapePalettes | | | [Zhang et al. 2001] | | | |
		No. of strokes on canvas	No. of patches	**Interaction time**	No. of normal constraints	No. of fairness curves	No. of discontinuity curves	**Interaction time**
Figure 1	274 × 284	14	0	**1m28s**	0	5	4	**3m46s**
Figure 2	220 × 250	11	0	**1m27s**	32	7	3	**6m57s**
Figure 5	244 × 342	38	0	**2m20s**	73	0	16	**5m45s**
Figure 6	306 × 324	75	0	**2m38s**	41	9	27	**20m27s**
Figure 7	491 × 307	23	0	**4m27s**	13	20	2	**15m41s**
Figure 8	225 × 334	15	3	**1m32s**	10	1	6	**5m32s**

Table 6.1 The table compares the interaction details between ShapePalettes and [Zhang et al. 2001]. As shown in Figure 6.11, ShapePalettes can produce visually better surfaces with shorter interaction time. Note that the normal constraints used in [Zhang et al. 2001] are specified in a pointwise manner, where each normal direction needs to be adjusted with a projected line using a series of mouse click-and-drag. Please refer to the accompanying video to compare the actual operation on results shown in Figures 1 and 5.

6.6 Summary

We have presented the shape palette metaphor for 3D markup and introduced an implementation based on normals. We have only begun to explore the potential of this approach to materialize 3D information from 2D marking, and can already demonstrate the immediate benefits from this approach on common tasks ranging from 3D markup over photos and sketches, image-based modeling and rendering, freehand 3D modeling, to quick 3D prototyping. This technique can lead to more, possibly complementary uses with other interaction techniques in traditional and image-based modeling.

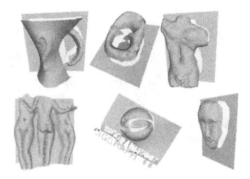

Fig. 6.11 Surface results produced by using [Zhang et al. 2001]. Interaction details are shown in Table 6.1.

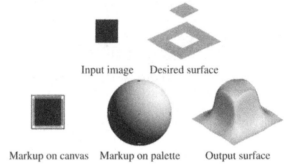

Fig. 6.12 This example shows a limitation of our system. Occlusion boundary with unknown depth difference cannot be handled.

Dense Normals from Sparse Normals

Denote a normal using $\frac{1}{\sqrt{p^2+q^2+1}}[-p \ -q \ 1]^T$ where $p = -\frac{x_i}{z_i}$ and $q = -\frac{y_i}{z_i}$ associated with a unit normal $[x_i \ y_i \ z_i]^T$ at pixel i. One typical implementation of estimating p_i is outlined for all pixels. Estimation of q_i is similar.

Let $\mathbf{G} = \{p_i | i \in 1 \cdots N\}$ be a set of p's and N is the total number of pixels. The goal is to estimate the optimal $\mathbf{G}$ given the sparse set of known gradient values, represented by the observation set $\mathbf{O} = \{\tilde{p}_k | k \in \mathscr{S}\}$, where $\tilde{p}_k$ is known and $\mathscr{S}$ is the set of corresponding pixel locations. The associated energy function is

$$E(\mathbf{G}) = \log(P(\mathbf{O}|\mathbf{G})) + \log(P(\mathbf{G})) \qquad (6.1)$$

where $P(\mathbf{O}|\mathbf{G})$ is the likelihood and $P(\mathbf{G})$ is the prior. The likelihood are defined as

$$P(\mathbf{O}|\mathbf{G}) = \prod_{k \in \mathscr{S}} \exp\left(-\frac{||p_k - \tilde{p}_k||^2}{2\sigma_1^2}\right) \qquad (6.2)$$

The prior $P(\mathbf{G})$ is defined as:

$$\prod_i \prod_j \exp\left(-\frac{||p_i - p_j||^2}{2\sigma_2^2}\right) \prod_i \exp\left(-\frac{||\Sigma_j p_j - 4p_i||^2}{2\sigma_3^2}\right) \qquad (6.3)$$

where $\sigma_1, \sigma_2, \sigma_3$ are the respective uncertainty measurements, and $j \in \mathscr{N}(i)$ is the pixel locations of the first-order neighbors of i. The first exponent in the prior energy (6.3) enforces the smoothness of the normal orientation, while the second minimizes the surface curvature. The energy function (6.1) is convex. Standard numerical optimization packages can be used to solve (6.1).

Acknowledgment

This research was supported in part by the Hong Kong Special Administrative Region under grant HKUST620006. We thank Zhang et al. for their single view modeling program, and Ying-Qing Xu and the anonymous SIGGRAPH reviewers for their constructive comments and recommendations.

6.7 References

BOOKSTEIN, F. 1989. Principal warps: Thin-plate splines and the decomposition of deformations. PAMI 11, 6 (June), 567C585.

CRIMINISI, A., REID, I., AND ZISSERMAN, A. 2000. Single view metrology. IJCV 40, 2 (November), 123C148.

DECARLO, D., FINKELSTEIN, A., RUSINKIEWICZ, S., AND SANTELLA, A. 2003. Suggestive contours for conveying shape. ACM Trans. Graph. 22, 3, 848C855.

FRANKOT, R., AND CHELLAPPA, R. 1988. A method for enforcing integrability in shape from shading algorithms. IEEE Trans. Pattern Anal. Mach. Intell. 10, 4, 439C451.

FUNKHOUSER, T., KAZHDAN, M., SHILANE, P., MIN, P., KIEFER, W., TAL, A., RUSINKIEWICZ, S., AND DOBKIN, D. 2004. Modeling by example. ACM Trans. Graph. 23, 3, 652C 663.

GOLDMAN, D., CURLESS, B., HERTZMANN, A., AND SEITZ, S. 2005. Shape and spatially-varying brdfs from photometric stereo. In ICCV05, I: 341C348.

HERTZMANN, A., AND SEITZ, S. 2005. Example-based photometric stereo: Shape reconstruction with general, varying brdfs. PAMI 27, 8 (August), 1254C1264.

HOIEM, D., EFROS, A. A., AND HEBERT, M. 2005. Automatic photo pop-up. ACM Trans. Graph. 24, 3, 577C584.

IGARASHI, T., MATSUOKA, S., AND TANAKA, H. 1999. Teddy: a sketching interface for 3d freeform design. In SIGGRAPH 99, 409C416.

JOHNSTON, S. F. 2002. Lumo: illumination for cel animation. In NPAR 02: Proceedings of the 2nd international symposium on Non-photorealistic animation and rendering, ACM Press, New York, NY, USA.

KARPENKO, O. A., AND HUGHES, J. F. 2006. Smoothsketch: 3d free-form shapes from complex sketches. ACM Trans. Graph. 25, 3.

KOENDERINK, J. 1998. Pictorial relief. Royal 356, 1740, 1071C 1086. KOVESI, P. 2005. Shapelets correlated with surface normals produce surfaces. In ICCV05, 994C1001.

MORTENSEN, E., AND BARRETT, W. 1995. Intelligent scissors for image composition. Proceedings of ACM SIGGRAPH95, 191C 198.

NALWA, V. 1993. A Guided Tour of Computer Vision. Addison- Wesley.

NEALEN, A., SORKINE, O., ALEXA, M., AND COHEN-OR, D. 2005. A sketch-based interface for detail-preserving mesh editing. ACM Trans. Graph. 24, 3, 1142C1147.

OHTAKE, Y., BELYAEV, A., AND SEIDEL, H.-P. 2004. Ridgevalley lines on meshes via implicit surface fitting. ACM Trans. Graph. 23, 3, 609C612.

OKABE, M., ZENG, G., MATSUSHITA, Y., IGARASHI, T., QUAN, L., AND SHUM, H.-Y. 2006. Single-view relighting with normal map painting. In Proceedings of Pacific Graphics, 27C34.

SLOAN, P. J., MARTIN, W., GOOCH, A., AND GOOCH, B. 2001. The lit sphere: A model for capturing NPR shading from art. In Proceedings of Graphics Interface 2001, B. Watson and J. W. Buchanan, Eds., 143C150.

VAN OVERVELD, C. W. A. M. 1996. Painting gradients: Freeform surface design using shading patterns. In Graphics Inter- face 96, Canadian Human-Computer Communications Society, W. A. Davis and R. Bartels, Eds., 151C158.

WU, T.-P., TANG, K.-L., TANG, C.-K., AND WONG, T.-T. 2006. Dense photometric stereo: A markov random field approach. PAMI 28, 11 (November), 1830C1846.

ZELEZNIK, R. C., HERNDON, K. P., AND HUGHES, J. F. 1996. Sketch: an interface for sketching 3d scenes. In SIGGRAPH 96, 163C170.

ZHANG, L., DUGAS-PHOCION, G., SAMSON, J., AND SEITZ, S. 2001. Single view modeling of free-form scenes. In CVPR01, I:990C997.

Chapter 7
Adaptive Directional Lifting-based Wavelet Transform for Image Coding[*]

Wenpeng Ding, Feng Wu, Xiaolin Wu, Shipeng Li and Houqiang Li

Abstract We present a novel two-dimensional wavelet transform scheme of adaptive directional lifting (ADL) in image coding. Instead of alternately applying horizontal and vertical lifting as in present practice, ADL performs lifting-based prediction in local windows in the direction of high pixel correlation. Hence, it adapts far better to the image orientation features in local windows. The ADL transform is achieved by existing one-dimensional wavelets and is seamlessly integrated into the global wavelet transform. The predicting and updating signals of ADL can be derived even at the fractional pixel precision level to achieve high directional resolution, while still maintaining perfect reconstruction. To enhance the ADL performance, a rate-distortion optimized directional segmentation scheme is also proposed to form and code a hierarchical image partition adapting to local features. Experimental results show that the proposed ADL-based image coding technique outperforms JPEG 2000 in both PSNR and visual quality, with the improvement up to 2.0 dB on images with rich orientation features.[2]

Key words: lifting wavelet transform, adaptive directional filtering, prediction, image segmentation, rate-distortion optimization

Wenpeng Ding
Department of Computer Science, University of Science and Technology of China, Hefei 230027, China
e-mail: wpding3@mail.ustc. edu.cn

Feng Wu and Shipeng Li
Microsoft Research Asia, Beijing 100080, China
e-mail: {fengwu,spli}@microsoft.com

Xiaolin Wu
Department of Electrical and Computer Engineering, Mc- Master University, Hamilton,ON L8S 4K1 Canada
e-mail: xwu@mail.ece.mcmaster. ca; xwu@ece.mcmaster.ca

Houqiang Li
Department of Electrical Engineering and Information Science, University of Science and Technology of China, Hefei 230027, China
e-mail: lihq@ustc.edu.cn

 * Source: IEEE Transactions on Image Processing Feb. 2007 Volume: 16, Issue: 2 Pages: 416-427
Copyright ©2007 IEEE. Reprinted, with permission. DOI Bookmark: 10.1109/TIP.2006.888341

[2] This work was done at Microsoft Research Asia and supported in part by the NSFC under Contract 60333020. The associate editor coordinating the review of this manuscript and approving it for publication was Dr. Amir Said.

7.1 Introduction

The past decade has seen increased sophistication and maturity of wavelet-based image compression technologies. Within the family of mathematical transforms for image coding, discrete wavelet transform has unseated discrete cosine transform (DCT)[1] [3]as the transform of choice. The wavelet-based JPEG 2000 interna-tional standard for still image compression [4] not only obtains superior compres-sion performance over the DCT-based old JPEG standard [3], but also offers sca-lability advantages in reconstruction quality and spatial resolution that are desirable features for many consumer and network applications.

However, the prevailing practice of 2D wavelet transform has a legacy from traditional 2D DCT transform in that it is implemented by separable 1D filtering in horizontal and vertical directions. This separable 2D wavelet transform is referred to as rectilinear 2D wavelet transform in this paper to distinguish it from another separable but adaptive 2D wavelet transform to be proposed, called adaptive di-rectional lifting (ADL). A serious drawback of rectilinear wavelet transforms is that they are ill suited to approximate image features with arbitrary orientation that is neither verti-cal nor horizontal. In these cases, rectilinear wavelets transform results in large-magnitude high-frequency coefficients. At low bit rates, the quantization noise from these coefficients is clearly visible, in particular causing annoying Gibbs artifacts at image edges with arbitrary directions. This problem has been identified by numerous researchers [1][2][5][6].

How to fully exploit the directional correlation in either the image or frequency domains has been a research topic for many years. Research on DCT-based image coding has converged at directional prediction. Feig et al. incorporate spatial pre-diction into a JPEG-like code in a manner similar to the fractal-based image com-pression [1]. Even though this method does not offer a better rate-distortion per-formance than pure DCT-based code, it has far fewer block artifacts and markedly better visual quality at very low bit rates. Kondo et al. perform directional prediction on DCT blocks. Their prediction is based on one of four coded neighboring DCT blocks [2]. The new video coding standard H.264 successfully applies the block-based spatial prediction technique to intra-frame coding. Significant coding gains are made over the version without spatial prediction [7].

Direction-aware wavelet/subband-based image coding methods fall into two major categories in their ways of using and coding directional information.

(1) **Directional filter and transform:** Ikonomopoulos et al. first propose a 2D filter bank that produces a one low-pass component image and N directional component images containing high-frequency components in a given direction [5]. Li et al. incorporate subband decomposition into the Ikonomopoulos' scheme [8], where each rectangular subband contains a given direction. Bam-berger et al. pro-pose a filter bank with critically sampled and wedge-shaped regions to describe directional information [9], which receives more attention for the virtues of max-imal decimation and perfect reconstruction. Some new directional filter banks based on Bamberger's method are recently reported in [10][11]. In addition, many new wavelet transforms have been proposed to preserve fine directional informa-tion in the wavelet domain, such as Ridgelet [12][13], Curvelet [14], directional wavelet transform [15], Contourlet [16], complex wavelet [17][18], BrushLet[19], and so on. These directional filters and transforms provide good presentations of directional data in the frequency domain. They are extensively applied in feature extraction, image enhancement, denoising, classification, and even retrieval. However, they are not suited for compression for lack of efficient entropy coding to exploit directional information in each wavelet region.

(2) **Directional prediction:** The key issue on applying directional prediction in wavelet de-composition is the conflict of global transform and local features. Nat-ural images usually contain rich orientation features. Partitioning an image into many small regions according to correlation direction may cause severe boundary effects and hurt coding efficiency. Taubman et al. propose a technique to resample an image before conventional subband decomposition [6]. The re-sampling process rotates image edges into horizontal or vertical directions so that following sub-band de-composition can gain accurate predictions from neighboring horizontal or ver-tical pixels. Wang et al. use a similar idea but further propose an overlapped ex-tension to prevent coding artifacts

around the boundaries of different directional regions [20]. A similar idea on wavelet packets is also reported in [21][22]. An additional method for directional prediction is to separate images into two or more parts, in which pixels of one part can be directionally predicted from other parts during wavelet decomposition [23][24]. Both of them are not appropriate to handle varying orientations of image features. Furthermore, 2D transform used in this category usually is unable to be separated as two 1D transforms.

This paper presents a new technique of seamlessly integrating directional pre-diction in arbitrary orientation into the familiar framework of lifting-based 2D wavelet transform. The lifting structure developed by W. Sweldens is an efficient and popular implementation of wavelet transform, in which each FIR (Finite Im-pulse Response) wavelet filter can be factored into several lifting stages [25]. A local spatial prediction can be readily incorporated into each lifting stage because the lifting stage only involves a few neighboring pixels in the calculation of predicting and updating signals.

Works in this line of thinking have been reported recently. Taubman proposes an orientation adaptive lifting transform for image compression [26]. Boulgouris et al. propose interpolative pyramids for lossless and progressive image coding [27] and an adaptive lifting scheme for lossless image coding [28]. Aiming to minimize the predicted error variance, this method derives four directional filters from the quincunx sampling scheme and selects one of them with a median operation. Claypoole et al. investigate the order of prediction and update in adaptive lifting transform in [29]. Li et al. propose a variance-normalized autocorrelation function of the difference image to reconstruct a linear predictor [30]. Gerek et a.l propose a 2-D orientation-adaptive prediction filter in lifting structure [31]. In all these schemes, feature directions are estimated from causal data of lower spatial resolution with limited accuracy. Moreover, most of them have only integer precision in directional lifting transform. These two drawbacks reduce coding efficiency.

The main contribution of this paper is a novel technique of ADL wavelet trans-form. Preliminary results of this work were first reported in [32], in which simple direction estimation is used on variable-size blocks similar to those in H.264. Chang et al. subsequently proposed to use quincunx sampling in directional lifting trans-form [33]. ADL is a general framework that allows the use of any 1D wavelet filter, such as the popular Haar, 5/3 and 9/7 wavelets, to perform 2D decomposition on images. The proposed ADL-based image transform is not a true 2D wavelet transform and can be implemented by two 1D transforms, but it has the following advantages not shared by rectilinear 2D wavelet transforms.

- In each lifting stage, the predicting or updating operations are carried out in the direction of image edges and textures in a local window, and are not necessarily horizontal or vertical. This adaptation can significantly reduce the signal energy of high-pass subbands.
- High angular resolution in prediction is achieved by the use of fractional pixels in prediction and update operations. The fractional pixels can be calculated by any existing interpolation method.
- In order to guarantee perfect reconstruction, the predicted and updated samples are always in integer pixel positions.
- When 2D transform is separated as two 1D transforms, the two 1D transforms are not necessarily performed in two perpendicular directions. But the split of the low and high subbands is in the horizontal and vertical directions, still generating rectangular subbands for operational convenience

Due to non-stationary orientation statistics of typical natural images, the pro-posed ADL image transform works best if coupled with an adaptive image segmentation that classifies the input image into regions of approximately uniform edge/texture orientations. In each of these homogeneous regions, ADL maximizes the compaction of signal energy into the low subband by adjusting the prediction and interpolation direction. To this end, we propose a quadtree-based segmentation technique to construct an adaptive image segmentation in a rate-distortion optimal sense. The rate-distortion optimization is done by the well-known BFOS optimal tree pruning algorithm [34].

Other than the replacement of conventional rectilinear wavelet transform by ADL and the adaptive segmentation component, the other components of the proposed image-coding system resemble their counterparts of JPEG 2000. The coefficient quantization is done by embedded bit plane coding, which preserves the scalability of our code stream. The entropy coding of coefficients is done by the EBCOT technique [35].

The remainder of this paper has the following presentation flow. In Section 7.2, the ADL technique is described in detail. We introduce the concept of ADL transform, and show how to integrate the directional spatial prediction into the conventional lifting framework. The problem of sub-pixel interpolation to facilitate spatial pre-diction in arbitrary angle is also discussed. Then in Section 7.3 we propose an R-D optimized image segmentation method to fit ADL transform to the orientations of local image features. The experimental results are presented in Section 7.4, followed by conclusion in Section 7.5.

7.2 2D Wavelet Transform via Adaptive Directional Lifting

This section presents a new adaptive directional lifting-based (ADL) 2D wavelet transform. The ADL-based transform can overcome the difficulty of rectilinear 2D wavelet transforms in approximating image signals of edges and textures in arbi-trary directions. Since the prediction of ADL uses the fractional pixels, the inter-polation methods are also described.

7.2.1 ADL structure

The fundamental difference between the conventional lifting and the proposed ADL lies in the prediction. Instead of always making the predictions in the hori-zontal or vertical direction, the ADL analyzes the local spatial correlations in all directions, and then chooses a direction of prediction in which the prediction error is minimal.

Consider a 2D signal $x(m,n)_{m,n\in Z}$. Without loss of generality, we assume that this signal is first decomposed into high and low subbands by a 1D wavelet trans-form in the vertical direction and then in the horizontal direction. With the technique given in [25], each 1D wavelet transform can be factored into one or multiple lifting stages. A typical lifting stage consists of three steps: split, prediction, and update.

Firstly, all samples are split into two parts: the even polyphase samples x_e and the odd polyphase samples x_o,

$$\begin{cases} x_e(m,n) = x(m,2n) \\ x_o(m,n) = x(m,2n+1) \end{cases} \tag{7.1}$$

In the prediction step, the odd polyphase samples located at integer positions are predicted from the neighboring even polyphase samples. The resulting prediction residuals, or high subband coefficients, are

$$h(m,n) = x_o(m,n) - p_e(m,n) \tag{7.2}$$

The prediction of each $x_o(m,n)$ is a linear combination of neighboring even coefficients with strong correlation. As shown in Fig.12.1, assume that the pixels have a strong correlation in the angle θ_V, where the integer pixels are marked by "o", the half pixels by "$+$" and the quarter pixels by "$\times$". The prediction of $x(m,2n+1)$ is taken as a linear combination of the even polyphase samples identified by the arrows in Fig.12.1, specifically,

$$P_e(m,n) = \sum_i \alpha_i x_e(m + sign(i-1)\tan\theta_V, n+i) \tag{7.3}$$

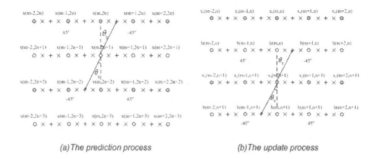

(a) The prediction process   (b) The update process

Fig. 7.1 The prediction process (a) and update processes (b) with the vertical angle θ_v in the proposed ADL, where the integer pixels are marked by "o", the half pixels by "+" and the quarter pixels by "×".

where $sign(x)$ is 1 for $x \geq 0$ and -1 otherwise. The weights α_i are given by the filter taps. Note that $x_e(m+sign(i-1)\tan\theta_v, n+i)$ is not necessarily sampled at an integer position. The corresponding finite impulse response function in z domain is

$$P(z_1, z_2) = \sum_{i=a}^{b} \alpha_i z_1^{sign(i-1)\tan\theta_v} z_2^i \qquad (7.4)$$

Here the indexes a and b delimit the finite support of the FIR wavelet filter. Since the prediction is still calculated from the even polyphase samples, if the angle is known, the ADL can still perfectly reconstruct the odd polyphase samples with Eq (7.2). In the updating step, the even polyphase samples are replaced with

$$l(m,n) = x_e(m,n) + u_h(m,n) \qquad (7.5)$$

Note $l(m,n)$ always locates at an integer position. The update step of the proposed ADL scheme is performed in the same angle as that in the prediction step. We stress that the ADL framework is very general, and it does not have any restriction on the update angle. We keep the prediction and update angles the same to save the side information of coding the angles, also for the fact that the optimal update angle is consistent with the prediction angle for most images. Consequently, in the update step of the proposed ADL, the even polyphase samples are predicted as

$$u_h(m.n) = \sum_{j} \beta_j h(m+sign(j)\tan\theta_v, n+j) \qquad (7.6)$$

The weights β_j are also given by the filter taps. $h(m+sign(j)\tan\theta_v, n+j)$ may not be integer high-pass coefficient due to $\tan\theta_v$. The corresponding finite impulse response function in z domain is

$$U(z_1, z_2) = \sum_{j=c}^{d} \beta_j z_1^{sign(j)\tan\theta_v} z_2^j \qquad (7.7)$$

Here the indexes c and d delimit the finite support of the FIR wavelet filter. This step is also trivially invertible. Given $l(m,n)$ and $h(m,n)$, one can perfectly reconstruct the even polyphase samples. In addition, in order to achieve perfect reconstruction of the original 2D signal, we impose the predicted and updated samples to be at integer pixel positions in Eqs. (7.2) and (7.5).

In summary we present in Fig.12.2 a schematic diagram of the proposed ADL-based wavelet transform. The proposed FIR functions of the extended Haar, 5/3 and 9/7 filters are given below, respectively

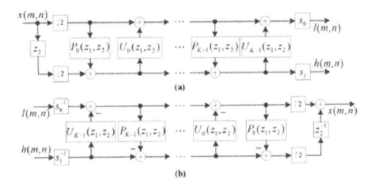

Fig. 7.2 The generic 1D ADL transform, (a) analysis side and (b) synthesis side.

$$
Harr: \begin{cases} P_0(z_1,z_2) = -z_1^{-tg(\theta_v)} \\ U_0(z_1,z_2) = z_1^{tg(\theta_v)}/2 \\ s_0 = s_1 = 1 \end{cases} \tag{7.8}
$$

$$
5/3: \begin{cases} P_0(z_1,z_2) = -(z_1^{-tg(\theta_v)} + z_1^{tg(\theta_v)}z_2)/2 \\ U_0(z_1,z_2) = (z_1^{tg(\theta_v)} + z_1^{-tg(\theta_v)}z_2^{-1})/4 \\ s_0 = s_1 = 1 \end{cases} \tag{7.9}
$$

$$
9/7: \begin{cases} -1.586134(z_1^{-tg(\theta_v)} + z_1^{tg(\theta_v)}z_2) \\ -0.05298(z_1^{tg(\theta_v)} + z_1^{-tg(\theta_v)}z_2^{-1}) \\ 0.882911(z_1^{-tg(\theta_v)} + z_1^{tg(\theta_v)}z_2) \\ 0.443506(z_1^{tg(\theta_v)} + z_1^{-tg(\theta_v)}z_2^{-1}) \\ s_0 = 1.230174 \\ s_1 = 1/s_0 \end{cases} \tag{7.10}
$$

We can view the conventional lifting as a special case of the ADL, when $\theta_v = 0$. Upon the completion of the 1D ADL wavelet transform running on index n, which can be viewed as a generalized vertical transform, the generalized horizontal transform is performed in the same way running on index m. Note that the prediction angle θ_h of generalized horizontal transform is not required to be perpendicular to the vertical counterpart θ_v. In other words, the generalized horizontal transform can optimize the prediction direction for its lifting decomposition. We would like to emphasize on the flexibility of the ADL scheme. When a 1D wavelet transform is factored into more than one lifting stage (e.g. the 9/7 filter), except for the first lifting stage, the spatial prediction may be disabled in subsequent stages by setting θ_v to zero if the previous lifting decomposition has removed the directional correlations.

Just like in conventional rectilinear 2D wavelet transform, the 2D ADL wavelet transform can decompose an image into multiple levels of different scales. Al-though the generalized vertical and horizontal transforms of the ADL technique do not necessarily have their lifting directions to be perpendicular to each other, they still generate a subband structure that is identical to that of the rectilinear 2D wavelet transform. This is because the 2D ADL wavelet transform splits the low and high subbands horizontally and vertically in turn in the exactly same way as conventional wavelet transform, creating LL, LH, HL, and HH subbands in one level of decomposition.

To visualize the effect of the 2D ADL wavelet transform we present in Fig.12.3 the four sub-bands of the test image of Fig.12.3 (a), which are the results of one level of ADL decomposition. In the HL subband, only the top row of horizontal stripes contains significant amount of energy after the generalized vertical transform. The adaptive directional prediction successfully removes the statistical redundancy in all other directional patterns, which is exhibited by uniformly small prediction errors in the bottom three rows of the HL subband. The HH subband has even less amount of energy with no recognizable signal structures remaining, after the generalized vertical and horizontal transforms. In the LH subband, the energy compaction is somewhat less effective than in HL and HH subbands. Besides the vertical stripes still remain, some high frequency diagonal textures also exist in LH subband. This is because the down-sampling process of the generalized vertical transform makes the spatial resolution insufficient for the ADL scheme to find accurate prediction direction. But even in this case, the signal energy left in the LH subband is far lower than that of the conventional lifting scheme. To see the advantage of ADL transform over rectilinear wavelet transform on real images, the reader is referred to Fig.8.6 for a quick preview.

7.2.2 Subpixel Interpolation

In order to perform directional prediction in an arbitrary angle θ_v, the proposed ADL scheme needs to know the intensity values at fractional pixel locations. In other words, $\tan \theta_v$ used in Eqs (7.3) and (7.6) are generally not an integer. Hence, the interpolation of subpixels becomes an issue.

We present an interpolation technique using Eq (7.3) as an example. For perfect reconstruction, the integer pixels used to interpolate the fractional pixel at angle θ_v have to be even polyphase samples $x_e(m,n)$. No odd polyphase samples $x_o(m,n)$ can participate in the prediction in this case. The interpolation can be generally described as

$$x_e(m + sign(i-1)tg(\theta_v), n+i) = \sum_k a_k x_e(m+k, n+i) \qquad (7.11)$$

Here the subscript k indexes the integers around $sign(i-1)tg(\theta_v)$, and a_k's are the interpolation filtering parameters. Based on Eq (7.3) and the z-transform of Eq (7.11), we have

$$z_1^{sign(i-1)tg(\theta_v)} = \sum_k a_k z_1^k \qquad (7.12)$$

In this paper, we adopt the popular Sinc interpolation technique [42]. The interpolation of Eq (7.6) is performed the same way.

The subpixel interpolation problem can also be cast into an optimal filter design problem. Since the interpolation filter can be generalized to any FIR filter, one can design the filter to minimize the energy of the high subband:

$$D = \sum_{m,n} |h(m,n)|^2 = \sum_{m,n} |x_0(m,n) - \sum_k a_k x(m, n+k)|^2 \qquad (7.13)$$

The minimization problem

$$\min_{\cdots a_{k-1}, a_k, a_{k+1} \cdots} \sum_{m,n} |x_0(m,n) - \sum_k a_k x(m, n+k)|^2 \qquad (7.14)$$

can be solved by the standard least-square method. The filter coefficients $\cdots a_{k-1}, a_k, a_{k+1}, \cdots$ can be optimized for a given input image or a set of training images. In the former case, the optimal

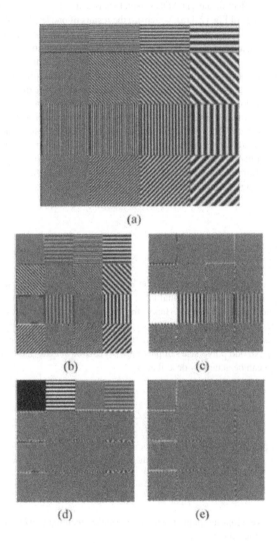

Fig. 7.3 The exemplified image and the resulted four subbands with the proposed ADL decomposition.

coefficients have to be sent as side information, whereas in the latter case the training set should have the same statistics of the input image.

In principle, the prediction angle θ_v can be a continuous variable. However, in practice, we found that nine uniformly quantized discrete angles, θ_i, $i = 0, \pm1, \pm2, \pm3, \pm4$, suffice to reap all the coding gains of ADL. Equivalently, the interpolation is done at the spatial resolution of quarter pixel.

7.3 R-D Optimized Segmentation for ADL

In order for an image codec to benefit from the adaptability of ADL to the edge/texture orientation, it has to segment an image into regions of textures and edges of clear directional bias. This poses the following rate-distortion optimization problem. For ease of implementation, we partition the image recursively into blocks of variable sizes by quad-tree. All pixels in a quad-tree block will be subject to the same ADL transform. The finer the segmentation, the greater degree of gradient uniformity in the resulting blocks. This leads to better directional prediction of the image signal, hence lower distortion. However, the improved signal approximation of ADL is achieved at the expense of increased side information to describe the segmentation tree and the lifting directions of individual blocks. To find the quad-tree of optimal balance between the cost of coding the segmentation tree and the cost of coding ADL transform coefficients, we apply the well-known BFOS algorithm for optimal tree pruning [34].

First, we build a full quad-tree T by recursively partitioning each block into four sub-blocks until reaching a pre-specified minimum block size. For a sub-tree $S \subset T$ we define its distortion

$$D(S) = \sum_{\tau \in S} \sum_{m,n} |h_{\tau,\vartheta}(m,n)| \tag{7.15}$$

where $h_{\tau,\vartheta}(m,n)$ is the high subband coefficient of the ADL decomposition in the optimal direction ϑ, and the subscript τ denotes a terminal (leaf) node of the sub-tree S. Also, we define the rate of the sub-tree S as

$$R(S) = \sum_{\tau \in S} r_C(\tau) + \sum_{\tau \in S} r_T(v) \tag{7.16}$$

where $r_C(\tau)$ is the rate of entropy-coding all high subband coefficients in terminal node τ, and $r_T(v)$ is the rate of coding the side information of the tree node $v \in S$.

Fig. 7.4 The prediction of lifting direction.

Recall from the previous section that ADL chooses the optimal prediction direction ϑ out of nine discrete angles θ_i, $i = 0, \pm1, \pm2, \pm3, \pm4$. We adopt a predictive coding scheme to code based on the observation that the image gradient changes smoothly. Referring to Fig.8.4, in a general location of a terminal quad-tree block related to its neighboring blocks of lifting angles α_n, α_w and α_d, we predict the optimal lifting direction ϑ to be

$$\hat{\vartheta} = \begin{cases} \alpha_n & |\alpha_d - \alpha_w| > |\alpha_d - \alpha_n| \\ \alpha_w & |\alpha_d - \alpha_w| \le |\alpha_d - \alpha_n| \end{cases} \tag{7.17}$$

Then, the prediction error $e_\vartheta = \vartheta - \hat{\vartheta}$ is arithmetic coded. The coded segment structure and predicted angle error are embedded in the user data part of JPEG2000.

If $v \in S$ is an internal node, then $r_T(v) = 1$, i.e., the bit to indicate the event of splitting the corresponding block; otherwise, for each leaf node $\tau \in S$, $r_T(\tau)$ is the number of bits to code the coefficients $h_{\tau,\vartheta}(m,n)$ in node τ and the optimal direction ϑ of the ADL, plus one bit to signal the terminal node. The rate of coding $h_{\tau,\vartheta}(m,n)$ is estimated by the entropy of ADL coefficients $h_{\tau,\vartheta}(m,n)$ in node τ, and the rate of coding ϑ is estimated by the entropy of prediction residual $e_{\vartheta} = \vartheta - \hat{\vartheta}$.

Among all the pruned sub-trees of T, an R-D optimal segmentation tree S^* is the one that minimizes the cost function

$$J = D(S) + \lambda R(S) \tag{7.18}$$

where λ is a Lagrangian multiplier that determines the total rate of coding the sub-tree S^* and the coefficients $h_{\tau,\vartheta}(m,n)$ of all the terminal nodes $\tau \in S$. Given a λ we apply the BFOS optimal tree pruning algorithm to compute S^*. In order to meet a target rate R_0 of coding an image, one can apply the BFOS algorithm iteratively in a binary search of the corresponding value of λ_0. However, this process is expensive. Alternatively, we find a simple fast trick to approximate the value of λ_0, using the JPEG 2000 image code as a reference. It is well known that the EBCOT technique of JPEG 2000 generates an almost convex operational R-D curve. The proposed ADL image coding method also adopts the EBCOT technique for entropy coding of $h_{\tau,\vartheta}(m,n)$, and hence has almost convex operational R-D curve as well. The only difference is in that the ADL scheme adapts to the image signal better than the rectilinear wavelet transform. Everything else being equal, the former method approximately translates the operational R-D curve of the latter. Based on this observation we run the JPEG 2000 code first to obtain its R-D slope $\lambda_J(R_0)$ at the target rate R_0. Then we estimate the Lagrangian multiplier of our method for the target rate R_0 to be $\lambda_0 = \lambda_J(R_0) - \delta$, where δ is an offset. Fig.8.5 shows the segmentation of the test image Barbara generated by the above algorithm and the optimal prediction directions of ADL in the quad-tree terminal nodes.

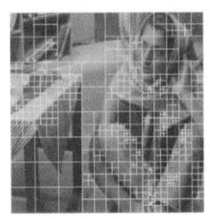

Fig. 7.5 The partition of Barbara and the directions for each block.

7.4 Experimental Results and observations

The proposed ADL wavelet transform is implemented. In order to evaluate the ADL performance only as objectively as possible, we simply replace the wavelet transform module of JPEG 2000 by the ADL transform and use the same bit-plane coding (quantization module) and EBCOT technique (entropy coding module) as in JPEG 2000. On a side note, the high modularity of the proposed ADL wavelet transform and its identical subband decomposition structure to other separable 2D transforms make our experiments very easy to conduct within the JPEG 2000 framework. This also means that the proposed ADL-based image codec can be made nearly compatible to JPEG 2000 standard.

Subbands	Methods	Barbara	Bike	Cafe	Foreman
LH	JPEG2000	5.31	3.01	5.01	1.3
	ADL	2.35 (55.8%)	2.25 (27.3%)	4.04 (19.2%)	0.92 (24.3%)
HL	JPEG2000	2.26	3.19	5.51	2.07
	ADL	1.44 (36.0%)	2.39 (25.1%)	4.4 (20.1%)	1.43 (31.5%)
HH	JPEG2000	1.48	1.05	1.56	0.6
	ADL	0.97 (34.6%)	0.88 (15.5%)	1.5 (4.5%)	0.51 (16.0%)

Table 7.1 AVERAGE COEFFICIENT MAGNITUDES IN THE LH, HL AND HH SUBBANDS AND THE NUMBERS IN BRACKETS REPRESENT THE PERCENTAGE OF REDUCTION.

We report the experimental results of six common testing images: Barbara (512x512), Lena (512x512), Baboon (512x512), Bike (2560x2048), Woman (2048x2560) and Cafe (2560x2048), plus the first frame of Foreman (352x288) video sequence from MPEG testing set. The reference software VM 9.0 of JPEG 2000 is used in our comparison study. We compare the abilities of the proposed ADL wavelet transform and that of JPEG 2000 in energy packing, or spatial de-correlation. The same 5/3 filter is used in two methods. Table 12.1 tabulates the average coefficient magnitudes of the LH, HL, and HH sub-bands. The ADL technique has a significant advantage over the conventional rectilinear wavelet transform on Barbara. This should be expected because this testing image contains strong directional textures. The reduction in average coefficient magnitude is 55.8% in the LH subband, 36% in the HL subband and 34.6% in the HH subband. On other test images the ADL technique also outperforms JPEG 2000. In parallel to Table 12.1, Fig.8.6 shows one level of wavelet decomposition of testing image Barbara by JPEG 2000 and the proposed ADL. For clear visualization the magnitudes of coefficients in the LH, HL and HH subbands are scaled into the range [0, 255] in the plot. We bring the reader's attention to the fact that the ADL technique not only has appreciably lowe r signal energy in the high frequency subbands in comparison with JPEG 2000, but also its residual signals in the high frequency subbands are much less correlated to the original spatial features of the image. This property contributes to superior visual quality of the reconstructed images by ADL as we will see in Fig.8.7.

To compare the coding performance of the two methods we present in Table 12.2 the PSNR results of all test images at 0.125bpp, 0.25bpp, 0.5bpp and 1.0bpp. For either method all images are decomposed by three-level 2D transform. Both the popular bi-orthogonal 9/7 and the 5/3 filters are tested. The Sinc interpolation is used by the ADL to generate subpixels. The coding gain can be up to 2.0dB for Barbara coded with the 5/3 filter. On the test set the gain of ADL ranged from 0.21dB to 1.36dB, depending on the presence or lack of orientation features in the image. But even on relatively smooth images like Lena, the ADL method still enjoys an advantage over the rectilinear 2D wavelet transform. The results with different prediction precisions are also given in Table 12.2. The results of sub-pixel prediction are significantly better than those of the integer prediction with both the 5/3 and 9/7 filters. However, the results of quarter pixel precision are only marginally better than those of half pixel prediction on images of strong edge features such as Barbara and Women. On relatively smooth images the angular prediction of quarter pixel precision can be even slightly worse than that of half pixel precision (see the case of Foreman at 1.0 bpp).

Fig. 7.6 The coefficient magnitudes of JPEG 2000 (left) and ADL (right) after one level of 2D de-composition

Fig. 7.7 Visual quality comparison of decoded Barbara at 0.3 bpp: JPEG 2000 (left) vs. ADL (right).

Table 12.3 shows the average number of side information bits for coding segmentation tree and associated directions, which depends on overall bit rates and image contents. One can see that the side information bits constitute only a small portion of total code length. The percentage of overhead bits at low bit rates is less than that at high bit rates because of the proposed RD optimized segmentation and direction estimation.

Due to its adaptability to directional signal features, the ADL wavelet transform tends to reconstruct image edges better than the rectilinear 2D wavelet transforms at the same bit rates. Since the human visual system is highly sensitive to edges, the former method should have superior visual quality than the latter method, which is indeed corroborated by our experimental results. As an example, Fig.8.7 presents the decoded Barbara images by the two methods, both at the rate 0.3 bpp and using the 5/3 filter. The image decoded by JPEG 2000 has severe moir patterns on the scarf and

Images	bpp	5/3 filter				9/7 filter			
		J2K	ADL Integer Pixel	ADL Half Pixel	ADL Quarter Pixel	J2K	ADL Integer Pixel	ADL Half Pixel	ADL Quarter Pixel
Barbara	0.125	24.59	25.69	26.07	25.95	25.02	26.16	26.32	26.45
	0.25	27.38	28.79	29.13	29.22	28.27	29.37	29.70	29.78
	0.5	30.95	32.35	32.87	32.95	32.15	33.10	33.50	33.58
	1	36.04	36.89	37.16	37.24	37.11	37.58	37.84	37.88
Lena	0.125	30.11	30.66	30.75	30.68	30.41	30.88	31.00	31.02
	0.25	33.22	33.76	33.90	33.88	33.78	34.13	34.18	34.25
	0.5	36.45	36.80	36.91	36.94	37.02	37.17	37.23	37.30
	1	39.51	39.68	39.74	39.73	40.06	40.09	40.17	40.20
Baboon	0.125	21.40	21.49	21.44	21.39	21.50	21.50	21.70	21.69
	0.25	22.87	23.03	23.05	23.04	23.10	23.10	23.25	23.23
	0.5	25.17	25.35	25.39	25.34	25.52	25.52	25.73	25.73
	1	28.62	28.79	28.83	28.88	29.02	29.02	29.29	29.32
Bike	0.125	25.74	26.62	26.66	26.61	25.93	26.77	26.78	26.78
	0.25	29.06	29.96	29.96	29.97	29.36	30.09	30.11	30.12
	0.5	33.09	33.80	33.79	33.76	33.38	33.98	33.99	34.00
	1	37.73	38.27	38.29	38.28	38.04	38.46	38.47	38.48
Café	0.125	20.42	20.42	20.57	20.55	20.70	20.80	20.83	20.84
	0.25	22.74	22.74	23.00	22.99	23.09	23.25	23.29	23.32
	0.5	26.42	26.42	26.66	26.67	26.78	26.93	27.02	27.06
	1	31.72	31.72	31.87	31.90	32.02	32.08	32.13	32.18
Women	0.125	26.59	26.77	26.96	27.00	26.94	27.16	27.33	27.35
	0.25	29.24	29.35	29.57	29.65	29.67	29.82	29.98	30.06
	0.5	33.00	33.03	33.14	33.24	33.42	33.51	33.60	33.72
	1	37.96	37.96	37.97	38.07	38.31	38.33	38.36	38.47
Foreman	0.125	28.71	29.82	29.85	29.94	29.15	30.06	30.11	30.16
	0.25	32.32	33.48	33.50	33.53	32.81	33.68	33.70	33.77
	0.5	35.89	37.19	37.19	37.25	36.33	37.27	37.44	37.43
	1	40.60	41.34	41.38	41.30	40.85	41.55	41.68	41.63

Table 7.2 THE COMPARISONS OF CODING PERFORMANCE (IN DB) BETWEEN JPEG2000 AND THE PROPOSED ADL-BASED CODING SCHEME WITH THE 5/3 AND 9/7 FILTERS

pants which even change the texture orientations of the original image. Also, edge ringing effects are clearly visible in the JPEG 2000 decoded image. In contrast, the ADL-based image code eliminates most of the above artifacts. It reproduces the high frequency scarf pattern almost perfectly, and greatly reduces the ringing effects around the edges.

The ADL wavelet transform retains the PSNR and spatial scalability of JPEG 2000. Although the segmentation tree for ADL is optimized for a given target rate as we discussed in Section 7.3, the rate-distortion performance of the proposed ADL-based image code still outperforms JPEG 2000 in a wide range of bit rates when operating progressively.

In Fig.8.8 we compare the rate-distortion performances of the scalable ADL code stream optimized for mid bit rate of 0.6 bpp vs. JPEG 2000 of four quality layers. Only when the bit rate is

Total bpp	Barbara	Lena	Baboon	Bike	Café	Woman	Forman
ADL 5/3							
0.125	0.015	0.009	0.008	0.007	0.006	0.004	0.017
0.25	0.019	0.020	0.012	0.013	0.009	0.007	0.021
0.5	0.034	0.040	0.021	0.031	0.021	0.021	0.033
1	0.034	0.040	0.021	0.031	0.021	0.021	0.033
ADL9/7							
0.125	0.008	0.005	0.004	0.003	0.002	0.002	0.011
0.25	0.013	0.009	0.007	0.006	0.003	0.003	0.013
0.5	0.018	0.018	0.008	0.013	0.007	0.005	0.021
1	0.018	0.018	0.008	0.013	0.007	0.005	0.021

Table 7.3 THE BITS FOR CODING SEGMENTATION TREE AND ASSOCIATED DIRECTIONS (IN BPP).

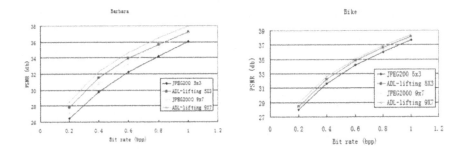

Fig. 7.8 The scalable rate-PSNR curves of ADL-based code optimized for 0.6 bpp vs. those of JPEG 2000.

extremely low (at or below 0.1 bpp), the ADL-based image code will have inferior performance to that of JPEG 2000 due to the fact that the side information for the segmentation tree has to be placed at the beginning of the code stream, and hence this part of the code stream is not scalable. We have incorporated the ADL wavelet transform into the SPIHT scheme to evaluate its performance when coupled with a different entropy coding scheme. Table 12.4 tabulates the coding results of the ADL-based SPIHT at quarter pixel precision and the original SPIHT. The parameters used are the same as those in the original SPIHT. Only the wavelet transform is replaced with the proposed ADL wavelet transform. One can see that the ADL approach makes similar gains with the zero-tree entropy coding technique of SPIHT as with EBCOT entropy coding technique of JPEG 2000.

Finally, let us discuss the computational complexity of the proposed ADL-based image codec in comparison with that of JPEG 2000. Clearly, the ADL-based image encoder has considerably higher complexity since it has to compute the image-dependent segmentation tree T, and then searches for the optimal prediction direction in each terminal node of T. However, the decoder complexity of an ADL-based image compression method can be made comparable to that of JPEG 2000. This is because the inverse ADL transform is only slightly more expensive than inverse rectilinear transform, once the optimal lifting direction is given as side information. The asymmetric design of the ADL technique makes it suitable for some internet and wireless applications that aim to achieve the highest possible rate-distortion performance by heavily optimizing the image code off-line once for all, while maintaining a reasonably low decoding complexity.

bpp	Barbara	Baboon	Lena	Bike	Café	Woman	Forman
				SPIHT			
0.125	24.83	21.69	31.04	25.89	20.67	27.33	29.34
0.25	27.56	23.24	34.03	29.13	23.03	29.95	32.76
0.5	31.38	25.61	37.07	33.02	26.49	33.59	36.33
1	36.40	29.16	40.18	37.71	31.73	38.28	40.95
				ADL-based SPIHT			
0.125	26.38	21.79	31.13	26.41	20.78	27.60	30.19
0.25	29.28	23.37	34.18	29.72	23.19	30.20	33.76
0.5	33.14	25.76	37.22	33.54	26.69	33.74	37.34
1	37.63	29.29	40.25	38.06	31.86	38.33	41.60

Table 7.4 AVERAGE COEFFICIENT MAGNITUDES IN THE LH, HL AND HH SUBBANDS AND THE NUMBERS IN BRACKETS REPRESENT THE PERCENTAGE OF REDUCTION.

7.5 Conclusions and future work

The rigidity of the existing rectilinear 2D wavelet transforms makes them ill suited for approximating image features of arbitrary orientations. This weakness can be overcome by the proposed new ADL technique. It can be seamlessly integrated into the conventional, global, and separable 2D wavelet transform, and can be implemented by any wavelet filter. In each ADL lifting stage, the prediction step can be performed in the direction of the strongest pixel correlation rather than stay mechanically fixed in the horizontal or vertical direction. Even though its prediction and update operations are based on fractional pixels, the ADL wavelet transform can guarantee perfect reconstruction without imposing any constraint on the interpolation method. A rate-distortion, optimized image-segmentation method is also developed so that ADL can efficiently approximate directional image features in local regions. Empirical results demonstrate the superior objective and perceived quality of the ADL-based image codec There are still several open issues to be investigated in the proposed ADL-based coding schemes. First, the interpolation used in the ADL wavelet transform is always performed in either the horizontal or vertical direction. It may blur the orientation property existing in raw images. Second, image blocks with different directions are continuously processed, which may cause boundary effects in the block boundaries. Third, the entropy coding does not take directional information into account, which should be used in the context model of arithmetic coding.

Acknowledgment

We would like to thank Dr. Jacky Shen, Jizheng Xu, Ruiqin Xiong, Prof. Shi Guangming and Prof. Xie Xuemei for many helpful discussions. The authors also wish to thank the associate editor and anonymous reviewers for their comments, which significantly helped improve this paper.

References

1. E. Feig, H. Peterson, V. Ratnakar, "Image compression using spatial prediction", In Proc. ICASSP, vol. 4, pp. 2339-2342, 1995.
2. H. Kondo, Y. Oishi, "Digital image compression using directional sub-block DCT", In Proc. Intl. Conf. on Comm. Technology, vol. 1, pp. 21-25, 2000.
3. W. B. Pennebaker and J. L. Mitchell, "JPEG still image data compression standard," New York: Van Nostrand, 1993.
4. D. Taubman and M. Marcellin, JPEG2000: Image Compression Fundamentals,Standards, and Practice, Kluwer Academic Publishers, 2001.
5. A. Ikonomopoulos and M. Kunt, "High compression image coding via directional filtering," Signal Processing, vol. 8, no 2, pp. 179-203, 1985.
6. D. Taubman and A. Zakhor, "Orientation adaptive subband coding of images," IEEE Trans. on Image Processing, vol. 3, no 4, pp. 421-437, April 1994.
7. T. Wiegand, G. J. Sullivan, G.Bjntegaard, A. Luthra, "Overview of the H.264/AVC video coding standard", IEEE Trans. CSVT, vol. 13, no. 7, pp. 557-559. 2003.
8. H. Li and Z. He, "Directional subband coding of images," In Proc.ICASSP, vol. 3, pp. 1823-1826, 1989.
9. R. H.Bamberger, M. Smith, "A filter bank for the directional decomposition of images: theory and design," IEEE Trans. on Signal Processing, vol. 40, no 4, pp. 882-893, 1992.
10. T. T. Nguyen, S. Oraintara, "A directional decomposition: theory, design, and implementation", In Proc. ISCAS, vol. 3, pp 281-284, 2004.
11. Y. Lu and M. N. Do, "The finer directional wavelet transform", In Proc. ICASSP, vol. 4, pp573-576, 2005.
12. E. J. Candes, "Monoscale ridgelets for the representation of images with edges," Dept. Statistic, Stanford Univ., Tech. Reporter, 1999.
13. M. N. Do and M. Vetterli, "The finite ridgelet transform for image representation", IEEE trans. on Image Processing, vol. 12, pp. 16-28, 2003.
14. E. J. Candes and D. L. Donoho, "Curvelets, multiresolution representation, and scaling laws," SPIE Wavelet Applications in Signal and Image Processing VIII, vol. 4119, 2000.
15. V. Velisavljevic, P. L. Dragotti, M. Vetterli, "Directional wavelet transforms and frames", In Proc. ICIP, vol. 3, pp 589-592,2002.
16. M. N. Do and M. Vetterli, "The contourlet transform: an efficient directional multiresolution image representation", IEEE trans. on Image Processing, vol. 14, 2091-2106, 2005.
17. Felix C. A. Fernandes, Rutger L. C. van Spaendonck, and C. Sidney Burrus, "A new framework for complex wavelet transforms", IEEE trans. on Signal Processing, vol.51, no 7, pp 1825-1837, 2003.
18. F. Fernandes, M. Wakin, R. Baraniuk, "Non-redundant, linear-phase, semi-orthogonal, directional complex wavelets", In Proc. ICASSP, vol. 2, pp 953-956, 2004.
19. F. G. Meyer and R. R. Coifman, "Brushlets: a tool for directional image analysis and image compression", Journal of Application and Computer Harmonic Analysis, vol. 5, pp 147-187, 1997.
20. D. Wang, L. Zhang and A. Vincent, "Curved wavelet transform for scalable video coding," ISO/IEC JTC1/SC29/WG11, MPEG doc M10535, Munich, 2004.
21. C. N. Zhang and X. Wu, "A hybrid approach of wavelet packet and directional decomposition for image compression," in Proc. IEEE Canadian Conf. on Electrical and Computer Engineering, vol. 2, pp.755-760, 1999.
22. P. Carre, E. Andres, C. F. Maloigne, "Discrete rotation for directional orthogonal wavelet packets," in Proc. Int. Conf. Image Processing, vol. 2, pp. 257-260,2001.
23. R. Vargic, "An approach to directional wavelet construction and their use for image compression", in Proc. IEEE Region 8 International Symposium on Video/Image Processing and Multimedia Communications, pp 201-204, 2002.
24. C.H. Kuo, T. C. Chou, and T. S. Wang, "An efficient spatial prediction-based image compression scheme", in IEEE trans. on CSVT, vol. 12, no 10, pp850-856, 2002.

25. W. Sweldens, "The lifting scheme: A custom-design construction of biorthogonal wavelets," Technical Report 1994:7, Industrial Mathematics Initiative, Department of Mathematics, University of South Carolina, 1994.
26. D. Taubman, "Adaptive, non-separable lifting transforms for image compression", In Proc. ICIP, vol. 3, pp 772-776, Oct. 1999.
27. N. V. Boulgouris and M. G. Strintzis "Orientation-sensitive interpolative pyramids for lossless and progressive image coding", IEEE Transactions on Image Processing, vol. 9, pp 710 -715, 2000.
28. N. V. Boulgouris, D. Tzovaras, M. G. Strintzis, "Lossless image compression based on optimal prediction, adaptive lifting, and conditional arithmetic coding", IEEE Trans. on Im-age Processing, vol. 10, no. 1, pp. 1-14, 2001.
29. R. L. Claypoole, G. M. Davis, W. Sweldens, and R. G. Baraniuk, "Nonlinear wavelet transforms for image coding via lifting", IEEE Transactions on Image Processing, vol. 12, pp 1449 - 1459, 2003.
30. H.Li, G. Liu, Z. Zhang, "Optimization of integer wavelet transforms based on difference correlation structures", IEEE Transactions on Image Processing, vol. 14, pp 1831-1847, 2005.
31. O.N.Gerek, A.E. Cetin, "A 2D Orientation-Adaptive Prediction Filter in Lifting Structures for Image Coding," IEEE Tran. on Image Processing, vol. 15, no. 1, Jan. 2006.
32. W. Ding, F. Wu, S. Li, "Lifting-based wavelet transform with directionally spatial prediction," Picture Coding Symposium, San Francisco, CA, 2004.
33. C. Chang, A. Maleki, B. Girod, "Adaptive wavelet transform for image compression via directional quincunx lifting,", In Prof. MMSP, Shanghai, 2005.
34. L.Breiman, J. H. Friedman, R. A. Olshen, and C. J. Stone, "Classification and regression trees", in The Wadsworth Statistics/Probability Series, Belmont, CA, 1984.
35. D.Taubman, "High performance scalable image compression with EBCOT", IEEE Trans. on Image Processing, vol. 9, no. 7, pp. 1158-1170, July 2000.
36. S.Mallat and F. Falzon, "Analysis of low bit rate image transform coding," IEEE Trans. Signal Processing, vol. 46, no. 4, pp. 1027-1042, April 1998.
37. A. Habibi, R. S. Hershel, "A unified representation of differential pulse-code modulation (DPCM) and transform coding systems," IEEE Trans. on Communications, vol. 22, no 5, pp. 692-696, 1974.
38. K. Ramchandran and M. Vetterli, "Best wavelet packet bases in a rate-distortion sense," IEEE Trans. Image Processing, vol. 2, no. 2, pp. 160-175, Apr. 1993.
39. A. Said and W. A. Pearlman, "A new fast and efficient image codec based on set partitioning in hierarchical trees," IEEE Trans. on CSVT, vol. 6, no 3, pp. 243-250, 1996.
40. J. M. Shapiro, "Embedded image coding using zerotree of wavelet coefficients," IEEE Trans. Signal Processing, vol. 41, no 12, pp. 3445-3462, 1993.
41. M. Vetterli and J.Kovacevic, Wavelets and Subband Coding, Prentice Hall Englewood Cliffs, NJ 1995.
42. L. Yaroslavsky, "Fast signal sinc-interpolation and its applications in signal and image processing", in Proc. IS&T/SPIE 14th Annual Symposium Electronic Image 2003, vol. 4667, January 2002.

Part II
Networking and Systems

Chapter 8
Low-Power Distributed Event Detection in Wireless Sensor Networks*

Yanmin Zhu, Yunhuai Liu, Lionel M. Ni and Zheng Zhang

Abstract In this paper we address the problem of energy-efficient event detection in wireless sensor networks (WSNs). Duty cycling is a fundamental approach to conserving energy in WSNs. However, it brings challenges to event detection in the sense that an event may be undetected or undergo a certain delay before it is detected, in particular when sensors are low duty-cycled. We investigate the fundamental relationship between event detection and energy efficiency. Based on a simplified network model, we quantify event detection performance by deriving the closed forms of detection delay and detectability. We also characterize the intrinsic tradeoff that exists between detection performance and system lifetime, which helps flexible design decisions for WSNs. In addition, we propose a completely localized algorithm, CAS, to cooperatively determine sensor wakeups. Without relying on location information, CAS is easy to implement and scalable to network density. Theoretical bounds of event detection are also studied to facilitate the comparative study. Comprehensive experiments are conducted and results demonstrate that CAS significantly improves detection performance.

8.1 Introduction

Continuous monitoring and event detection are two major classes of applica-tions for wireless sensor networks (WSNs) [1]. In monitoring applications, sensor nodes regularly report sensory readings. Event detection applications, however, are concerned with detecting events and sensor nodes report data only when an event is detected. In this paper, we focus on WSNs for event detection. Many ap-pealing applications, such as fire surveillance, pollution detection and radiation prevention [2], fall in the class of event detection.

Tiny sensor nodes are very resource-constrained and the most severe constraint is limited energy. It has been a great challenge to obtain long-lived operational WSNs with short-lived sensor nodes. The most effective way to approach longevity is duty cycling (or, putting sensors into power-save mode). Duty cycling, how-ever, brings challenges to the design of WSNs. It degrades event detection since at any time only a fraction of the sensor nodes is active, in particular, when sensor nodes are low duty-cycled. Detection performance concerned by detection applications includes detectability and detection delay. With duty-cycled sensor nodes, an event may be undetected, or is detected but the detection is associated with a certain latency.

Yanmin Zhu, Yunhuai Liu and Lionel M. Ni
The Hong Kong University of Science and Technology
e-mail: {zhuym, yunhuai, ni}@cse.ust.hk

Zheng Zhang
Microsoft Research Asia, e-mail: zzhang@microsoft.com

* Source: Proceedings of INFOCOM 2007, Alaska, March 2007. 26th IEEE International Conference on Computer Communications. IEEE 6-12 May 2007 Pages:2401-2405 Copyright ©2007 IEEE. Reprinted with permission. DOI: 10.1109/INFCOM.2007.289

We leverage two essential properties of event detection applications to design energy-efficient detection protocols. First, physical events are usually persistent, rather than ephemeral, which can last for seconds or even minutes after their occurrence Examples for such events are fire, pollution, and radiation. Second, a broad class of applications accepts a certain detection delay. After all, application-level delays for a detected event are inevitable since it takes time for the network to report the event through hop-by-hop transmissions. In our approach, each sensor node sleeps most of the time and wakes up every τ_{cycle} time units. While in active mode, a sensor detects any potential event that occurs in its vicinity. Let τ_{on} denote the active time in every cycle of τ_{cycle}. The duty cycle of the sensor node is

$$\delta = \tau_{on}/\tau_{cycle}. \tag{8.1}$$

It suggests two ways in (12.1) to reduce the duty cycle of sensor nodes: either shorten τ_{on} or lengthen τ_{cycle}. In practice, on is assigned the minimum time needed for detecting and processing of one event. on is usually very small, on the order of tens of milliseconds [1]. It is apparent that when τ_{on} is fixed, a longer sensor cycle implies a lower duty cycle. The key, however, is the setting of τ_{cycle} for a given WSN because it directly influences detection delay and detectability. A longer sensor cycle leads to a longer delay and a lower detectability. In other words, it controls the tradeoff between event detection and energy efficiency.

There are several key issues before such a scheme can be applied in real applications. First, we need to quantify detection delay and detectability given the net-work parameters. Second, we need a distributed algorithm to schedule sensor wakeups so that detection performance can be optimized. The maximum detection delay for an event is τ_{cycle}. However, a WSN is usually densely deployed, and it has been reported that as many as 20 sensors can be deployed in one square meter [3]. With dense deployment, detection delay can be much less than τ_{cycle} if the wakeups of the sensor nodes are elaborately scheduled.

This paper has made the following contributions. First, we investigate in detail the fundamental relationship between event detection and energy efficiency, and characterize the intrinsic tradeoff between detection performance and lifetime extension. Second, we quantify detection performance of a random independent wakeup network by deriving the closed forms of detection delay and detectability. Third, we propose a completely distributed algorithm CAS to schedule sensor wakeups, which significantly reduces detection delay and improves detectability.

8.1.1 Related Work

Many valuable research efforts have been made for energy conservation in WSNs through duty cycling. Energy-quality tradeoffs for objecting tracking were studied in [4]. Probabilistic coverage in WSNs has been studied in the context of object tracking [5]. A testbed of 70 sensor nodes was deployed to detect and track the positions of moving vehicles [6]. In this system, 5% of deployed motes serve as sentries and non-sentries operates at a 4% duty cycle.

A number of algorithms were proposed to turn off redundant sensor nodes while maintaining the sensing coverage. In PEAS [7], a sensor node probes neigh-bors to find if there is active neighbors. If receiving acknowledgement from an ac-tive neighbor, it goes to sleep. Network-provisioning [8] identifies a redundant sensor node whose sensing coverage is jointly covered by its active neighbors. Tian and Georgana [9] noted the underestimation problem that exists in [8] and proposed a randomized algorithm to determine the active schedule of the sensor nodes. Several efforts [10] take both sensing coverage and network connectivity into account. These algorithms provide full sensing coverage and meanwhile maintain network connectivity.

8.1.2 Paper Organization

The rest of the paper is organized as follows. In Section 8.2, we analyze event detection delay and lifetime extension based on a simplified network model. We describe the design of CAS in Section 8.3. Experimental results are presented in Section 8.4. Finally, we conclude the paper in Section 8.5.

8.2 Analysis of Detection and Lifetime

In this section we present the analytical model, and analyze event detection and the tradeoff between detection performance and energy efficiency.

8.2.1 System Model

We consider that n sensor nodes are randomly deployed in a unit square field. A sensor node is composed of three major units: *processor*, *sensing device* and *radio transceiver*. Ideally, each unit can have separate power control [11]. We assume that the duty cycle of the transceiver is given, which is subject to the control of communication protocols. We only study the duty cycling of the sensing device. The transceiver does not necessarily have the same duty cycle with the sensing device. The consequent advantage is the increased flexibility for our protocol to work with different communication protocols. It is important to note that a sensor node can actually be attached with multiple sensing devices of different types. For simplification, however, we assume that a sensor node is equipped with a single sensing device throughout the analysis and the protocol design. Later, we call a sensor node just a sensor for short if it is not confused with the sensing device.

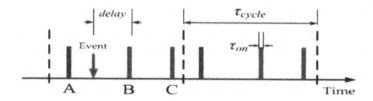

Fig. 8.1 The timing of three example sensors using the RIW algorithm.

In the analysis, we consider a simple algorithm, in which each sensor wakes up periodically, once in every cycle. In the rest of the cycle, the sensor stays in power-save mode. The wakeup selection is random and independent of other sensors. We refer to this algorithm as RIW. We are interested in low duty-cycled WSNs. Thus, we can safely assume that $\tau_{on} \ll \tau_{cycle}$. The example timing of three sensors with RIW is shown in Fig. 12.1.

The detection delay of an event, denoted by D, is defined as the amount of time elapsed from the instant when the event occurs to the instant when the first sensor detects it. D is a random variable because the factors that determine the delay, such as event arrival time, covering sensors and their wakeups, are all unpredictable. The detectability of an event with duration t is the probability that it can be detected by at least one sensor. The detectability of an event is 100% if its duration exceeds the sensor cycle. Although events are usually persistent, we still study the detectability of an event whose duration is shorter than the sensor cycle since it reflects the capability of the network to capture events. We study the detection of any event that occurs anywhere within the field and arrives at any time.

In the rest of this paper, we make the following assumptions.

- **Binary detection model** Each sensor has a sensing range (R_s). An event is reliably detected by an active sensor if its distance to the sensor is less than the sensing range.
- **Time synchronization** We assume the time synchronization mechanism is available for loose time synchronization. Protocols for clock synchronization in WSNs can be found in [12], which achieves accuracy on the order of milliseconds.
- **Stationary events** After an event has occurred, it remains at the location where it happens.

8.2.2 Detection Analysis

We analyze detection delay and detectability given a fixed sensor cycle. Since τ_{on} is much smaller than τ_{cycle}, we firstly assume that τ_{on} is negligible for analysis simplicity. The complete analysis with consideration of τ_{cycle} follows. Due to page limitation, we omit proof details.

Lemma 8.1. *A point is covered by k sensors, and their wakeups are fixed values w_i, and $w_i \geq w_{i+1}$,$1 \leq i \leq k-1$. The expected delay of any event at this point is*

$$E[D] = \frac{1}{\tau_{cycle}} \left(\sum_{i=1}^{k} w_i^2 - w_i w_{(i+1) \mod k} - (w_1 - w_k - \tau_{cycle}/2) \tau_{cycle} \right). \tag{8.2}$$

Note that in Lemma 8.1, we fix both the set of covering sensors and their wakeups. Next, we relax the assumption of fixed wakeups and give Lemma 8.2.

Lemma 8.2. *A point is covered by k sensors, whose wakeups are randomly and uniformly selected over $[0, \tau_{cycle}]$. The expected delay of any event at this point is $\tau_{cycle}]/(k+1)$.*

The proof of Lemma 8.2 involves integral calculation and uses the following probability knowledge. Let W_i, $1 \leq i \leq k$, denote the sensor wakeups which is a uniform random variable.

Lemma 8.3. *In a unit square field of n sensors deployed according to random uniform deployment, any point is covered by M sensors. The probability mass function of M is given by*

$$P\{M = k\} = \binom{n}{k} (\pi R_s^2)^k (1 - \pi R_s^2)^{n-k}. \tag{8.3}$$

M is a random variable having binomial distribution with parameters πR_s^2 and n. Next, we relax the assumption in Lemma 2 that the point is covered by a fixed set of k sensors.

Theorem 8.1. *In a unit square field, n sensors with R_s are deployed according to random uniform deployment. The expected delay in the whole field is given by*

$$\mu = \frac{\tau_{cycle}(1 - (1 + n\pi R_s^2)(1 - \pi R_s^2)^n)}{(n+1)\pi R_s^2}. \tag{8.4}$$

To derive a more accurate analysis of expected delay, we relax the assumption that the length of τ_{on} is negligible. Let $h(i)$ denote the following function

$$h(i) = \begin{cases} \tau_{cycle} - i\tau_{on}, & \text{if } 0 \leq i \leq d \\ 0, & \text{otherwise} \end{cases} \text{, where } d = \lfloor \frac{\tau_{cycle}}{\tau_{on}} \rfloor. \tag{8.5}$$

Corollary 8.1. *In a unit square field, n sensors with R_s are deployed according to random uniform deployment. The active time of the sensing device in each cycle is τ_{on}. The expected delay in the field is bounded by*

$$\mu = \sum_{i=1}^{n} \left(\frac{h(i)}{i+1} \times \binom{n}{i} (\pi R_s^2)^i (1 - \pi R_s^2)^{n-i} \right). \tag{8.6}$$

In what follows, we analyze the detectability. Notice that when the density is low some parts in the field may not be covered by any sensor. As a result, events falling into these parts are never detected. As this phenomenon inherently results from the initial deployment of the sensors, we exclude such events in calculating the expected detectability. We define the detectability as the conditional probability of event detection on the condition that at least one sensor covers the event.

Theorem 8.2. *In a unit square field, n sensors with R_s are deployed according to random uniform deployment. The detectability of an event with duration t, $t < \tau_{cycle}$, is given by*

$$\chi(t) = 1 - (1 - t\pi R_s^2 / \tau_{cycle})^n + (1 - \pi R_s^2)^n. \tag{8.7}$$

Corollary 8.2. *In a unit square field, n sensors with R_s are deployed according to random uniform deployment. The active time of the sensing device in each cycle is τ_{on}. The detectability of an event with duration t, $t < \tau_{cycle}$, is bounded by*

$$\chi(t) = 1 - \sum_{i=1}^{n} \binom{n}{i} (1 - \pi R_s^2)^{n-i} \left(\pi R_s^2 (1 - t/h(i)) \right)^i. \tag{8.8}$$

8.2.3 Tradeoff Characterization

In general, when the sensing device or the transceiver is active, the processor should also be active to execute appropriate programs. Let Φ_P, Φ_S, and Φ_R denote the power rates of processor, transceiver, and sensing device, respectively. The duty cycle of the transceiver is denoted by Ψ. The lifetime, Γ_{life}, is computed as follows

$$\Gamma_{life} = \xi \cdot (\psi \times \Phi_R + (\psi + \delta)\Phi_P + \delta \times \Phi_S)^{-1}. \tag{8.9}$$

Note that in (12.9), we do not consider the situation where the active time of the transceiver overlaps with that of the sensing device. The power consumption of the processor is computed twice while it should have been counted only once. This implies that the above Γ_{life} is a little smaller than the real lifetime.

The relationship between network lifetime and event detection is very useful for understanding the intrinsic tradeoff between energy efficiency and detection performance. This helps flexible design decisions of different WSNs. We derive tradeoff formulas by combining (12.4), (12.7) and (12.9). We prefer closed formulas as they ease the combination.

Theorem 8.3. *For a network with n randomly deployed sensors whose sensing range is R_s, the network lifetime as a function of the expected delay is*

$$\Gamma_{life}(\mu) = \xi \cdot (\psi(\Phi_R + \Phi_P) + y(\mu))^{-1}, where$$
$$y(\mu) = \frac{\tau_{on}(\Phi_S + \Phi_P)\left(1 - (1 + n\pi R_s^2)(1 - \pi R_s^2)^n\right)}{\mu(n+1)\pi R_s^2}. \tag{8.10}$$

and the network lifetime as a function of the expected detectability is

$$\Gamma_{life}(\chi) = \xi \cdot (\psi(\Phi_R + \Phi_P) + \eta(\chi))^{-1}, where$$
$$\eta(\chi) = \tau_{on}(\Phi_S + \Phi_P)\left(1 - \sqrt[n]{1 + (1 - \pi R_s^2)^n - \chi}\right)(t\pi R_s^2)^{-1}. \tag{8.11}$$

8.3 CAS: Coordinated Wakeup Scheduling

The analysis of RIW in the previous section reveals that there is a fundamental tradeoff between energy efficiency and detection performance. The network life-time can be significantly extended by exploiting detection delays. RIW provides us a baseline of event detection with low duty-cycled sensors. It is simple and easy to implement but does not provide optimal detection performance. This is because the sensors that are close to each other may wakeup at about the same time due to the lack of awareness about their neighboring sensors. It is apparent for applications that smaller delay and higher detectability are more preferable when the duty cycle is fixed. Thus, the key issue is the scheduling of sensor wakeups that can produce minimal delay and maximal detectability when the sensor cycle is fixed. However, wakeup scheduling for a distributed WSN is highly challenging. The sensing coverage of each sensor is different and may partly overlap with those of others. This suggests that an optimal schedule of sensor wakeups at a point may not necessarily be optimal for other points. Our goal is optimal detection within the whole field. In spite of the challenges, we have the instructive observation that the sensors that reside closely should separate their wakeups as much as possible. In light of the observation, we propose CAS, a fully distributed wakeup scheduling algorithm for event detection optimization.

8.3.1 Overview

Before the system starts detecting events, CAS is executed to schedule sensor wakeups at the initialization stage. After CAS finishes, each sensor has deter-mined its wakeup and enters the detecting stage, in which the sensor is alternatively in active mode and sleep mode. In each cycle, a sensor wakes up once at the wakeup time determined at the initialization stage and detects any potential event within its sensing vicinity. CAS is a fully localized algorithm and every sensor determines its wakeup through multiple rounds of wakeup adjustments based on a joint effort with its neighbors. CAS consists of two components: *distributed scheduling coordination* and *aggressive wakeup adjustment*. The former component defines the protocol for distributed coordination and the latter one is the algorithm executed at each sensor to adjust its wakeup. The design details are described in the next subsections. CAS assumes that every sensor is aware of the distance to each of its neighbors.

8.3.2 *Distributed Scheduling Coordination*

To separate wakeups of nearby sensors, it is essential for each sensor to cooperate with its neighbors. To this end, we need design the protocol defining the distributed coordination among sensors. The key issues here are twofold. First, we need determine for each sensor the set of neighboring sensors that it needs to cooperate with. Second, we need design the coordination protocol through which sensors carry on distributed cooperation.

We introduce a design parameter, *cooperative range*, denoted by CR. It defines, for every sensor, the set of neighbors, which is within the range of CR from the sensor, to cooperate with in determining its wakeup. It is clear that $0 < CR \leq 2R_s$. If two sensors are further than $2R_s$ from each other, they do not have overlapped sensing coverage, and therefore need not to cooperate. Apparently, CR impacts on detection performance. The impact of CR is studied with simulations in Section 8.5. Here, we assume that the communication range (R_t) is greater than $2R_s$, which holds for most sensors. The CAS state transition diagram is illustrated in Fig. 12.2. CAS consists of an initial wakeup-exchange phase and multiple rounds of wakeup adjustments. At the initial phase, every sensor randomly selects a wakeup time and informs it to its neighbors using an INIT broadcast. The length of the exchange phase should be such set that every sensor is able to successfully broadcast its INIT. Each sensor maintains a table of the wakeups of its cooperative neighbors. Upon receiving an INIT from a cooperative neighbor, a sensor extracts the wakeup of this sender, and stores it in the table.

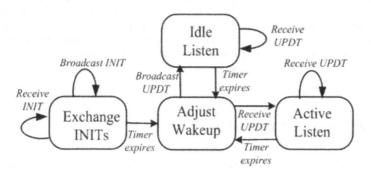

Fig. 8.2 CAS state transition diagram

Multiple rounds of wakeup adjustments follow the exchange phase and each round takes the same period. In each round, a sensor can make at most once wa-keup adjustment. At the beginning of each round, a new wakeup is computed based on the wakeups of its cooperative neighbors. How the new wakeup is computed will be discussed in the next subsection. An adjustment request on its wa-keup is formed if the new wakeup helps reduce detection delay within its vicinity. Next, sensors should contend for wakeup adjustment to avoid parallel adjustments because of computation dependency of new wakeups.

A simple backoff technique is employed to realize the contention. A timer is started upon the generation of the adjustment request. When the timer fires a sen-sor broadcasts the UPDT if it holds an adjustment request, and then commits the adjustment on its wakeup. Upon receiving an UPDT, a sensor checks the ID list in this message. If it is included in the list, it suppresses its own timer and hence can-cels its adjustment request. Meanwhile, it updates the sender's wakeup in its local table. The ID list mitigates the problem of asymmetric distance estimation.

The number of adjustment rounds, denoted by NR, is a system design parameter. A small NR incurs less message exchanges but results in a lower degree of optimization. NR should be adaptive to the density of sensors. A higher density needs a larger *NR*. In simulations, we find that the *NR* that allows on average two UPDTs per sensor leads to a steady system status.

8.3.3 Aggressive Wakeup Adjustment

Given the wakeups of its cooperative neighbors, a sensor needs to determine whether it should adjust its wakeup and what the new wakeup is. CAS regards the cooperative neighbors as equally important in detecting events within its coverage. It is because they are all close to it and their sensing coverage highly overlaps with its own. This suggests that an event that occurs within its vicinity can probably be detected by any of them.

CAS is a completely localized algorithm, in which each sensor can only manipulate its own wakeup time. For each sensor, it is desirable to evenly distribute the wakeups of its cooperative neighbors and itself over τ_{cycle}, which produces the least expected delay and the highest detectability. A wakeup separation is the time difference of two consecutive wakeups. The fundamental property of the evenly distributed wakeups is that the variance of the separations formed by the wakeups is zero. A smaller variance indicates more even distribution of the wakeups. In light of this, each sensor tries to reduce the variance of the wakeup separations seen by it.

The key issue here is how to select the new wakeup so that the variance of the separations can be reduced as much as possible. According to CAS, each sensor takes an aggressive approach to adjusting its wakeup. We consider a sensor G and suppose that it has m cooperative neighbors. CAS considers the wakeup separations formed by the m cooperative neighbors (excluding itself). G identifies the maximum separation and then selects the new wakeup by placing its wakeup in the middle of the maximum wakeup separation. If the resulting new variance is less than the previous one, G will generate a request to update its wakeup.

8.4 Performance Evaluation

In this section, we introduce the evaluation methodology and present performance results.

8.4.1 Experiment Setting

To evaluate the performance of CAS, we conducted comprehensive simulations. The performance metrics are detection delay and detectability. We adopt the configuration data based on the eXtreme Scale Mote [1]. The simulation setting is shown in Table 12.1. Event arrival follows the Poisson process. The sensing field is a square with the side length L. To have different deployment densities of sensors, we fix the length of L and vary the number of sensors deployed in the sensing field.

8.4.2 Results

To study the impact of cooperative range, we vary CR from $0.1R_s$ to $2R_s$. Fig. 12.3 and Fig. 8.4 plot detection delay and detection percentage against CR, respectively. At first, both the mean and the standard deviation of delays decrease gradually as CR increases. They both reach the

Parameter	Value	Parameter	Value
R_t	20m	L	300m
R_s	8m	ξ	100J
Φ_S	19.4mW	τ_{cycle}	10s
Φ_P	24mW	τ_{on}	0.1s
Φ_R	24mW	n	3600

Table 8.1 Simulation Settings

minimum when CR is around $1.3R_s$. Afterwards, the mean and the standard deviation increase as CR increases. This is reasonable because when CR is zero CAS falls back to RIW and when CR is large a sensor over considers those sensors whose coverage actually overlaps little with its own. We ob-serve that the detection percentage increases with increasing CR and reaches the maximum when CR is around $1.3R_s$ The two experiments suggest that a good choice for CR is between $[1.1R_s, 1.4R_s]$.

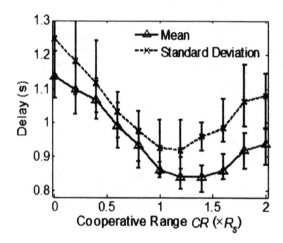

Fig. 8.3 Detection delay vs. cooperative range

We present a comparative study, comparing CAS with the theoretical lower bound (LOB), and RIW. It is very difficult to derive the actual lower bounds. We present the lower bounds based on an optimistic model. A point in the field is covered by on average $n\pi R_s^2/L^2$. For this point, the optimal scheduling for these sensors is to evenly separate the wakeups. This results in

$$\mu_{LOB} = \tau_{cycle}L^2/2n\pi R_s^2, \sigma_{LOB} = \sqrt{\tau_{cycle}L^2/12n\pi R_s^2},$$

$$\chi_{LOB}(t) = \begin{cases} tn\pi R_s^2/\tau_{cycle}L^2, & \text{if } t < \tau_{cycle}L^2/n\pi R_s^2 \\ 1, & \text{otherwise} \end{cases}, \tag{8.12}$$

where μ_{LOB}, σ_{LOB}, and χ_{LOB} denote the lower bounds of expected delay, standard deviation and detectability, respectively. The lower bounds are over optimistic and can never be achieved in reality because it is impossible to have such real deployment.

We compare three algorithms in terms of detection delay and detectability under different sensor density configurations in Fig. 8.5 and Fig. 8.6, respectively. When studying detectability, we set a short event duration, $t = 2s$. We can see CAS is much superior to RIW and the improvement

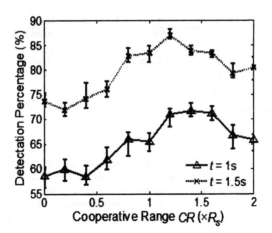

Fig. 8.4 Detectability vs. cooperative range

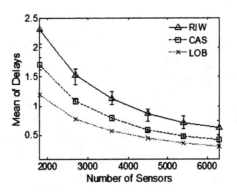

Fig. 8.5 Delay comparison with different densities

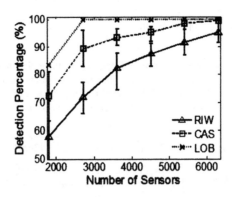

Fig. 8.6 Detectability comparison with different densities, t=2s

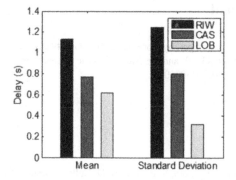

Fig. 8.7 Delay comparison

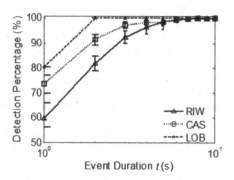

Fig. 8.8 Detectability comparison

of CAS over RIW becomes more significant when sensor density is high. To have a more careful look at the improvement, we further show detection delay and detectability for the configuration of 3600 sensors in Fig. 8.7 and Fig. 8.8. CAS reduces as high as 35% of the mean of delays compared with RIW. The mean of delays achieved by CAS is only 24% higher than that of LOB. We vary event duration from 1s to 10s in Fig. 8.8. When the event duration is 1s, CAS increases as high as 25% of detectability compared with RIW.

8.5 Conclusion

In this paper, we have studied low-power event detection in WSNs. The analysis of event detection and lifetime extension quantifies the detection performance of low duty-cycled detection protocols and reveals the potential lifetime extension by exploiting detection delay. RIW is simple but does not provide optimal detection performance. To improve detection performance, we proposed CAS, which is a fully localized algorithm for detection optimization. CAS only requires minimal knowledge of distances to its neighbors and is scalable to network density. Comprehensive evaluation results demonstrate that CAS significantly improves detection performance in terms of detection latency and detectability.

Acknowledgement

This research was supported in part by Hong Kong RGC Grant HKUST6183/05E, the Key Project of China NSFC Grant 60533110, and the National Basic Research Program of China (973 Program) under Grant No. 2006CB303000.

References

[1] P. Dutta, M. Grimmer, A. Arora, S. Bibyk, and D. Culler, "Design of a Wireless Sen-sor Network Platform for Detecting Rare, Random, and Ephemeral Events," in Pro-ceedings of IPSN, 2005.

[2] S. Brennan, A. Mielke, and D. Torney, "Radioactive Source Detection by Sensor Networks " IEEE Transactions on Nuclear Science, vol. 52, 2005.

[3] E. Shih, S. H. Cho, N. Ickes, R. Min, A. Sinha, A. Wang, and A. Chandrakasan, "Physical Layer Driven Protocol and Algorithm Design for Energy-Efficient Wireless Sensor Networks," in Proceedings of MobiCom, 2001.

[4] C. Gui and P. Mohapatra, "Power Conservation and Quality of Surveillance in Target Tracking Sensor Networks," in Proceedings of MobiCom, 2004.

[5] S. Ren, Q. Li, H. Wang, X. Chen, and X. Zhang, "Probabilistic Coverage for Object Tracking in Sensor Networks," in Proceedings of MobiCom poster, 2004.

[6] T. He, S. Krishnamurthy, J. Stankovic, T. Abdelzaher, L. Luo, T. Yan, L. Gu, J. Hui, and B. Krogh, "Energy-efficient surveillance systems using wireless sensor networks," in Proceedings of Mobisys'04, 2004.

[7] F. Ye, G. Zhong, J. Cheng, S. Lu, and L. Zhang, "PEAS: A Robust Energy Conserv-ing Protocol for Long-lived Sensor Networks," in Proceedings of ICDCS, 2003.

[8] D. Tian and N. D. Georganas, "A Node Scheduling Scheme for Energy Conservation in Large Wireless Sensor Networks," Wireless Communication and Mobile Compu-ting, vol. 3, pp. 271-290, 2003.

[9] T. Yan, T. He, and J. A. Stankovic, "Differentiated Surveillance for Sensor Networks," in Proceedings of SenSys, 2003.

[10] X. Wang, G. Xing, Y. Zhang, C. Lu, R. Pless, and C. Gill, "Integrated Coverage and Connectivity Configuration in Wireless Sensor Networks," in Proceedings of SenSys, Los Angeles, CA, USA, 2003.

[11] V. Shnayder, M. Hempstead, B.-r. Chen, G. Werner-Allen, and M. Welsh, "Simulating the Power Consumption of Large-Scale Sensor Network Applications," in Proceedings of SenSys, Baltimore, MD, 2004.

[12] J. Elson, L. Girod, and D. Estrin, "Fine-Grained Network Time Synchronization using Reference Broadcasts," in Proceedings of OSDI, Boston, MA, 2002.

Chapter 9
Understanding User Behavior in Large-Scale Video-on-Demand Systems[*]

Hongliang Yu, Dongdong Zheng, Ben Y. Zhao and Weimin Zheng

Abstract Video-on-demand over IP (VOD) is one of the best-known examples of next-generation Internet applications cited as a goal by networking and multimedia researchers. Without empirical data, researchers have generally relied on simulated models to drive their design and developmental efforts. In this paper, we present one of the first measurement studies of a large VOD system, using data covering 219 days and more than 150,000 users in a VOD system deployed by China Telecom. Our study focuses on user behavior, content access patterns, and their implications on the design of multimedia streaming systems. Our results also show that when used to model the user-arrival rate, the traditional Poisson model is conservative and overestimates the probability of large arrival groups. We introduce a modified Poisson distribution that more accurately models our observations. We also observe a surprising result, that video session lengths has a weak inverse correlation with the videos popularity. Finally, we gain better understanding of the sources of video popularity through analysis of a number of internal and external factors.[2]

Key words: Video-on-demand, User behavior, modeling, Poisson distribution

9.1 Introduction

Streaming Video-on-Demand (VOD) over the Internet is the next major step in the evolution of media content delivery. For several years, cable and satellite providers (Comcast, Dish Networks), video rental companies (Netflix) and other media companies (TiVo) have been developing online streaming video systems for an increasingly demanding and growing consumer population [?]. By leveraging the increasing availability of broadband access, VOD systems offer users the ability to browse, select, view, and scan through media content from a large content repository on an on-demand basis, all from the comfort of their homes. With recent studies [15, 17, 19] that show

Hongliang Yu, Dongdong Zheng and Weimin Zheng
Computer Science Department, Tsinghua University, Beijing, China,
e-mail: {hlyu@,zdd03@mails.,zwm-dcs@}tsinghua.edu.cn

Ben Y. Zhao
Computer Science Department, U. C. Santa Barbara, CA, USA
e-mail: ravenben@cs.ucsb.edu

[*] Source: ACM SIGOPS Operating Systems Review, Volume 40, Issue 4 (October 2006), Proceedings of the 2006 EuroSys conference, Pages: 333 - 344, 2006 Copyright ©2006 Association for Computing Machinery, Inc. Reprinted by permission. DOI Bookmark: http://doi.acm.org/10.1145/1217935.1217968

[2] This work is supported by the National Natural Science Foundation of China under Grant No.60433040. This work is also partially supported by DARPA BAA04-11 and by the NSF under CAREER Award CNS-0546216.

a significant shift in Internet traffic from the web to multimedia content, it is clear that both the necessary capacity and demand for streaming multimedia have arrived.

While current VOD systems remain in the prototype or design stages, a key challenge companies face is how to design an architecture that scales smoothly to a large number of customers, all while maintaining low access latency, high video quality and reasonable operational costs. Designers use simulations based on common assumptions to evaluate and drive their architectures. Unfortunately, the lack of deployed VOD systems meant few of these assumptions have been validated on real measurement data.

In this paper, we present one of the first measurement studies of a large deployed VOD system. Our data set comes from detailed logs of a video-on-demand system deployed by China Telecom, covering a total of 1.5 million unique users for a period of seven months in 2004. Our analysis seeks to validate and adapt existing assumptions about streaming media, focusing on user behavior and content access patterns. More specifically, we examine the accuracy of existing models for user arrival rates and request patterns. By comparing and contrasting our analysis with existing models, we rectified some of the common misunderstandings about VOD users and their access patterns. In addition, we derived more accurate models of user behavior and access patterns based on our analysis, which will not only increase the accuracy of existing simulations, but also serve as building blocks in more sophisticated experiments.

Initial analysis revealed several key facts. First, user distributions follow clear patterns with respect to time and arrival rates match a modified form of the Poisson distribution. Second, the average session is quite short, due to users sampling movies by "scanning" through them, much like the "intro-sampling" mode supported by portable CD-players. In addition, session lengths are influenced by file popularity. But surprisingly, the correlation is an inverse one, where less popular videos actually see longer session times. Third, our system does not follow the "fetch-at-most-once" model, and our file popularity matches the Zipf's distribution much better than prior work suggested. Finally, we find the change of file popularity over time is greatly influenced by external factors such as highly visible "recommended videos" and "most popular videos" lists, suggesting that system designers can use them as predictable guidance metrics for near-future user access requests.

The rest of this paper is organized as follows. We begin by first describing the China Telecom video-on-demand system and our source data in Section 9.2. Then in Section 9.3, we present our detailed analysis on user behavior characteristics and content access patterns. Next, we compare our approach study to related work in Section 9.6. Finally, we summarize our results and conclude in Section 9.7.

9.2 The PowerInfo VOD System

Measurement data used in our study come from logs collected during daily operation of the PowerInfo Video-on-demand system. Currently deployed VOD systems are mainly operated as a free value-added services by telecommunication companies in China. Paying customers can access the large video libraries free of charge on an unlimited basis. Many of these are Internet Service Providers with large bandwidth resources, whose primary goal is to attract new users. PowerInfo is one of the leading video streaming software providers in China. Its system provides service to over 20 cities in China, most of which are generally managed by regional branches of China Telecom. To date, the PowerInfo system user base exceeds 1.5 million, the large majority of whom are connected using broadband (512 kb/s) to the home.

The PowerInfo Video-on-Demanding system uses a distributed architecture for media streaming. Customers are divided into regional networks, each served by one or more server clusters known as Units. Nodes in each VOD Unit cluster serve one of three different roles: *application servers*, *management servers* and *media servers*. In each unit, one application server caches video metadata, performs authentication, and interacts directly with users to schedule streaming requests.

Role	# of Servers	Functionality
Application server	1	Task scheduling, load balancing
Management server	1	System monitoring, management, accounting
Media server	⩾ 1	Media streaming

Table 9.1 Components in the Powerinfo VOD system

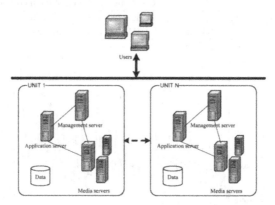

Fig. 9.1 Architecture of the PowerInfo VOD system

Prog #	Starttime (s)	Endtime (s)	Traffic	MS	AS
2884	1097397599	1097400153	764192	22	1
16742	1097397600	1097397619	3980	21	1
2021	1097397600	1097400053	357888	22	1
...	...	...	...	...	...

Table 9.2 Log Samples

Tasks route to one or more media servers, which stream video directly to the user. Application servers load balance tasks appropriately across media servers. Finally, a management server monitors all servers in the VOD Unit, and perform accounting functions based on user requests. Statistics gathered on user requests are used to determine the optimal number and placement of replicates for each individual video file. We list these components and their responsibilities in Table 9.2.

For the analysis presented in this paper, we used a complete segment of the PowerInfo system log ranging from May 16th to December 20th of 2004. The system log includes both an extensive record of user accesses and a full metadata listing of available video files. For each streaming session, the user log includes the user's IP address, ID number of video requested, timestamps for the start and end of the session, and the media and application servers used. A sample of the user log is shown in Table 9.2.

We focus our analysis to logs from a single representative city with a total user base of 150,000 users served by 3 VOD Units. We list the hardware configuration of this regional system in Table 9.3. Note that like many other regions, all servers in these Units are connected to the main bone of China Telecom through a gigabyte network.

We summarize the logged statistics for our representative city in Table 9.4. During the logged period of 219 days, users in our representative city issued more than 21 million video requests covering a total of over 6700 unique video files. The total length of videos streamed is more than 317,000 minutes, or roughly 5300 hours. Figure 9.2 shows the daily user distribution during our

UNIT	Components	Num	Hardware configurations
1	Application server	1	HP DL360 G2 (2*PIII XEON 1.4G, 1G RAM)
	Management server	1	HP DL580 (2*PIII XEON 700, 1G RAM)
	Media server	4	HP DL580 (8*PIII XEON 1.4G, 2G RAM)14*73G SCSI HD
2	Application server	1	Co-located with one of the media servers
	Management server	1	Co-located with one of the media servers
	Media server	3	HP DL5807(8*PIII XEON 1.4G, 2G RAM) 10*73G SCSI HD
3	Application server	1	Co-located with one of the media servers
	Management server	1	Co-located with one of the media servers
	Media server	2	Compaq DL380 G3(4*XEON 3G, 1G RAM)10*36G SCSI HD

Table 9.3 Hardware configurations

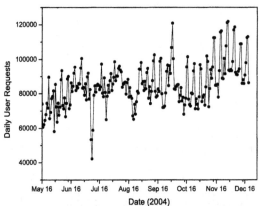

Fig. 9.2 Number of daily user accesses across the entire log period of 219 days.

Sessions	Length	Files Avail.	Files accessed
21,498,338	219 days	7036	6716

Table 9.4 Statistics summary of logs

tracking period. In addition, the first week of May and October are both Chinese national holidays, and we were able to isolate user behavior changes during these two vacation weeks.

Finally, we briefly describe the types of videos available in the PowerInfo system. The large majority of videos in the library are recordings of older television shows and Chinese movies, encoded via MPEG1, MPEG2 and MPEG4 codecs at relatively low resolution. A typical file is an older movie, roughly 100 minutes in length, and stored as a 300 MByte MPEG1 file. We note that while PowerInfo is a commercially deployed VOD system, videos can be accessed by members free of charge on an unlimited basis. Note that this value-added service model is also being adopted by Comcast Cable as they begin their video-on-demand service deployment in the US [?].

9.3 User Access Patterns

In this section, we discuss the basic characteristics of user behavior in our large scale VOD system. Understanding how users access the system can help system designers optimize resources in order to produce the best user experience at minimal cost. We begin our analysis with user access patterns

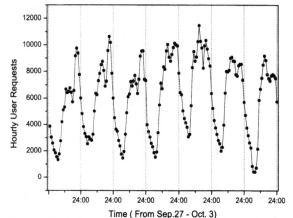

Fig. 9.3 Hourly distribution of user accesses during the course of a single week. (China's week-long national holiday begins annually on October 1st.)

over time, then discuss the modeling of the user arrival distribution, and conclude with a study of user session length distributions.

9.3.1 User Accesses over time

We begin by trying to gain a basic understanding of user access patterns in the system. The distribution of user accesses can be characterized as a function of time. We examine its distribution first across hours of the day, and then across days of the week.

9.3.1.1 Daily Access Patterns

Looking at how user accesses change during the course of a day, we found that as expected, the user accesses follow a clear daily pattern. While our data shows a consistent pattern across most days, we focus specifically on the days with the highest traffic volume. Therefore, we focused on seven days during the first week of October 2004, when the PowerInfo system experienced its highest number of user accesses due to the arrival of the week-long national holiday.

Figure 9.3 shows a time-series plot of the total number of users. As expected, within one single day the number of users drops gradually during the early morning (12AM-7AM) and the afternoon (2PM-5PM), while it climbs up to a peak when users are in noon break (Noon-2PM) or after work (6PM-9PM). This pattern reflects the expected behavior as users entertain themselves during breaks and after work hours. Naturally, the second daily peak in the number of users usually arrives after the "prime time" (7PM-10PM) of the commercial television industry.

9.3.1.2 Weekly Access Patterns

To get a broader view of the user distribution over time, we chose data for a period of seven consecutive weeks from our records. We plot the daily access count in Figure 9.4, with the division

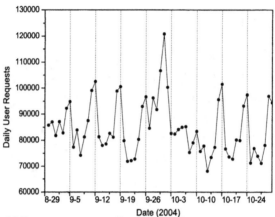

Fig. 9.4 A view of daily user requests covering a period of seven weeks, including the week-long national holiday from 10/1 to 10/7.

into weeks shown as vertical lines marking each Sunday night at midnight. As we can see, while the daily number of user requests can fluctuate during the first three workdays of the week, the average number of daily requests increases steadily in the second half of the week, reaching its peak on Sunday. As expected, this shows a direct correlation with users' work habits during the week, and more relaxed time at home during the weekends.

We observe an interesting phenomenon just days before the start of the national holiday on October 1, 2004. There is a substantial increase in user requests starting on September 30th, the day before vacation starts. Clearly, worker productivity is impacted by employees watching more videos at work in anticipation of the arriving holiday week. While requests hit an all-time daily high on the first day of vacation (10/1/2004), they quickly drop to below-normal levels for the next two weeks. This is consistent with the traditional annual boom in domestic travel that occurs every year during and following the national holiday. While the average subscriber is vacationing on the road, active requests on PowerInfo drop significantly.

9.3.2 User Arrival Rates

User arrival distributions in multimedia systems are often modeled using a Poisson distribution. Here, we study the validity of that model applied to our usage data. First, we look at the general user arrival rate. We measure user arrival by counting the number of arrivals in 5 second buckets. Figure 9.5 shows the results of this measurement across the entire log period. From this simple result, we can draw two conclusions. First, the number of arrivals usually ranges from 0 to 27 users per 5 seconds, or 0 to 5 users per second. Second, this arrival rate does not match a Poisson distribution.

One of the main challenges in the design of a VOD system is how to handle a large number of simultaneous users. Therefore, we take a closer look at user arrival patterns under periods of heavy load. We isolate the user arrival data from 6PM-9PM for each day of our log period. As shown in Figure 9.3, this is the daily period with the heaviest user traffic. When we try to match this arrival distribution with one derived from the Poisson distribution, we get Figure 9.6. It seems that while the heavy-load user arrival distribution looks similar to the Poisson distribution, the two do not match well. From the analysis, we see that the Poisson distribution underestimates the possibility

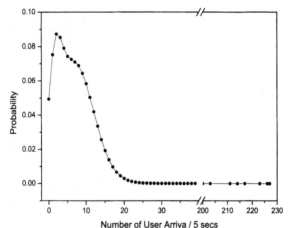

Fig. 9.5 User arrival distribution showing the number of arrivals per 5 second intervals across the entire log period.

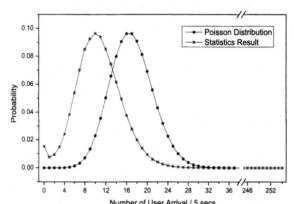

Fig. 9.6 Statistics of user arrival versus Poisson distribution (with lambda=15)

of small arrival cases and it over-estimates the probability of large arrivals. So any VOD system or simulation model based on a Poisson distribution will result in an over-provisioned system.

To provide a more accurate model, we introduce a modified version of the Poisson distribution by replacing the independence variant x with $(N - x)$, where N is the maximum number of user arrivals in our records. As Figure 9.7 shows, our tracking results match the modified Poisson distribution very well. This modified version of Poisson distribution can be defined as:

$$P(X) = \frac{\lambda^{(N-X)}e^{-\lambda}}{(N-X)!}, X = 0, 1, 2...$$ (9.1)

Here, N is the maximum number of user arrivals in a target system. In Figure 9.7, we used the values $\lambda = 17$ and $N = 27$. Clearly, our modified Poisson distribution can be used as a reference model to study the user behavior of large scale streaming services in a heavy workload.

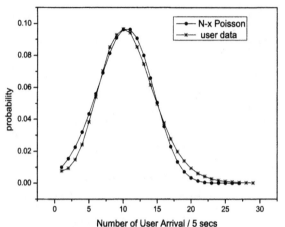
Fig. 9.7 Statistics of user arrival versus modified Poisson distribution

Session length	5 min	10 min	25 min	50 min
percentage	37.44%	52.55%	75.25%	94.23%

Table 9.5 Statistics of session length

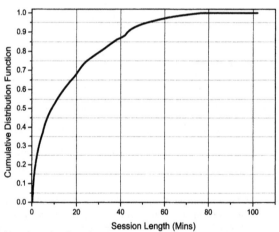
Fig. 9.8 Distribution of session length

9.3.3 Session Lengths

We now turn our attention to an analysis of the lengths of streaming sessions measured on the PowerInfo VOD system. In particular, we wish to better understand why and how users terminate a streaming session. We first present general results on session lengths across all videos. Next, we examine session length statistics for two representative video streams to explain user behavior artifacts. Finally, we explore the relationship between session length and video popularity.

We first note that the videos in the VOD library span a wide range of lengths, including everything from television shows that range between 30 to 60 minutes to a large number of movies that range from 90 to more than 120 minutes. To adjust for this large variance, we use as our metric

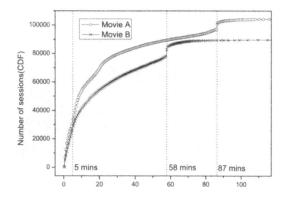

Fig. 9.9 The session length distribution for two popular movies. Movie A has a total length of 87 minutes, while movie B has a total length of 58 minutes.

the *normalized session length* (NSL), the proportion of the video viewed before the session terminated (*SessionLength/VideoLength*). In addition, because we are using session length data to help us better understand user behavior, we focus on sessions proactively terminated by the user, and remove from our dataset sessions that ran to completion. Specifically, we examine for Table 9.5 and Figure 9.8 sessions that lasted less than 85% of their video lengths. This accounts for roughly 86.33% of the entire dataset.

We summarize some session length statistics in Table 9.5, and plot the cumulative distribution function (CDF) of session lengths in Figure 9.8. As shown in both, the majority of partial sessions (52.55%) are terminated by the user within the first 10 minutes. In fact, 37% of these sessions do not last past the first five minutes. Within 25 minutes, more than three-quarters of all sessions have been terminated. Note that since this dataset covers nearly 90% of the entire dataset, we expect similar results to hold across the full dataset.

These results show an extremely "impatient" audience, who despite the availability of program guides and movie information, often scan through the beginning of videos to quickly determine their interest. This evidence suggests that prefix cache systems such as [20] can significantly improve user response time by caching the beginning of a large portion of videos in easily accessible memory or disk. Our results predict that caching the first 10 minutes of videos will be sufficient to serve 50% of all user sessions. While we can attribute some of this user impatience to the fact that users do not pay per video, this evidence also suggests that even pay-per-video VOD systems can significantly improve user satisfaction if they can offer users the ability to scan through the beginning of movies for free. This approach is currently offered by some Pay-Per-View movie services such as DirecTV.

To shed additional light on this phenomenon, we next examine in detail session lengths for two popular videos. We collect the lengths of all sessions that streamed these two videos, and show the session length distribution in Figure 9.9. Note that for clarity between the lines, we used a "non-normalized" CDF. We note the presence of two large spikes in sessions terminated within the first 10 minutes. A large number of sessions end within the first minute. We can only speculate that these users quickly determined they had ordered the wrong video after seeing the initial title screen. This suggests that VOD systems need to do a good job of providing information about movies in order to reduce the frequency of these types of "fruitless" sessions. Another major spike occurs around the five minute mark, when a large number of sessions end. We can presume that these users are "scanning" through videos, and having seen enough of the movie, decided to move on to the next video. Finally, the rest of the user sessions are spread out in length, except for two clusters of user sessions that match the length of each video (58 minutes for *B* and 87 minutes for *A*). Those account for users who watched the entire length of the video. The small portion of

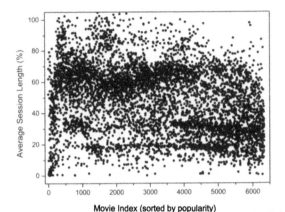

Fig. 9.10 A comparison of session lengths to video popularity. Average session lengths for videos are sorted by the video's popularity from least popular to most popular.

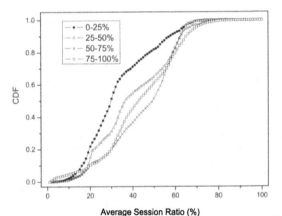

Fig. 9.11 A CDF comparison of session lengths to video popularity, with four lines representing the four quartiles of popularity. 0-25% represent the most popular quartile, and 75-100% represent the least popular quartile.

sessions that go over the video length are users who have extended the session by rewinding and replaying certain segments of the video.

Finally, we explore the relationship between session length and the popularity of a video. One might assume that the video with the highest demand will have the best chance of holding on to its audience for the duration of the video. Surprisingly, our data shows the opposite result.

We first plot the average NSL of each video with videos sorted in order from least to most popular. Here popularity is measured by the total number of user accesses throughout the log period. As seen in Figure 9.10, results are fairly scattered, showing a weak correlation. However, we do see a general trend showing that more popular videos often have lower NSL values than less popular videos.

To more clearly detect any possible correlation between the two, we partitioned all movies from Figure 9.10 into four quartiles according to their popularity. We then plotted the CDF of all NSL values of each quartile in Figure 9.11, where the line 0-25% indicates the most popular quartile of movies and 75-100% denotes the least popular movies. We see that while weak, there is a distinct inverse relationship between popularity and session lengths. Note that the session lengths for videos of different popularity are similar at the beginning and end of videos. The main difference occurs in the middle of videos, where less popular videos do a better job of keeping the user's attention.

This inverse correlation is an interesting result that may provide insight into the way users watch videos. We hypothesize that the highly popular videos suffer from loss of interest after repeat viewings. In other words, people watching the most popular videos are likely to have seen them before, either in another medium (theater or DVD) or in a prior VOD session. Therefore, they lose interest more easily during the movie, resulting in shorter session times.

9.3.4 Implications

These results on file popularity and session times suggest a number of guidelines for optimizing performance in VOD systems. First, as expected, the clear diurnal patterns in user access patterns mean that maintenance and upgrade operations should be scheduled for early morning hours (5-8AM) in order to minimize impact on users. Note that we do not observe any effects of different timezones, since all of China operates on a single timezone. For systems deployed in the USA or Europe, we would expect a more even distribution of accesses in the morning hours. Next, our observation of short session times suggest that a high proportion (70%) of sessions are terminated in the first 20 minutes. Therefore, system caches can maximize their effectiveness by allocating the majority of their capacity to storing beginning segments of movies. Finally, our initial results show shorter sessions for popular movies, suggesting that beginning segments of popular movies should be prioritized over latter segments in any caching scheme. Clearly, VOD systems need to exploit time-varying user interest patterns by intelligently partitioning videos into segments and taking their time index in replica and cache management.

9.4 Popularity and User Interest

We now examine the issue of user interest and video popularity. Having an accurate model of how user requests spread across videos can help system designers choose system parameters such as cache size and replication factors for popular items. In this section, we look at how a static snapshot of video popularity compares to the Pareto principle, explore the applicability of the Zipf distribution to VOD requests, and examine how video popularity changes over time.

9.4.1 Pareto Principle

The Pareto Principle, or 80-20 rule, is the most popular rule used to describe the skew of user interest distributions. To test the accuracy of the Pareto principle on our data, we analyze user logs for the entire 219 days, and sort all objects who were accessed at least once according to how often they were requested. The results are plotted in Figure 9.12.

As we see from the figure, given the opportunity to choose from a wide selection of videos, user requests are spread more widely than predicted by the Pareto principle, with 10% of the most popular objects accounting for approximately 60% of all accesses while 23% of the objects account for 80% of the accesses. This is a more moderate result than the frequently referred to 80/20 or 90/10 rule. We believe that this moderate Pareto principle is relevant to VOD systems with relatively large libraries. Consequently, VOD systems are likely to require larger than expected caches in order to achieve the same hit rates predicted by the traditional Pareto Principle.

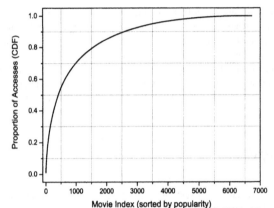

Fig. 9.12 CDF of videos accessed sorted by popularity. A total of 6716 videos were requested at least once.

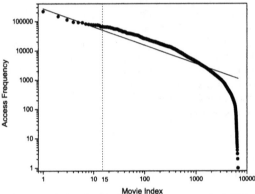

Fig. 9.13 Fitting the video popularity distribution of videos across the 219 day log period to a Zipf distribution using a log-log graph.

9.4.2 Request (Popularity) Distribution

In examining video popularity, one of our main goals is to explore the applicability of Zipf-like distribution to VOD requests. Zipf's law is commonly used as a sound model to capture the distribution of media accesses. Early in 1994, Dan and Sitaram [9] considered the distribution of hits on the available videos and chose Zipf distribution to model video popularity. Wolf and Yu, in 1997, noticed that in their study that Zipf-like distribution roughly matched their access pattern, with a varying degrees of skew week by week. Breslau et al. [4] confirmed this result when analyzing characteristics of webpage request distribution. Later in 2000, Acharya and Smith [1] showed that Zipf distribution with a fixed parameter α does not accurately model the video file popularity distribution. In 2002, Cherkasova and Gupta [6] argued that although the distribution of client accesses to media files can be approximated by a Zipf-like distribution, the time scale plays an important role in this approximation. Finally, measurements by Gummadi *et al.* [12] showed that file downloads on the Kazaa [?] network did not follow the Zipf distribution, and instead proposed a *fetch-at-most-once* model.

In this subsection, we set out to determine how accurately Zipf-like distributions apply to our data and the characteristics of the varying skew factor. The Zipf-like distribution is defined as

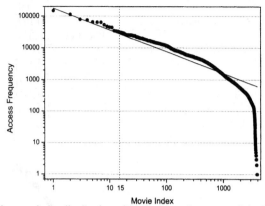

Fig. 9.14 Fitting the popularity distribution of 3969 videos that were originally introduced at the launch date of PowerInfo.

N	Min.	Max.	Mean	Std. Dev.
209	0.000	0.348	0.199	0.070

Table 9.6 Statistic summary of skew factors

$$\sum_{i=1}^{N} P_i = 1, P_k = \frac{\lambda}{K^{1-\alpha}}, \lambda = \frac{1}{\sum_{i=1}^{N} \frac{1}{i^{1-\alpha}}} \qquad (9.2)$$

In this formula, N is the number of available movie titles, i is the index of a movie title in the list of N movies sorted in order of decreasing popularity, and α is the skew factor. Setting $\alpha = 0$ corresponds to a so-called pure Zipf distribution, which is highly skewed. Setting $\alpha = 1$ corresponds to a uniform distribution. So Zipf-like distributions model a wide range of skew alternatives. It is also noteworthy that this distribution, typically used as the basis for investigations on video server operations, is completely independent of the number of users in the system.

In prior work by Gummadi *etal*. [12], the authors used a log-log plot to argue that popularity data in VOD systems did not in fact fit the Zipf distribution. The log-log graph showed that accesses for both the most and least popular items were lower than those predicted by Zipf. Instead, they proposed a "fetch-at-most-once" model to fit existing VOD data from a 1992 video-rental data set. To verify the applicability of Zipf distribution to our data, we plot the access frequency of videos in a log-log graph against a Zipf distribution. The results in Figure 9.13 show that unlike the 1992 video rental data set, most of our data fit the Zipf distribution well, with the exception of a heavy tail of unpopular items. This contradicts the "fetch-at-most-once" model, but fits within a video-on-demand model, where users cannot store streamed movies locally and must re-fetch the video for repeat viewing.

We speculated that the long tail of low popularity items might be due to the aging of old videos. To test this hypothesis, we identify the 3969 videos that were introduced into PowerInfo at the launch of the system on January 9, 2004. When we plot the log-log graph of their accesses through our log period in Figure 9.14, we see that the result is very similar to the overall data set, and does not confirm our hypothesis. We performed further analysis by plotting the log-log graph of all videos introduced *after* the launch date, and again the results are similar.

While popularity statistics across the entire log fit Zipf well, daily segments show Zipf fits with highly variable skew factors, as shown in Table 9.6. To determine the characteristics of the constantly-changing skew factor, we use the Kolmogorov-Smirnov Goodness-of-Fit Test [5]. The Kolmogorov-Smirnov test is useful in deciding if a sample comes from a population with a specific distribution, and it is defined as

N		209
Normal Parameters (a,b)	Mean	0.199
	Std. Dev.	0.070
Most Extreme Differences	Absolute	0.037
	Positive	0.028
	Negative	-0.037
Kolmogorov-Smirnov Z		0.531
Asymptotic Significance (2-tailed)		0.940

Table 9.7 One-Sample Kolmogorov-Smirnov Test

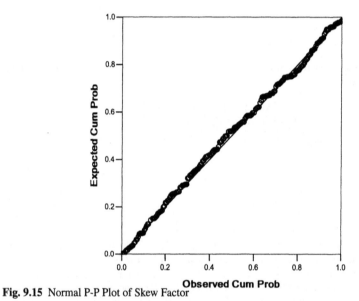

Fig. 9.15 Normal P-P Plot of Skew Factor

Skewness	Std. Error	Kurtosis	Std. Error
-0.253	0.168	0.048	0.335

Table 9.8 Descriptive statistics of skew factor

$$Z = \sqrt{N} \cdot D, D = \max_{1 \leq i \leq N} |F(Y_i) - \frac{i}{N}| \qquad (9.3)$$

Here F is the theoretical cumulative distribution of the distribution being tested. The Z test statistic is the product of the square root of the sample size (N) and the largest absolute difference between the empirical and theoretical CDFs (D). Also, we calculated the two-tailed significance level (Asymptotic Significance), testing the probability that the observed distribution would not deviate significantly from the expected distribution in either direction. If the significance level result is above 0.05, then it was safe for us to assume that the data tested was not significantly different from the hypothesized (*e.g.* normal) distribution.

Using Kolmogorov-Smirnov Goodness-of-Fit, we tested our skew factor values against different distributions, and found that the normal distribution matched our data best. As shown in Table 9.7, the Asymptotic Significance value (0.940) was well above 0.05, indicating that the normal distribution is a good fit for the skew factors we observed in fitting Zipf's law.

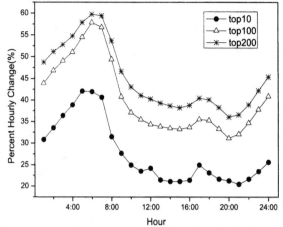

Fig. 9.16 Rate of change in user interest, as seen over hours in a single day.

Further, the Normal Probability-probability Plot, or Normal P-P Plot, plots the cumulative proportion of a single numeric variable against the cumulative proportion expected if the sample were from a normal distribution. If the sample is from a normal distribution, the points will cluster around a straight line. This is one method of assessing whether a variable is normally distributed. As shown in Figure 9.15, our data points are well represented by a straight line. This together with our Kolmogorov-Smirnov result above, shows that the Zipf's skew factor is normally distributed in our VOD system.

Table 9.8 also presents the descriptive statistics of all of the 209 skew factors we collected during our analysis. Here, a negative skewness value means that our data has a long left tail, but it still can be taken as a symmetrical distribution since the skewness value is not more than twice its standard error. Meanwhile, the positive kurtosis indicates that our observations cluster more and have longer tails than those in the normal distribution.

9.4.3 Rate of Change in User interest

Our analysis of video popularity shows user interest is spread widely across a number of videos. We now examine the rate at which user interest changes, an important design consideration for VOD system architects. To optimize the performance of VOD systems, a commonly used approach is to move popular objects around the network based on the transfer of user interest. So it is essential to consider how frequently the content in the buffer or peer server should be refreshed. This subsection analyzes the rate of change in user interest by examining the videos that make up the top-10, top-100 and top-200 in accesses for different time periods.

Figures 9.16, 9.17 and 9.18 show the percentage of change in the top 10/100/200 videos over different time scales. From Figure 9.16, we see that user interest varies significantly on an hourly basis. The highest rates of change seem to occur near the morning, when the rate of change almost reaches 30% in the top 10 videos, and around 50% in the top 100. It is noteworthy that the top 10 is significantly more stable compared to the top 100, and only changes an average of 10-20% for most hours of the day. Note that during the most busy hours from 11AM to midnight, the top-10 list is remarkably stable. We hypothesize that the increased variance in the top 10 between midnight and 8AM is due to the more varied and unpredictable access patterns of a smaller user set between

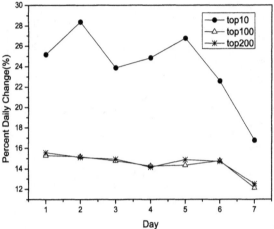

Fig. 9.17 Rate of change in user interest, seen over days in a single week. Day 1 represents Monday while day 7 represents Sunday.

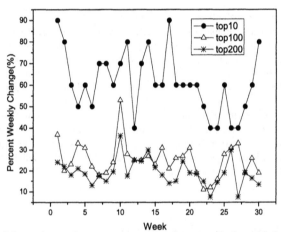

Fig. 9.18 Rate of change in user interest, seen over weeks across the log period.

those hours. In general, these results suggest that an adaptive cache that focuses on storing the top 10 accessed videos will be able to serve the top 80-90% of the most frequently requested videos.

In order to get some idea of how fast users' interest changes day by day, we calculate the daily change across the course of a week, and average those results for all weeks during our log period. The result shown in Figure 9.17 shows that the top-10 list fluctuated significantly through the week, while the top-100 and top-200 lists were much more stable with a steady change rate between 12 and 15 percent. The underlying reason for this result is that our system inserts some new objects into the content server every day, and that the latest video files usually supplant the current favorites within a day of being released.

Finally, Figure 9.18 shows the rate at which the top movies changed week by week. Here we can draw the same conclusion as from the daily change pattern. The only difference is that the top-10 list fluctuates more radically at this time scale. Note that in the top 200 videos on Figure 9.17 and Figure 9.18, the rate of change closely matches the top 100 curve. This suggests that there is likely very little performance gain between caching the top 200 videos and caching the top 100.

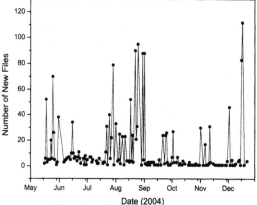

Fig. 9.19 New video files introduced on a daily basis.

The key implication of these results is that the top 10 and top 100 most popular videos exhibit churn on different time scales. The top-10 lists exhibits relative stability on an hourly basis, but shows high churn on a daily or weekly basis. The top 100 videos however, shows stability over the long term. This suggests a two level caching model, where a fast but relatively small adaptive cache focuses on capturing a small number (~ 10) of the most popular videos, while a potentially slower but larger secondary cache serves content based on the second tier of popular videos.

9.5 Understanding Popularity

Our analysis has shown that a small number of videos account for a large proportion of total user accesses. It is unclear whether this is purely a social phenomenon, or whether it has been influenced by external factors. In this section, we seek to understand this issue by analyzing data on the introduction of new videos into the system, and examining the impact of external factors such as official recommended movie lists or lists of most popular videos.

9.5.1 Introduction of New Content

Tang[22] introduced a new file introduction process in HP corporate media servers. He argued that the time gap between two introduction days followed a Pareto distribution. However, the data in our system shows no such distribution. In fact, new movies are generally added to system on a daily basis.

While PowerInfo launched in January 2004 with an initial video library of 3969 videos, our log of new file introductions began on May 16, 2004. Figure 9.19 presents the overview of the new file introduction process in our VOD system on a daily level (from May 16th, 2004 to December 22nd, 2004). Note that on some days more than 30 new files are introduced into the system. In such cases, those clusters of files are usually TV mini-series movies or cartoons. From the user interest perspective, multiple episodes of the same TV mini-series are similar to a single movie, and usually do not result in the same disruption of user interest as would if the same number of independent videos were added to the system.

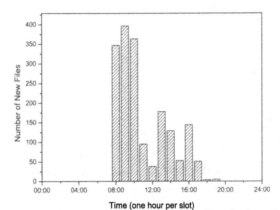

Fig. 9.20 Hourly histogram of when new videos are introduced into the PowerInfo system.

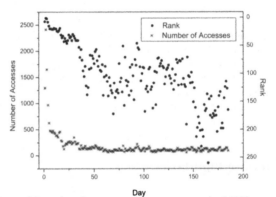

Fig. 9.21 The "life span" in rank and accesses of an average movie: 14102.

The next logical question we answer is what time of the day is new content most often introduced. Figure 9.20 shows a cumulative histogram showing when new videos were introduced into the system. We see that most new content is introduced during the morning hours (8AM-10AM), when the system is lightly loaded. If we revisit our data on the rate of change in user interest shown in Figure 9.16, this corresponds to the relatively high rate of change between 9AM and 11AM. Clearly, the availability of new content captures users' attention and requests, thereby changing the distribution of user requests.

These results demonstrate the direct impact new content introduction has on user requests. Correlation to fluctuations in user interest suggests that dynamic caches should be re-calibrated shortly after a large amount of new content is introduced to the system. This way, users can quickly adapt to new video popularity patterns emerging after the integration of new material.

9.5.2 *Impact of Recommendations*

To enhance the user experience, the PowerInfo web interface includes some user-friendly features, including two features. One is a list of the 15 most popular movies of the month, the top-15 hot list, with a link to each movie. The other is a list of 20 movies recommended by the system. Most

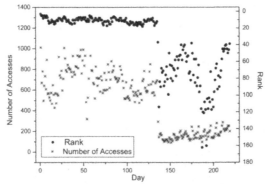

Fig. 9.22 The "life span" of one of the most popular movies, 116, showing the impact membership on top-15 hot lists.

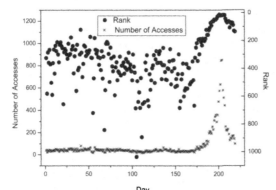

Fig. 9.23 The "life span" of an older movie, 9757, showing the impact of a movie remake rekindling interest.

of these are recent additions to the system. As our analysis will show, the appearance of movies on these two lists has a significant impact on their popularity within the VOD system.

We start our analysis by taking a closer look at the rise and fall of a typical video in our system, movie 14102. We choose movie 14012 because its history of popularity is quite representative of most videos in our system. In Figure 9.21, we plot both its rank in terms of video popularity and also its number of user requests against time. When it is first introduced into the system on June 19, 2004, 14102 became the 7th most popular video in the system. On the next day, it became the most frequently requested video with 2413 daily accesses. But in the next few days, its popularity rank decreased rapidly.

We observed that while most videos share a similar burst of popularity, their ability to maintain popularity is what sets them apart from each other. While some movies stay consistently popular, others exit the limelight quickly, dropping from 1000 daily accesses to 50 in one week.

The effect of the hot movie list can be seen from the life span of movie 116, shown in Figure 9.22. This movie is one of the top 5 in total accesses across our entire log period, and maintains its popularity ranking in the top 15 for a significant amount of time. But once 116 dropped out of the ranks of the top 15, it was never able to recover its popularity, and both accesses and rank dropped significantly. What makes the story of movie 116 even more interesting is the unusual way that it dropped out of the top-15 hot list. We found out from the system administrator that on day 136 of our log, he saw movie 116 had been on the top-15 list for several months, and manually

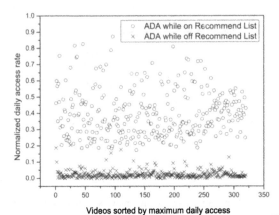

Fig. 9.24 The impact of membership on the recommendation list on normalized average daily accesses.

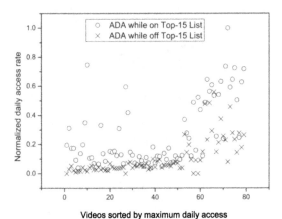

Fig. 9.25 The impact of membership on the Top-15 list on normalized average daily accesses.

removed it from the top-15 hot list in favor of more recent popular movies. While the top-15 list is usually generated monthly by the system, this rare external intervention explains the drastic change in 116's popularity.

In another case study, Figure 9.23 shows the lifetime of movie #9757. Based on an old Chinese novel, 9757 is an older movie in the video library on PowerInfo's launch date. However, the later release of a new film based on the same book dramatically increased interest in this older version, accounting for a dramatic rise in ranking and requests near the end of our log period.

While these individual case studies prove interesting, we need to further quantify the impact of the recommendation list and the top-15 hot list on the access popularity of videos. To show this for each movie, we plot the movie's average daily access rate while it is on and off the manager's recommend list, and plot both as a normalized ratio of its maximum daily access rate. For example, a video might reach a maximum daily access rate of 3000 requests on a particular day. We would calculate the average daily access rate for all days when it was on the recommend list, and normalize that against 3000.

In Figure 9.24, we plot this pair (on/off) of normalized average daily access (ADA) rates for all videos that have ever appeared on the recommend list. sorted by its maximum daily access rate. We observe that the inclusion on the recommend list drastically increases the average daily access rate, generally by an order of magnitude or more. Most videos only average less than 5% of their maximum daily access rate when they are not included in the recommend list, but can average anywhere from 20% to 90% of their maximum rate while listed on the recommend list. Clearly, an external opinion, or perhaps just membership on an "official" list, can dramatically influence users on their choice of video selections. This is likely a social phenomenon that applies to movie rental outlets in general, and not specific to the PowerInfo VOD system. We also note that this impact appears to be independent of the actual video popularity. Thus we would expect the same relative "burst of popularity" from recommending a title, regardless of how popular it was originally.

Next, we use the same technique to analyze the impact of membership on the top-15 hot list, and show the results in Figure 9.25. Note that because the top-15 list is calculated on a monthly basis, only a small number (< 80) of videos have ever been listed. Because videos have to sustain their popularity for a month in order to enter the top-15 list, our sample set only includes highly popular videos, and the relative impact of membership is less significant. In contrast, popularity-independent lists like the recommendation list covers a greater selection of videos, and is likely to achieve greater impact. Finally, we note that the largest difference between membership and non-membership occurs for videos with lower popularity, suggesting a scenario where removal from the list resulted in a significant drop in daily access rates similar to the history of movie 116 as shown in Figure 9.22.

9.6 Related Work

Many studies have been carried to analyze the user behaviors in different media services, including web services, file sharing services, media broadcasting services and on-demand video streaming services.

Due to the lack of a real deployed large-scale VOD streaming system, previous VOD studies mainly relied on data from video rentals, small-scale systems or web-based Internet streaming services. While studies of web-based video streaming is similar in scale to a large VOD system, such services were deployed on lower bandwidth links compared to the broadband connections used in VOD systems. As observed in [7] and [13], lower bandwidth connections resulted in lower quality of service and impatient users. Another implication of the lower bandwidth is seen in the relatively smaller object sizes. Finally, these systems did not provide features like movie recommendation or top-ranked video lists. These features not only make the user experience more enjoyable, but as our results have shown, also have significant impact on user access patterns. In comparison, we believe our study provides results much more relevant to the design of future large-scale VOD systems.

The pioneer study on video-on-demand services models user behavior according to a week's worth of empirical data on video rentals in various video stores [9]. Later, Griwodz [11] introduced a model of movies' long-term life cycle using data from a video store and movie magazine. Conclusions such as the Zipf assumption from these offline data sets were highly influential.

Acharya [1] presented the analysis of a little more than six months of trace data from a multicast media on demand (mMOD) system which had a mix of educational and entertainment videos. Its analysis was based on a small scale system covering only 139 videos, and had a much larger average request inter-arrival time of 400 seconds.

The sequence of studies in [2], [3] and [8] focused on user behavior and data access patterns in video streaming systems. Their studies included two kinds of video streaming services. The first is a small scale VOD system named eTeach and BIBS, and include a small number of files being accessed by a specific group of users: undergraduate students. The difference in content, size and audience probably accounts for the difference in results between our studies. Since our log data provided relatively little information about specific users, we believe our studies can be viewed as complementary. The second was a study of web-based streaming services, which as we described above, are significantly different from VOD systems.

Cherkasova [6] and Tang [22] explored workload characteristics based on logs from two internal media servers at Hewlett-Packard. The servers were limited in delivering company-related content to employees. We believe the limited choice of topics limit the applicability of their results on general VOD systems. Finally, these services only observed a light workload of less than 1 million sessions in 29 months. In contrast to these studies, the system used to gather our data served more than 150,000 users and 21 million requests under varying amount of load.

Veloso [23] and Sripanidkulchai [21] characterized live Internet streaming media workloads. Veloso showed that the object-driven nature of interactions between users and objects for live streaming is fundamentally different from stored objects. Sripanidkulchai affirmed the feasibility of application level multicast with enough resources and nonlethal dynamics.

While most of the above works used media server logs, Mena [16], Chesire [7] and Guo [13] used different traffic tracing methods to trace the user accessing data in Internet streaming systems. They gathered data across multiple sites and multiple media types, but cannot detect properties specific to a single site or media type. Gummadi et al. [12] used tracing at the network border of Univ. of Washington to gather data on multimedia file-sharing in Kazaa, and extended their results to VOD systems.

Finally, Paxson [18] investigated a number of wide-area TCP arrival processes to determine the error introduced from modeling them using Poisson processes, and showed that not all network arrivals are well-modeled by Poisson distributions. We show that even user-initiated session arrivals could not be modeled by pure Poisson distribution, but instead, by a modified version of it.

9.7 Conclusion

Multimedia streaming has become a dominant factor in today's Internet, and Video-on-Demand is one of the most promising killer applications for the Internet of the future. The lack of data from deployed VOD systems has limited researchers to relying on assumptions about user behavior and content access patterns. In this study we tracked, analyzed and modeled user behavior and relevant access patterns in a large scale VOD environment. Our results show that the timing of user accesses are predictable, but user arrival rates do not match the Poisson distribution. Instead, we propose a modified version of the Poisson distribution which matches our empirical data. We also found low but significant correlation between a video's average session length and its popularity.

Our analysis showed that video popularity matched the Zipf distribution better than predicted using the "fetch-at-most-once" model. In addition, we found change in video popularity was strongly influenced both by the introduction of new content as well as external factors such as recommendation lists and popularity rankings. Results of our analysis should help VOD system designers make intelligent decisions about resource allocation and techniques for performance optimization. Finally, we are working to make our data set publicly available to researchers worldwide.

Acknowledgments

We wish to thank Yi Li, CTO of Powerinfo Software Co. of China for helping us collect log data from the Powerinfo streaming servers. We also thank our shepherd Thomas Gross and the anonymous reviewers for their valuable feedback.

References

1. ACHARYA, S., SMITH, B., AND PARNE, P. Characterizing user access to videos on the world wide web. In Proc. of ACM/SPIE Multimedia Computing and Networking (January 2000).
2. ALMEIDA, J., KRUEGER, J., AND VERNO, M. Characterization of user access to streaming media files. In Proc. of ACM SIGMETRICS/Performance (2001).
3. ALMEIDA, J. M., KRUEGER, J., EAGER, D. L., AND VERNON, M. K. Analysis of educational media server workloads. In Proc. of NOSSDAV (Port Jefferson, NY, June 2001).
4. BRESLAU, L., CAO, P., FAN, L., PHILLIPS, G., AND SHENKER, S. Web caching and zipf-like distributions: Evidence and implications. In Proc. of INFOCOM (New York, NY, March 1999).
5. CHAKRAVARTI, I. M., LAHA, R. G., AND ROY, J. Handbook of Methods of Applied Statistics, Vol. I. John Wiley and Sons, 1967.
6. CHERKASOVA, L., AND GUPTA, M. Characterizing locality, evolution, and life span of accesses in enterprise media server workloads. In Proc. of NOSSDAV (May 2002).
7. CHESIRE, M., WOLMAN, A., VOELKER, G. M., AND LEVY, H. M. Measurement and analysis of a streaming-media workload. In Proc. of USITS (San Francisco, CA, March 2001).
8. CRISTIANO, C., CUNHA, I., BORGES, A., RAMOS, C., ROCHA, M., ALMEIDA, J., AND RIBERIO-NETO, B. Analyzing client interactivity in streaming media. In Proc. of WWW (New York, NY, 2004).
9. DAN, A., SITARAM, D., AND SHAHABUDDIN, P. Scheduling policies for an on-demand video server with batching. In Proc. of ACM Multimedia (October 1994).
10. GOUGH, P. J. Comcast video-on-demand hits 1 billion mark. http://news.yahoo.com/s/nm/20051014/tv_nm/comcast_dc, October 2005.
11. GRIWODZ, C., BAR, M., AND WOLF, L. C. Long-term movie popularity models in video-on-demand systems. In Proc. of ACM Multimedia (1997).
12. GUMMADI, K. P., DUNN, R. J., SAROIU, S., GRIBBLE, S. D., LEVY, H. M., AND ZAHORJAN, J. Measurement, modeling, and analysis of a peer-to-peer file-sharing workload. In Proc. of SOSP (October 2003).
13. GUO, L., CHEN, S., XIAO, Z., AND ZHANG, X. Analysis of multimedia workloads with implications for internet streaming. In Proc. of WWW (Chiba, Japan, May 2005).
14. KaZaa media desktop. http://www.kazaa.com. Using Fasttrack: http://www.fasttrack.nu.
15. Managing peer-to-peer traffic with cisco service technology. http://www.cisco.com, 2005.
16. MENA, A., AND HEIDEMANN, J. An empirical study of real audio traffic. In Proc. of INFOCOM (March 2000).
17. P-cube white paper. approaches to controlling peer-to-peer traffic: A technical analysis. http://www.p-cube.com/new_solutions/traffic_P2P.shtml, 2003.
18. PAXSON, V., AND FLOYD, S. Wide-area traffic: The failure of poisson modeling. IEEE/ACM Transactions on Networking, 3(3), pp.226-244, June 1995.
19. SAROIU, S., GUMMADI, K. P., DUNN, R. J., GRIBBLE, S. D., AND LEVY, H. M. An analysis of internet content delivery systems. In Proc. of OSDI (December 2002), ACM, pp. 315C328.
20. SEN, S., REXFORD, J., AND TOWSLEY, D. Proxy prefix caching for multimedia streams. In Proc. of INFOCOM (New York, NY, March 1999).
21. SRIPANIDKULCHAI, K., GANJAM, A., MAGGS, B. M., AND ZHANG, H. The feasibility of supporting large-scale live streaming applications with dynamic application end-points. In Proc. of SIGCOMM (Portland, OR, August 2004).
22. TANG, W., FU, Y., CHERKASOVA, L., AND VAHDAT, A. Medisyn: Synthetic streaming media service workload generator. In Proc. of NOSSDAV (2003).
23. VELOSO, E., ALMEIDA, V.,MEIRA, W., BESTAVROS, A., AND JIN, S. Hierarchical characterization of a live streaming media workload. In Proc. of Internet Measurement Workshop (Marseille, France, November 2002).
24. ZATZ, D. Tivo inches towards video on demand. RealTechNews Article, September 2005. http://www.realtechnews. com/posts/1834

Chapter 10
A representation theorem for minmax regret policies [*]

Sanjiang Li

Abstract Decision making under uncertainty is one of the central tasks of artificial agents. Due to their simplicity and ease of specification, qualitative decision tools are popular in artificial intelligence. Brafman and Tennenholtz (*J. ACM* 47(2000)452–482) model an agent's uncertain knowledge as her local state, which consists of states of the world that she deems possible. A policy determines for each local state a total preorder of the set of actions, which represents the agent's preference over these actions. It is known that a policy is `maximin` representable if and only if it is closed under unions and satisfies a certain acyclicity condition.
In this paper we show that the above conditions, although necessary, are insufficient for `mregret` and `cratio` policies. A complete characterization of these policies is obtained by introducing the best-equally strictness.[2]

Key words: Qualitative decision; Policy; maximin; minmax regret; competitive ratio

10.1 Introduction

Decision making under uncertainty is one of the central tasks of artificial agents. Due to their simplicity and ease of specification, qualitative decision tools are popular in artificial intelligence (see e.g. [1, 2, 3, 7]).

Brafman and Tennenholtz [2] defined a model of a situated agent, where an agent is described by the set of her local states and the set of actions. For the current purpose, we identify the agent's local state as the set of states of the world she deems possible. Therefore an agent can be defined as a pair (S, A), where S is the (finite) set of states of the world in which the agent is situated, and A is the (finite) set of actions from which the agent can choose. The agent ranks the set of actions in a total preorder based on her state of information (i.e. her local state).

This choice of ranking of actions is called a *policy* in this paper, which corresponds to the notion of *generalized s-policy* of [2].

Note that this naive description of policy is space-consuming. Brafman and Tennenholtz proposed an implicit way for specifying policies that uses value functions, where a value function assigns to each action-state pair a real value.

Sanjiang Li
State Key Laboratory of Intelligent Technology and Systems, Department of Computer Science and Technology, Tsinghua University, Beijing 100084, China
Institut für Informatik, Albert-Ludwigs-Universität Freiburg D-79110 Freiburg, Germany
e-mail: lisanjiang@tsinghua.edu.cn

[*] Source: Artificial Intelligence, Volume 171, Issue 1, January 2007, Pages 19-24 Copyright ©2007 with permission from Elsevier. DOI: 10.1016/j.artint.2006.11.001

[2] This work was partly supported by the Alexander von Humboldt Foundation, the National Natural Science Foundation of China (60305005, 60673105), and a Microsoft Research Professorship.

Many decision criteria can be defined using value functions. Of particular importance are the three qualitative ones: maximin, mregret, and cratio. While maximin and mregret are well known in decision theory [6], cratio is popular in theoretical computer science [5].

Brafman and Tennenholtz [2] carried out an axiomatic treatment of these three decision criteria. They gave representation theorems for maximin policies. As for mregret and cratio, it is easy to see that (i) a policy is mregret representable iff it is cratio representable; (ii) each mregret policy is maximin representable.

In this paper we first show by an example that, unlike what was claimed in [2, Theorem 5, page 466], maximin policies are not necessarily mregret representable. Then we find a necessary and sufficient condition, called *best-equally strictness*, for a maximin policy to be mregret representable. Roughly speaking, this condition allows the agent to adopt a value function which has the same best value for all singleton local states.

The rest of this paper is structured as follows. Section 10.2 formalizes the three qualitative decision criteria. Section 10.3 gives an example that shows maximin policies are not necessarily mregret representable, followed by a complete characterization of mregret (cratio) policies. Conclusions are given in Section 10.4.

10.2 Three qualitative decision criteria

A binary relation $\preceq$ is called a *preorder* if it is reflexive and transitive. A preorder $\preceq$ is *total* if $x \preceq y$ or $y \preceq x$ for all x and y. For a total preoder $\preceq$, we define two associated relations $\prec$ and $\approx$ as follows:

$$x \prec y \Leftrightarrow \neg(y \preceq x)$$
$$x \approx y \Leftrightarrow (x \preceq y) \wedge (y \preceq x)$$

Definition 10.1. [2] A *policy* for an agent (S,A) is a function $\wp$ that assigns to each local state $X \subseteq S$ a total preorder $\preceq_X^\wp$.

In what follows, we denote $\wp = \{\preceq_X^\wp: \varnothing \neq X \subseteq S\}$, and if no confusion can occur, we often omit the superscript $\wp$ in the notation $\preceq_X^\wp$.

A policy may also be implicitly prescribed by using a value function.

Definition 10.2. [2] A *value function* u assigns to each action-state pair a real value, i.e. $u : A \times S \to \mathbb{R}$.

For convenience, we call a value function $u : A \times S \to \mathbb{R}$ *positive* if $u(a,s) > 0$ for all $(a,s) \in A \times S$.

Given a value function u on $A \times S$, we define the *regret function* $\mathrm{reg}_u : A \times S \to \mathbb{R}$ as $\mathrm{reg}_u(a,s) = \max_{a' \in A} u(a',s) - u(a,s)$. If u is positive, then we define the *competitive ratio function* $\mathrm{cmpr}_u : A \times S \to \mathbb{R}$ as $\mathrm{cmpr}_u(a,s) = \max_{a' \in A} u(a',s)/u(a,s)$.

Now, we can formalize the three qualitative decision criteria as follows.

Definition 10.3. [2] A policy $\wp = \{\preceq_X: \varnothing \neq X \subseteq S\}$ has a maximin representation if there exists a value function u on $A \times S$ such that for any local state X and any two actions a, a',

$$a \prec_X a' \text{ iff } \min_{s \in X} u(a,s) < \min_{s \in X} u(a',s). \tag{10.1}$$

Definition 10.4. [2] A policy $\wp = \{\preceq_X: \varnothing \neq X \subseteq S\}$ has a mregret (cratio, resp.) representation if there exists a (positive) value function u on $A \times S$ such that the condition specified in (10.2) ((10.3), resp.) is satisfied for any local state X and any two actions a, a', where

$$a \prec_X a' \text{ iff } \max_{s \in X} \text{reg}_u(a,s) > \max_{s \in X} \text{reg}_u(a',s). \tag{10.2}$$

$$a \prec_X a' \text{ iff } \max_{s \in X} \text{cmpr}_u(a,s) > \max_{s \in X} \text{cmpr}_u(a',s). \tag{10.3}$$

Noticing that `mregret` and `cratio` are very similar, the following result is clear.

Proposition 10.1. *[2] A policy is* `mregret` *representable if and only if it is* `cratio` *representable.*

10.3 When does a policy have minmax regret representation?

Brafman and Tennenholtz [2] and Hesselink [4] gave representation theorems for `maximin` policies. This section gives a representation theorem for `mregret` (`cratio`) policies. Note that by Proposition 10.1 we need only consider `mregret` policies.

We begin with the following proposition.

Proposition 10.2. *[2] A* `mregret` *policy is* `maximin` *representable.*

Proof. Suppose $\wp$ is `mregret` represented by $\bar{u}$. Set u to be the value function that is specified by $u(a,s) = -\text{reg}_{\bar{u}}(a,s) = \bar{u}(a,s) - \max_{a' \in A} \bar{u}(a',s)$. For any local state X and any two actions a, a', we have

$$a \prec_X a' \text{ iff } \max_{s \in X} \text{reg}_{\bar{u}}(a,s) > \max_{s \in X} \text{reg}_{\bar{u}}(a',s)$$
$$\text{iff } \min_{s \in X} -\text{reg}_{\bar{u}}(a,s) < \min_{s \in X} -\text{reg}_{\bar{u}}(a',s)$$
$$\text{iff } \min_{s \in X} u(a,s) < \min_{s \in X} u(a',s)$$

This means $\wp$ is `maximin` represented by u.

The following example shows, however, the inverse of the above proposition is not true.

Example 10.1 (A counter-example). Suppose $S = \{s,s'\}, A = \{a,a'\}$. Consider the following policy $\wp$ that is specified as follows:

$$a \approx^{\wp}_{\{s\}} a', \ a' \prec^{\wp}_{\{s'\}} a, \ a \approx^{\wp}_{\{s,s'\}} a'. \tag{10.4}$$

$\wp$ is `maximin` representable but not `mregret` representable (see Table 10.1). In fact, set $u(a,s) = u(a',s) = u(a',s') = 0$ and $u(a,s') = 1$. Then $\wp$ is `maximin` represented by u. Suppose we also have a value function $\bar{u}$ that `mregret` represents $\wp$. Write $\bar{u}(a,s) = p_1, \bar{u}(a',s) = p_2, \bar{u}(a,s') = q_1$, and $\bar{u}(a',s') = q_2$. Then by $a \approx^{\wp}_{\{s\}} a'$ we know $\max\{p_1,p_2\} - p_1 = \max\{p_1,p_2\} - p_2$, i.e. $p_1 = p_2$; and by $a' \prec^{\wp}_{\{s'\}} a$ we know $\max\{q_1,q_2\} - q_1 < \max\{q_1,q_2\} - q_2$, i.e. $q_1 > q_2$. Therefore

$$\text{reg}_{\bar{u}}(a,s) = \text{reg}_{\bar{u}}(a',s) = \text{reg}_{\bar{u}}(a,s') = 0 < q_1 - q_2 = \text{reg}_{\bar{u}}(a',s').$$

We also have

$$\max\{\text{reg}_{\bar{u}}(a,s), \text{reg}_{\bar{u}}(a,s')\} = 0 < q_2 - q_1$$
$$= \max\{\text{reg}_{\bar{u}}(a',s), \text{reg}_{\bar{u}}(a',s')\}.$$

$\wp$	{s}	{s'}	{s,s'}
	$a \approx a'$	$a' \prec a$	$a \approx a'$

u	s	s'
a	0	1
a'	0	0

$\bar{u}$	s	s'
a	p_1	q_1
a'	p_2	q_2

$\mathrm{reg}_{\bar{u}}$	s	s'
a	0	0
a'	0	$q_1 - q_2$

Table 10.1 A maximin policy that has no mregret representation

According to the mregret criterion, the agent would prefer a to a'. This contradicts the assumption $a \approx^{\wp}_{\{s,s'\}} a'$. Consequently, $\wp$ is not mregret representable.

So a maximin policy is not necessarily mregret representable.

The following lemma identifies a necessary and sufficient condition for a maximin policy to be mregret representable.

Lemma 10.1. *A policy $\wp$ is* mregret *representable iff it can be* maximin *represented by a value function* $u : A \times S \rightarrow \mathbb{R}$ *such that* $\max_{a \in A} u(a,s) = 0$ *for any* $s \in S$.

Proof. Suppose $\wp$ is mregret represented by $\bar{u} : A \times S \rightarrow \mathbb{R}$. Set u to be the value function that is specified by $u(a,s) = -\mathrm{reg}_{\bar{u}}(a,s) = \bar{u}(a,s) - \max_{a' \in A} \bar{u}(a',s)$. By the proof of Lemma 10.2, we know $\wp$ is maximin represented by u. It is also clear that $\max_{a \in A} u(a,s) = 0$ for any $s \in S$.

On the other hand, suppose $\wp$ is maximin represented by a value function u such that $\max_{a \in A} u(a,s) = 0$ for any $s \in S$. We show $\wp$ is also mregret represented by u. In fact, since $\mathrm{reg}_u(a,s) = \max_{a' \in A} u(a',s) - u(a,s) = -u(a,s)$, we have

$$a \prec_X a' \text{ iff } \min_{s \in X} u(a,s) < \min_{s \in X} u(a',s)$$

$$\text{iff } \max_{s \in X} \mathrm{reg}_u(a,s) > \max_{s \in X} \mathrm{reg}_u(a',s).$$

Therefore $\wp$ is mregret representable.

The above lemma suggests that, in order to characterize mregret policies, we need only to characterize those maximin policies that have a value function u such that $\max_{a \in A} u(a,s) = 0$ for all $s \in S$.

The following example gives a clue.

Example 10.2. Suppose $S = \{s,s'\}$, $A = \{a,a'\}$. Consider the following policy $\hat{\wp}$ that is specified as follows:

$$a \approx^{\hat{\wp}}_{\{s\}} a', \ a' \prec^{\hat{\wp}}_{\{s'\}} a, \ a' \prec^{\hat{\wp}}_{\{s,s'\}} a. \tag{10.5}$$

$\hat{\wp}$ is mregret represented by the value function u which is specified by $u(a,s) = u(a',s) = u(a,s') = 0 > -1 = u(a',s')$.

Note the two policies given in Examples 10.1 and 10.2 differ only in the local state $\{s,s'\}$.

Definition 10.5. A policy $\wp$ is *best-equally strict* if, for any pair of states s and t, and any pair of best choices a and b at s such that a is better than b at t, we have that a is better than b at $\{s,t\}$. Or more formally, $\wp$ is best-equally strict if, for all $s,t \in S$ and all $a,b \in A$ we have

$$a \approx_{\{s\}} b \wedge (\forall c \in A)c \preceq_{\{s\}} a \wedge b \prec_{\{t\}} a \rightarrow b \prec_{\{s,t\}} a. \tag{10.6}$$

Note that while the policy given in Example 10.2 is best-equally strict, the one given in Example 10.1 is not. The next proposition gives a characterization of the *best-equally strict* maximin policies.

Proposition 10.3. *For a* maximin *policy $\wp$, the following two conditions are equivalent:*

1. $\wp$ is best-equally strict;

2. $\wp$ is maximin *represented by a value function* $u : A \times S \to \mathbb{R}$ *which satisfies* $\max_{a \in A} u(a,s) = 0$
for all $s \in S$.

Proof. (*Necessity*) Suppose $\wp$ is maximin represented by a value function u such that $\max_{a \in A} u(a,s) = 0$ for all $s \in S$. For any a, a' and any s, s', suppose a, a' are two best choices at $\{s\}$, and a is better than a' at $\{s'\}$. We now show a is also better than a' at $\{s, s'\}$.

Since a, a' are two best choices at $\{s\}$, we have $u(a,s) = u(a',s) = 0$. Moreover, $a' \prec_{\{s'\}} a$ implies $u(a',s') < u(a,s') \leq \max_{\bar{a} \in A} u(\bar{a},s') = 0$. Now, by $\min\{u(a',s), u(a',s')\} = u(a',s') < u(a,s') = \min\{u(a,s), u(a,s')\}$, we know a is better than a' at $\{s, s'\}$, i.e. $a' \prec_{\{s,s'\}} a$. Hence $\wp$ is best-equally strict.

[*Sufficiency*] Suppose $\wp$ is a best-equally strict policy that is maximin represented by a value function u. We next define a new value function $\bar{u}$ such that $\max_{a \in A} \bar{u}(a,s) = 0$ for all $s \in S$ and show that $\wp$ is maximin represented by $\bar{u}$.

For $(a,s) \in A \times S$, define

$$\bar{u}(a,s) = \begin{cases} 0, & \text{if } u(a,s) = \varphi(s); \\ u(a,s) - k, & \text{otherwise.} \end{cases}$$

where $\varphi(s) = \max_{a \in A} u(a,s)$, and $k = \max_{s \in S} \varphi(s) = \max_{(a,s) \in A \times S} u(a,s)$. Note that $u(a,s) - k \leq \bar{u}(a,s) \leq 0$ for all $(a,s) \in A \times S$.

In order to show that $\wp$ is also maximin represented by $\bar{u}$, we need only show the following condition (10.7) holds for any local state X, and any actions a, a'.

$$\min_{s \in X} u(a',s) < \min_{s \in X} u(a,s) \Leftrightarrow \min_{s \in X} \bar{u}(a',s) < \min_{s \in X} \bar{u}(a,s) \tag{10.7}$$

($\Rightarrow$) Suppose $\min_{s \in X} u(a',s) < \min_{s \in X} u(a,s)$. Take $s_1 \in X$ such that $u(a',s_1) = \min_{s \in X} u(a',s)$. Clearly, $u(a',s_1) < u(a,s)$ for each $s \in X$. In particular, by $u(a',s_1) < u(a,s_1) \leq \varphi(s_1)$ we know $\bar{u}(a',s_1) = u(a',s_1) - k$. For any $s \in X$, since $u(a,s) - k \leq \bar{u}(a,s)$, we have $\bar{u}(a',s_1) = u(a',s_1) - k < u(a,s) - k \leq \bar{u}(a,s)$. This means $\bar{u}(a',s_1) < \bar{u}(a,s)$ for all $s \in X$. Therefore $\min_{s \in X} \bar{u}(a',s) < \min_{s \in X} \bar{u}(a,s)$.

($\Leftarrow$) Suppose $\min_{s \in X} \bar{u}(a',s) < \min_{s \in X} \bar{u}(a,s)$. Take $s_1 \in X$ such that $\bar{u}(a',s_1) = \min_{s \in X} \bar{u}(a',s)$. Clearly, $\bar{u}(a',s_1) < \bar{u}(a,s)$ for all $s \in X$. We next show $u(a',s_1) < u(a,s)$ for all $s \in X$.

We note that $\bar{u}(a',s_1) = u(a',s_1) - k$ because $\bar{u}(a',s_1) < \bar{u}(a,s_1) \leq 0$. Moreover, for each $s \in X$, we have either $u(a,s) < \varphi(s)$ or $u(a',s) < u(a,s) = \varphi(s)$ or $u(a',s) = u(a,s) = \varphi(s)$.

Suppose $u(a,s) < \varphi(s)$. Then we have $\bar{u}(a,s) = u(a,s) - k$. Therefore, by $\bar{u}(a',s_1) < \bar{u}(a,s)$, we know $u(a',s_1) < u(a,s)$.

Suppose $u(a,s) = \varphi(s)$ and $u(a',s) < u(a,s)$. Then by $\bar{u}(a',s_1) = u(a',s) - k$ and $\bar{u}(a',s_1) \leq \bar{u}(a',s)$, we know $u(a',s_1) \leq u(a',s) < u(a,s)$.

Suppose $u(a,s) = u(a',s) = \varphi(s)$. Recall that $\wp$ is maximin represented by u. This means a and a' are two best choices of $\wp$ at $\{s\}$. By $\bar{u}(a',s_1) < \bar{u}(a,s_1)$ we know $u(a',s_1) < u(a,s_1)$, i.e. $a' \prec_{\{s_1\}} a$. Since $\wp$ is best-equally strict, we know $a' \prec_{\{s,s_1\}} a$. This means $\min\{u(a',s), u(a',s_1)\} < \min\{u(a,s), u(a,s_1)\}$, i.e. $\min\{\varphi(s), u(a',s_1)\} < \min\{\varphi(s), u(a,s_1)\}$. This is possible if and only if $u(a',s_1) < \varphi(s) = u(a,s)$.

In summary, $u(a',s_1) < u(a,s)$ holds for all $s \in X$. Therefore, $\min_{s \in X} u(a',s) < \min_{s \in X} u(a,s)$.

As a corollary of Lemma 10.1 and Propositions 10.1.1 and 10.3.2, we have

Theorem 10.1. *A* maximin *policy is* mregret (cratio) *representable iff it is best-equally strict.*

Note that if $\wp$ has a strictly best choice at each singleton local state, then $\wp$ is best-equally strict. In particular, a deterministic policy is best-equally strict, where a policy is *deterministic* if $\preceq_X$ is a total order for each local state X. This proves the next two corollaries.

Corollary 10.1. *Suppose* $\wp$ *is a* maximin *policy such that at each singleton local state* $\{s\}$ *the agent has a strictly best choice. Then* $\wp$ *is* mregret *representable.*

Corollary 10.2. *A determinate policy $\wp$ is* maximin *representable iff $\wp$ is* mregret *representable.*

10.4 Conclusions

Axiomatic approach is the prominent approach for understanding and justifying the rationality of decision criteria. This paper showed that, unlike what was claimed in [2, Theorem 5, page 466], there are policies that are maximin representable, but not mregret representable. We then identified a necessary and sufficient condition for a maximin policy to be mregret (cratio) representable, which allows the agent to take the same value for all best choices at all singleton local states.

Recall that Brafman and Tennenholtz [2] and Hesselink [4] have obtained representation theorems for maximin policies. We therefore conclude that a policy is mregret (cratio) representable if and only if it satisfies (1) the closure under unions property [2], (2) the acyclicity condition [4], and (3) the best-equally strictness.

Acknowledgement

We thank the anonymous reviewers for their invaluable suggestions that greatly improved the paper. In particular, the term "best-equally strict" is suggested by one referee for replacing the debatable term "best-equal."

References

1. C. Boutilier, Toward a logic for qualitative decision theory, in: KR, 1994, pp. 75C86.
2. R.I. Brafman, M. Tennenholtz, An axiomatic treatment of three qualitative decision criteria, J. ACM 47 (3) (2000) 452C482.
3. D. Dubois, H. Fargier, P. Perny, Qualitative decision theory with preference relations and comparative uncertainty: An axiomatic approach, Artificial Intelligence 148 (1C2) (2003) 219C260.
4. [4] W.H. Hesselink, Preference rankings in the face of uncertainty, Acta Inf. 39 (3) (2003) 211C231.
5. C.H. Papadimitriou, M. Yannakakis, Shortest paths without a map, Theoret. Comput. Sci. 84 (1) (1991) 127C150.
6. L.J. Savage, Foundations of Statistics, John Wiley & Sons, New York, 1954.
7. S. Tan, J. Pearl, Qualitative decision theory, in: AAAI, 1994, pp. 928C933.

Chapter 11
A Note on the Cramer-Damgård Identification Scheme*

Yunlei Zhao, Shirley H. C. Cheung, Binyu Zang and Bin Zhu

Abstract In light of the recent work of Micali and Reyzin on showing the subtleties and complexities of the soundness notions of zero-knowledge (ZK) protocols when the verifier has his public-key, we re-investigate the Cramer-Damgård intended-verifier identification scheme and show two man-in-the-middle attacks in some reasonable settings: one simple replaying attack and one ingenious interleaving attack. Our attacks are independent of the underlying hardness assumptions assumed.

Key words: cryptography, identification scheme, Σ_{OR}, man-in-the-middle attacks

11.1 Introduction

Identification protocol is one of the major cryptographic applications, especially in E-commerce over the Internet. Feige, Fiat and Shamir introduced a paradigm for identification (ID) schemes based on the notion of zero-knowledge (ZK) proof of knowledge [8, 7]. In essence, a prover identifies himself by convincing the verifier of knowing a given secret. Almost all subsequent ID schemes followed this paradigm. But, all previous Fiat-Shamir-like ZK-based ID schemes suffer from a weakness, as observed by Bengio et al [3]. Specifically, a malicious verifier may simply act as a moderator between the prover and yet another verifier, thus enabling the malicious verifier to pass as the prover. In [4] Cramer and Damgård presented a simple yet efficient ZK-based (specifically, Σ_{OR}-based) solution for preventing aforementioned man-in-the-middle attacks. Essentially, beyond the novel use of Σ_{OR} in the identification setting, in the Cramer-Damgård ID scheme not only the identification prover but also the identification verifier are required to have public-keys. In other words, the Cramer-Damgård scheme is an *intended-verifier* ID scheme. Though the intended-verifier property is necessary to prevent aforementioned man-in-the-middle attacks, it brings other security issues, as we shall observe in this paper, in light of the recent work of Micali and Reyzin

Yunlei Zhao and Binyu Zang
Software School, Fudan University, Shanghai 200433, P. R. China.
e-mail: {990314, byzang}@fudan.edu.cn

Shirley H. C. Cheung
Department of Computer Science, City University of Hong Kong, Hong Kong.
e-mail: hccheung@cs.cityu.edu.hk

Bin Zhu
and Microsoft Research Asia, Beijing, P. R. China.
e-mail: binzhu@microsoft.com

* Source: Internet and Network Economics, Volume 3828/2005, Pages 385-390, Copyright ©2005 Springer Science+Business Media, Inc. Manufactured in the United States. DOI: 10.1007/11600930

[12] on showing the subtleties and complexities of the soundness notions of zero-knowledge (ZK) protocols when the verifier has his public-key.

11.2 Description of the Cramer-Damgård Intended-Verifier ID Scheme

In this section, we first present the basic tools used in the Cramer-Damgård ID scheme and then give the protocol description of the Cramer-Damgård ID scheme.

We assume the following form of *3-round protocol* is considered. Suppose P and V are probabilistic polynomial-time (PPT) machines, on common input x to P and V, and a w such that $(x, w) \in R$ is the only advantage of P over V that he knows w. The *conversation* of a 3-round protocol $\langle P, V \rangle$ is defined as a 3-tuple, say (a, e, z), where a is the first message sent from P to V, e is a random string sent from V to P, and z is replied by P to V. After this 3-round conversation, V would decide to accept or reject based on the conversation.

11.2.1 Σ-protocol and Σ_{OR}-protocol

Definition 11.1 (Σ-protocol). A 3-round protocol $\langle P, V \rangle$ is said to be a Σ-protocol for a relation R if the following holds:

- **Completeness.** If prover P and verifier V follow the protocol, the verifier always accepts.
- **Special soundness.** From any common input x of length n and any pair of accepting conversations on input x, (a, e, z) and (a, e', z') where $e \neq e'$, one can efficiently compute w such that $(x, w) \in R$. Here a, e, z stand for the first, the second and the third message respectively, and e is assumed to be a string of length k (that is polynomially related to n) selected uniformly at random from $\{0, 1\}^k$.
- **Perfect Special honest verifier zero-knowledge (SHVZK).** There exists a probabilistic polynomial-time (PPT) simulator S, which on input x (where there exists a w such that $(x, w) \in R$) and a random challenge string $\hat{e}$, outputs an accepting conversation of the form $(\hat{a}, \hat{e}, \hat{z})$, with the same probability distribution as that of the real conversation (a, e, z) between the honest $P(w)$, V on input x.

The OR-proof of Σ-protocols [5]. One basic construction with Σ-protocols allows a prover to show that given two inputs x_0, x_1, it knows a w such that either $(x_0, w) \in R_0$ or $(x_1, w) \in R_1$, but without revealing which is the case. Specifically, given two Σ-protocols $\langle P_b, V_b \rangle$ for R_b, $b \in \{0, 1\}$, with random challenges of, without loss of generality, the same length k, consider the following protocol $\langle P, V \rangle$, which we call Σ_{OR}. The common input of $\langle P, V \rangle$ is (x_0, x_1) and P has a private input w such that $(x_b, w) \in R_b$.

- P computes the first message a_b in $\langle P_b, V_b \rangle$, using x_b, w as private inputs. P chooses e_{1-b} at random, runs the SHVZK simulator of $\langle P_{1-b}, V_{1-b} \rangle$ on input (x_{1-b}, e_{1-b}), and let $(a_{1-b}, e_{1-b}, z_{1-b})$ be the simulated conversation. P now sends a_0, a_1 to V.
- V chooses a random k-bit string e and sends it to P.
- P sets $e_b = e \oplus e_{1-b}$ and computes the answer z_b to challenge e_b using (x_b, a_b, e_b, w) as input. He sends (e_0, z_0, e_1, z_1) to V.
- V checks that $e = e_0 \oplus e_1$ and that both (a_0, e_0, z_0) and (a_1, e_1, z_1) are accepting conversations with respect to (x_0, R_0) and (x_1, R_1), respectively.

Theorem 11.1. [6] *The above protocol Σ_{OR} is a Σ-protocol for R_{OR}, where $R_{OR} = \{((x_0,x_1),w)|(x_0, w) \in R_0$ or $(x_1,w) \in R_1\}$. Moreover, for any malicious verifier V^*, the probability distribution of conversations between P and V^*, where w satisfies $(x_b,w) \in R_b$, is independent of b. That is, Σ_{OR} is perfectly witness indistinguishable.*

11.2.2 Description of protocol

Let X and Y be two parties, and let f_X and f_Y be two one-way functions that admit Σ-protocols. The following description of protocol is taken from [6, 4], in which X plays the role of identification prover and Y plays the role of identification verifier.

Key Generation. On a security parameter n, randomly select x_X and x_Y of length n each in the domains of f_X and f_Y respectively, compute $pk_X = f_X(x_X)$ and $pk_Y = f_Y(x_Y)$. pk_X and pk_Y are the public-keys of X and Y respectively and x_X and x_Y are their corresponding secret-keys.

The ID Protocol. In order to identify himself to the *intended* verifier Y with public-key pk_Y, X proves to Y that he knows either the preimage of pk_X (i.e. x_X) or the preimage of pk_Y (i.e. x_Y), by executing the Σ_{OR}-protocol on common input (pk_X, pk_Y). We denote by a_{XY}, e_{XY}, z_{XY} the first, the second and the third message of the Σ_{OR}-protocol respectively.

11.3 Two Man-in-the-Middle Attacks

In this section, we show two attacks on the Cramer-Damgård ID scheme in some reasonable settings: one replaying attack and one interleaving attack.

11.3.1 The replaying attack

As shown in [4, 6], the intended-verifier property of the Cramer-Damgård ID scheme prevents a malicious verifier to pass as the prover to another *different* verifier. But, we observe that a simple replaying attack enables an adversary (the man-in-the-middle) to identify himself as the (honest) verifier to the (honest) prover. In other words, the Cramer-Damgård ID scheme suffers from the man-in-the-middle attack when it is used for mutual identification purpose between two players X and Y, in which both X and Y identify themselves to each other concurrently with reversed playing role in the two concurrent protocol executions.

Now, suppose X (with public-key pk_X) is identifying himself to Y (with public-key pk_Y) and an adversary A (i.e. the man-in-the-middle) controls the communication channel between X and Y and wants to identify himself as Y to X. The following is the message schedule of the adversary:

Move-1: After receiving a_{XY} from X, A sets $a_{YX} = a_{XY}$ and sends a_{YX} back to X.

Move-2: After receiving the random challenge e_{YX} from Y, A sets $e_{XY} = e_{YX}$ and sends back e_{XY} as the random challenge to X.

Move-3: After receiving z_{XY} from X, A sets $z_{YX} = z_{XY}$ and sends z_{YX} back to X.

Clearly, if X can successfully identify himself to Y (which means (a_{XY}, e_{XY}, z_{XY}) is an accepting conversation on (pk_X, pk_Y) with X playing the role of identification prover and Y playing the role of identification verifier), then (a_{YX}, e_{YX}, z_{YX}) is also an accepting conversation on (pk_Y, pk_X) with X playing the role of identification verifier and the adversary A playing the role of identification prover (which means that A has successfully impersonated himself as Y to X).

11.3.2 The interleaving attack

We consider a scenario in which two parties X (with public-key pk_X) and Y (with public-key pk_Y) identify each other internally, but they *externally* identify themselves as a group with public-key (pk_X, pk_Y) to outside parties (say, a third party T with public-key pk_T). That is, when X (or Y) identifies himself to an outsider party T, X (or Y) just convinces T that he is either X or Y without revealing exactly who he is. Specifically, X (or Y) convinces T that he knows the preimage of either pk_X or pk_Y or pk_T, by executing the Σ_{OR} on (pk_X, pk_Y, pk_T) with pk_X (or pk_Y respectively) as his private witness. We remark that this scenario is meaningful in certain applications. Now, suppose the honest player X is identifying himself to the honest player Y, then we show an interleaving attack that enables an adversary A (i.e. the man-in-the-middle who controls the communication channel between X and Y) to convince T that he is one member of the player group $\{X, Y\}$ (i.e. he is either X or Y). The following is the specification of the interleaving message schedule of A who is the man-in-the-middle between X and Y. We remark the interleaving attack is ingenious in comparison with the above simple replaying attack.

Move-1:   After receiving a_{XY} from X, A first generates a simulated conversation that he knows the preimage of pk_T (by running the SHVZK simulator as shown in the description of Σ_{OR}). Denote by $(\hat{a}_T, \hat{e}_T, \hat{z}_T)$ the simulated transcript, where $\hat{e}_T$ is a random string. Then, A sends $(a_{XY}, \hat{a}_T)$ to T.

Move-2:   After receiving the random challenge e_T from T, A sets $e_{XY} = e_T \oplus \hat{e}_T$, and sends e_{XY} to X as the random challenge in the protocol execution between X and Y.

Move-3:   After receiving z_{XY} from X, A sends $(z_{XY}, \hat{z}_T)$ to T.

Note that from the point view of T: $(\hat{a}_T, \hat{e}_T, \hat{z}_T)$ is an accepting conversation on pk_T, (a_{XY}, e_{XY}, z_{XY}) is an accepting conversation on (pk_X, pk_Y) for proving the knowledge of the preimage of either pk_X or pk_Y, and furthermore $e_{XY} \oplus \hat{e}_T = e_T$. This means A has successfully identified himself to T as one member of the player group $\{X, Y\}$.

11.4 Concluding Remarks

Identification protocol is one of the major cryptographic applications, especially in E-commerce over the Internet, and the Cramer-Damgård intended-verifier ID scheme is a famous one (due to its conceptual simpleness and highly practical efficiency) that may have been employed in practice. Though the intended-verifier property is necessary to prevent man-in-the-middle attacks of certain types, but as shown in this work, the intended-verifier property (i.e. letting the verifier also have his public-key) brings other security issues. Note that the two attacks shown in this work are all related to the intended-verifier property. In particular, if the identification verifier (e.g. Y) has no public-key (say, pk_Y), but, rather *freshly* generates and sends the "public-key message" (i.e. pk_Y) to the identification prover in each invocation, then our attacks will not work. But a verifier without a public-key suffers from other security vulnerabilities, as we mentioned in Section 11.1. We note that, by subsequent works [15, 16, 17, 14], the security vulnerabilities we reported in this paper are not an incidental phenomenon. Actually, the underlying reason behind the above two attacks is just the subtleties and complexities of the fundamental notion of proof-of-knowledge [11, 7, 1, 9, 2] for interactive cryptographic protocols *running concurrently in public-key models when players possess public-keys*, which are further studied in the subsequent works [15, 16, 17, 14][1].

In particular, it is shown there that, in the public-key setting, concurrent interactions render *strictly stronger* power/advantages (over only sequential interactions) to an attacker against knowledge provers.

---

[1] Actually, it is this work that motivated the subsequent studies in [15, 16, 17, 14]

Acknowledgements

The first author is indebted to Andrew C. C. Yao, Frances F. Yao and Moti Yung for many valuable discussions and comments. This work was supported in part by a grant from the Research Grants Council of the Hong Kong Special Administrative Region, China (No. CityU 122105), CityU Research Grant (No. 9380039) and a grant from the Basic Research Development (973) Program of China (No. 2007CB807901). The first author is also supported by a grant from the National Natural Science Foundation of China (NSFC No. 60703091).

References

1. M. Bellare and O. Goldreich. On Defining Proofs of Knowledge In *E. F. Brickell (Ed.): Advances in Cryptology-Proceedings of CRYPTO 1992, LNCS 740*, pages 390-420, Springer-Verlag, 1992.
2. M. Bellare and O. Goldreich. On Probabilistic versus Deterministic Provers in the Definition of Proofs Of Knowledge. Electronic Colloquium on Computational Complexity, 13(136), 2006. Available also from Cryptology ePrint Archive, Report No. 2006/359.
3. S. Bengio, G. Brassard, Y. Desmedt, C. Goutier and J. J. Quisquater. Secure Implementation of Identification Systems. *Journal of Cryptology*, 1991(4): 175-183, 1991.
4. R. Cramer and I. Damgård. Fast and Secure Immunization Against Adaptive Man-in-the-Middle Impersonation. In *Wa. Fumy (Ed.): Advances in Cryptology-Proceedings of EURO-CRYPT 1997, LNCS 1233*, pages 75-87. Springer-Verlag, 1997.
5. R. Cramer, I. Damgård and B. Schoenmakers. Proofs of Partial Knowledge and Simplified Design of Witness Hiding Protocols. In *Y. Desmedt (Ed.): Advances in Cryptology-Proceedings of CRYPTO 1994, LNCS 839*, pages 174-187. Springer-Verlag, 1994.
6. I. Damgård. On Σ-protocols. A lecture note for the course of Cryptographic Protocol Theory at Aarhus University, 2003. Available from: http://www.daimi.au.dk/~ivan/CPT.html
7. U. Feige, A. Fiat and A. Shamir. Zero-knowledge Proof of Identity. *Journal of Cryptology*, 1(2): 77-94, 1988.
8. A. Fiat and A. Shamir. How to Prove Yourself: Practical Solutions to Identification and Signature Problems. In *A. Odlyzko (Ed.): Advances in Cryptology-Proceedings of CRYPTO'86, LNCS 263*, pages 186-194. Springer-Verlag, 1986.
9. O. Goldreich. *Foundation of Cryptography-Basic Tools*. Cambridge University Press, 2001.
10. L. Guillou and J. J. Quisquater. A Practical Zero-Knowledge Protocol Fitted to Security Microprocessor Minimizing both Transmission and Memory. In *C. G. Gnther (Ed.): Advances in Cryptology-Proceedings of EUROCRYPT 1988, LNCS 330* , pages 123-128, Springer-Verlag, 1988.
11. S. Goldwasser, S. Micali and C. Rackoff. The Knowledge Complexity of Interactive Proof-Systems In *ACM Symposium on Theory of Computing*, pages 291-304, 1985.
12. S. Micali and L. Reyzin. Soundness in the Public-Key Model. In *J. Kilian (Ed.): Advances in Cryptology-Proceedings of CRYPTO 2001, LNCS 2139*, pages 542–565. Springer-Verlag, 2001.
13. C. Schnorr. Efficient Signature Generation by Smart Cards. *Journal of Cryptology*, 4(3): 24, 1991.
14. A. Yao, M. Yung and Y. Zhao. Concurrent Knowledge Extraction in the Public-Key Model. Electronic Colloquium on Computational Complexity, 14(2), 2007.
15. M. Yung and Y. Zhao. Concurrently Knowledge-Extractable Resettable-ZK in the Bare Public-Key Model. Electronic Colloquium on Computational Complexity, 12(48), 2005. Extended abstract appears [17].
16. M. Yung and Y. Zhao. Interactive Zero-Knowledge with Restricted Random Oracles. In *S. Halevi and T. Rabin (Ed.): Theory of Cryptography (TCC) 2006, LNCS 3876*, pages 21-40, Springer-Verlag, 2006.

17. M. Yung and Y. Zhao. Generic and practical resettable zero-knowledge in the bare public-key model. In *M. Naor (Ed.): Advances in Cryptology-Proceedings of EUROCRYPT 2007, LNCS 4515*, pages 116-134, Springer-Verlag, 2007.

Appendix A. Σ-Protocols for DLP and RSA

The contents described in this Appendix is only to facilitate submission review. It will not be included in the formal publication due to space limitation.

The idea of Σ-protocols as an abstract concept was introduced by Cramer in his Ph.D thesis (University of Amsterdam, 1996). Informally, a Σ-protocol is itself a 3-round public-coin special honest verifier zero-knowledge protocol with special soundness in the knowledge-extraction sense. Σ-protocols have been proved to be a very powerful cryptographic tool and are widely used in numerous important cryptographic applications including digital signatures, identification schemes, efficient electronic payment and voting systems. We remark that a very large number of Σ-protocols have been developed in the literature (mainly in the field of applied cryptography). The following are Σ-protocol examples for DLP and RSA. For a good survey of Σ-protocols and their applications, readers are referred to [6].

Σ-Protocol for DLP.

The following is a Σ-protocol $\langle P, V \rangle$ proposed by Schnorr [13] for proving the knowledge of discrete logarithm, w, for a common input of the form (p, q, g, h) such that $h = g^w \bmod p$, where on a security parameter n, p is a uniformly selected n-bit prime such that $q = (p-1)/2$ is also a prime, g is an element in $\mathbf{Z}_p^*$ of order q. It is also actually the first efficient Σ-protocol proposed in the literature.

- P chooses r at random in $\mathbf{Z}_q$ and sends $a = g^r \bmod p$ to V.
- V chooses a challenge e at random in $\mathbf{Z}_{2^t}$ and sends it to P. Here, t is fixed such that $2^t < q$.
- P sends $z = r + ew \bmod q$ to V, who checks that $g^z = ah^e \bmod p$, that p, q are prime and that g, h have order q, and accepts iff this is the case.

Σ-Protocol for RSA.

The following Σ-protocol for RSA is proposed by Guillou and Quisquater [10]. Let n be an RSA modulus and q be a prime. Assume we are given some element $y \in Z_n^*$, and P knows an element w such that $w^q = y \bmod n$. The following protocol is a Σ-protocol for proving the knowledge of q-th roots modulo n.

- P chooses r at random in Z_n^* and sends $a = r^q \bmod n$ to V.
- V chooses a challenge e at random in Z_{2^t} and sends it to P. Here, t is fixed such that $2^t < q$.
- P sends $z = rw^e \bmod n$ to V, who checks that $z^q = ay^e \bmod n$, that q is a prime, that $gcd(a, n) = gcd(y, n) = 1$, and accepts iff this is the case.

Part III
Natural User Interface

Chapter 12
A Tree-based Kernel Selection Approach to Efficient Gaussian Mixture Model - Universal Background model based Speaker Identification*

Zhenyu Xiong, Thomas Fang Zheng , Zhanjiang Song, Frank Soong and Wen-hu Wu

Abstract We propose a tree-based kernel selection (TBKS) algorithm as a computationally efficient approach to the Gaussian mixture modelCuniversal background model (GMMCUBM) based speaker identification. All Gaussian components in the universal background model are first clustered hierarchically into a tree and the corresponding acoustic space is mapped into structurally partitioned regions. When identifying a speaker, each test input feature vector is scored against a small subset of all Gaussian components. As a result of this TBKS process, computation complexity can be significantly reduced. We improve the efficiency of the proposed system further by applying a previously proposed observation reordering based pruning (ORBP) to screen out unlikely candidate speakers. The approach is evaluated on a speech database of 1031 speakers, in both clean and noisy conditions. The experimental results show that by integrating TBKS and ORBP together we can speed up the computation efficiency by a factor of 15.8 with only a very slight degradation of identification performance, i.e., an increase of 1% of relative error rate, compared with a baseline GMMCUBM system. The improved search efficiency is also robust to additive noise.

Key words: Speaker Recognition, Speaker Identification; Tree-based Kernel Selection; GMM-UBM

12.1 Introduction

Speaker recognition (Campbell, 1997), including both speaker identification and verification, has been an active research area for several decades. The goal of speaker recognition is to automati-

Zhenyu Xiong, Thomas Fang Zheng and Wen-hu Wu
Center for Speech Technology, State Key Laboratory of Intelligent Technology and Systems,
Department of Computer Science and Technology, Tsinghua University, Beijing, 100084, China,
e-mail: xiongzhy@cst.cs.tsinghua.edu.cn, {fzheng,wuwh }@tsinghua.edu.cn

Zhanjiang Song
Beijing d-Ear Technologies Co., Ltd., http://www.d-Ear.com
e-mail: zjsong@d-Ear.com

Frank Soong
Microsoft Research Asia, Beijing China, http://research.microsoft.com/asia/
e-mail: frankkps@microsoft.com

* Source: Speech Communication, Volume 48, Issue 10, October 2006, Pages 1273-1282 Copyright ©2006 with permission from Elsevier. DOI: 10.1016/j.specom.2006.06.011

cally identify a particular person in a pre-specified set of speakers or to verify a claimed speaker identity from his/her own voice. Wide applications of speaker recognition have been tried, including: access control, telephone-based account transactions, automatic labeling of a talking speaker for indexing or archiving audio recordings of multi-party meetings, etc. In terms of the operation mode, speaker recognition can be in a text-independent or a text-dependent mode, based on whether utterances of specific words or sentences are used in the recognition process. The former one is more commonly used in monitoring a speaker continuously while the later one is more frequently adopted in applications like access control due to its higher performance. The focus of this study is on text-independent speaker identification applications.

While the aim of speech recognition is on how to extract the linguistic content (e.g., words) out of a spoken utterance, speaker recognition is on how to recognize the identity of the speaker. Speaker recognition generally uses the same short-time spectral features used in speech recognition, e.g., the mel-frequency cepstral coef-ficients (MFCC), linear prediction cepstral coefficients (LPCC) or perceptual linear prediction (PLP) cepstral coefficients, etc. MFCC have been shown to yield the best and robust performance, comparing with all other features (Reynolds, 1994) and they are also used as the exclusive features in this paper.

Many classifier approaches, such as vector quantization (VQ) (Soong et al. 1985), Bayesian discriminant, dynamic time warping (DTW), Gaussian mixture models (GMMs), hidden Markov models (HMMs) and neural networks (NN) (Ramachandran et al., 2002; Reynolds, 2002), have been tried for speaker recognition and GMMs yield the best performance, especially for text-independent applications (Reynolds, 1997; Reynolds et al, 2000). GMM is a powerful approach to modeling a speaker's characteristics for its flexibility to approximate the underlying probability distribution in a high dimensional space (Reynolds, 1995; Reynolds and Rose, 1995). To obtain a high resolution characterization of the underlying acoustic space for good recognition performance, the number of Gaussian mixture components should be adequately large. This is especially true when only diagonal covariance matrices are used. Generally, a universal background model with a large number of Gaussian mixture components is created first, based on hours of speech data from many non-target speakers and speaker specific models are created by adapting the UBM in a *maximum a posteriori* (MAP) sense with speaker specific speech data (Gauvain and Lee, 1994). This GMM-UBM based approach has been shown to yield the best performance, compared with other modeling techniques, and is cur-rently the most predominant approach in text-independent speaker verification (Reynolds et al, 2000). In this paper, the GMM-UBM is used as our baseline system.

In the recognition phase, for a given input feature vector, not all but a smallèr subset, or the N nearest neighbors, of the Gaussian kernels in a UBM need to be scored. Thus in such a GMM-UBM based speaker identification system, the major computational load is on computing the likelihoods of all mixture Gaussian kernel components of the UBM to select the N best components and also computing the likelihoods of all speaker models in the system.

There have been various approaches proposed to reduce the computation com-plexity of GMM-UBM based text-independent speaker recognition. A hash GMM was proposed and applied (Auck-enthaler and Mason 2001). In the paper a small hash GMM is first trained with the entire training data set and a shortlist indices of mixture components in the large UBM is generated for each hash GMM component. Based on the occurring frequencies of the best scoring components in the hash GMM and the UBM, for each test vector, only a short list of components with the highest scoring hash will be evaluated. A computation reduction of ten-fold was achieved with only minor degradation of verification performance. Other approaches have also been proposed like lowering model order or decreasing frame rate (Mclaughlin et al, 1999), where the computation cost can be reduced by a factor of four with a negligible degradation of performance. In the paper (Xiang and Berger, 2003) where a structural Gaussian mixture model (SGMM) was proposed, a structured background model (SBM) is constructed based on the UBM and the feature space is partitioned hierarchically. For each target speaker, a SGMM is generated through a multilevel MAP adaptation of the SBM. In verifi-cation, the computation cost can be reduced significantly by searching down the SBM tree and scoring only a small subset of the Gaussian mixture components in the SBM and SGMM. Furthermore, multiple scores from different layers of the SGMM-SBM are combined via a neural network to make the final decision. This method reduces the computation load by a factor of seventeen at a price of 5% relative equal error rate degradation.

In this paper, we propose a tree-based kernel selection (TBKS) method to select the N-best Gaussian kernels in the UBM. A tree structure is built first based on the UBM, and the N-best components are then obtained by searching down the tree. To achieve both efficiency and accuracy, the top K nodes with highest likelihood scores in each non-leaf layers are preserved in the search to find the N-best leaf-node components. The speaker identification experiments were conducted on a database of 1 031 speakers and the results show that the computation load in the N-best selection can be reduced by a factor of 14.7 with only 1% increase of the relative error rate.

The other computation load is on the likelihood calculation of all speaker mod-els in the system. Although only N components in each speaker Gaussian mixture model need to be scored for each test vector, nevertheless, a large number of speakers still needs to be evaluated. Approaches have been proposed to prune out unlikely candidates in speech recognition, such as the beam search in Viterbi decoding (Ney and Ortmanns, 1999). In GMM-UBM based text-independent speak-er recognition, since the order of the test vectors to be evaluated does not affect the final decision, an reordering the observations was proposed to screen out un-likely candidate speakers efficiently (Pellom and Hansen, 1998). It can speed up the pruning process by a factor of six compared to the conventional sequential processing without it. In this paper, our TBKS is used in conjunction with the test vector reordering for more efficient, higher performance speaker identification.

This paper is organized as follows. In Section 12.2 we review the GMM-UBM based speaker identification. We then present our tree-base kernel selection (TBKS) algorithm in detail in Section 12.3. The observation reordering based pruning (ORBP) is reviewed in Section 12.4. In Section 12.5 the experimental setups and corresponding results are presented. Finally we give our conclusions in the last section.

12.2 GMM-UBM identification system

In GMM-UBM based speaker identification system, a speaker-independent UBM of M Gaussian mixture components is trained via the EM algorithm using hours of speech data from many non-target speakers (Dempster et al, 1977; Reynolds et al, 2000). For a D-dimensional feature vector x, a probability density function (pdf), parametrized in a mixture of Gaussian kernels, is used:

$$p(\mathbf{x}|\lambda_{ubm}) = \sum_{i=1}^{M} w_i g_i(\mathbf{x}) \tag{12.1}$$

where w_i is the weight of the i-th component, and $g_i(.)$ is the Gaussian kernel with corresponding mean vector, μ_i , and covariance matrix, Σ_i

$$g_i(\mathbf{x}) = \frac{1}{(2\pi)^{D/2}|\Sigma_i|^{1/2}} \exp\{-\frac{1}{2}(\mathbf{x} - \mu_i)^T \Sigma_i^{-1}(\mathbf{x} - \mu_i)\} \tag{12.2}$$

For each speaker, a GMM can be created through an MAP adaptation of the UBM. It has been shown that adapting only the means of Gaussian components yields the best speaker verification performance (Reynolds et al, 2000). Our experimental results confirmed that this is also the case for speaker identification and it is used in this study. The mean $\hat{u}_i$ of the i-th Gaussian component of the GMM is obtained as

$$\hat{\mu}_i = \frac{n_i}{n_i + r} E_i(\mathbf{X}) + \frac{r}{n_i + r} \mu_i \tag{12.3}$$

where $\mathbf{X} = \{\mathbf{x}_1, \mathbf{x}_2, ..., \mathbf{x}_T\}$ is the whole set of observed feature vectors and μ_i is the mean of the i-th Gaussian component in the UBM.

Here n_i and $E_i(x)$ are computed in the expectation step of EM algorithm as

$$n_i = \sum_{t=1}^{T} P(i|\mathbf{x_t}) \tag{12.4}$$

and

$$E_i(\mathbf{X}) = \frac{1}{n_i} \sum_{t=1}^{T} P(i|\mathbf{x_t})\mathbf{x_t}, \tag{12.5}$$

where r is a fixed relevance factor and $P(i \mid \mathbf{x_t})$ is the posteriori probability of the i-th component, given the feature vector $\mathbf{x}$,

$$P(i \mid \mathbf{x_t}) = \frac{w_i g_i(\mathbf{x_t})}{\sum_{j=1}^{M} w_i g_i(\mathbf{x_t})} \tag{12.6}$$

The speaker identification system is a maximum a posterior (MAP) classifier. For a group of S speakers, $\varphi = 1, 2, ..., S$, represented by the corresponding speaker models, $\lambda_1, \lambda_2, , \lambda_S$, the objective is to find the speaker model which has the maximum posterior probability, given the input feature vector sequence, $X = x_1, x_2, ..., x_T$. The minimum error Bayesian decision rule is:

$$\hat{S} = \arg \max_{1 \le s \le S} P(\lambda_s \mid X) = \arg \max_{1 \le s \le S} \frac{p(\mathbf{X} \mid \lambda_s)}{p(\mathbf{X})} P(\lambda_s) \tag{12.7}$$

Assuming equal priors for all speakers, the terms $P(\lambda_s)$ and $p(X)$ are the same for all speakers and can be ignored. Using logarithms and the assumed independence between observations, the decision rule then becomes

$$\hat{S} = \arg \max_{1 \le s \le S} \sum_{t=1}^{T} \log p(x_t|\lambda_s) \tag{12.8}$$

A block diagram of the speaker identification system is show in Figure 12.1.

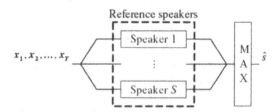

Fig. 12.1 Speaker identification.

It has been observed that only a few Gaussian mixture components in the whole GMM contributes to the final likelihood scores. Based on this fact and the correspondence between the speaker GMM and the UBM, an efficient scoring approach was proposed (Reynolds et al, 2000). For each test vector, the top N Gaussian components out of the entire M components in the UBM are found first and the corresponding N components in the speaker GMM are evaluated. Usually N is much smaller than M and the likelihood computation can be significantly streamlined.

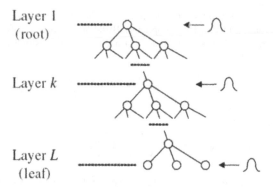

Fig. 12.2 Tree structure.

12.3 Tree-based kernel selection

In a GMM-UBM based speaker recognition system, generally all mixture com-ponents of the UBM need to be scored to find the N-best components for each test feature vector, which is a heavy computation load for the system. Based on the UBM, an L-layer tree, as shown in Figure 12.2, can be generated to model the acoustic space hierachically. Through a top-down clustering, each node in the upper L-1 layers represents a cluster of the Gaussian components in the UBM and is modeled by a single Gaussian pdf. Each leaf node corresponds to a separate Gaussian mixture component in the UBM. In this way, the tree structure models the acoustic space with different level of acoustic resolution and the top N components in the UBM can be selected more effectively by searching down the tree.

12.3.1 Distortion measure & cluster centroid

In order to build the tree, a distortion measure between any two Gaussian com-ponents needs be defined. Two widely used distortion measures are the Kullback-Leibler (KL) divergence (Shinoda and Lee, 2001; Watanabe et al, 1994; Xiang and Berger, 2003) and Bhattacharyya distance (Xiang and Berger, 2003). The KL divergence has been shown to give a slightly better performance in speaker verification (Xiang and Berger, 2003) and is used in this paper. In a diagonal covariance matrix based Gaussian model, the symmetric KL distance $d(i, j)$ between two Gaussians, $g_i(.)$ and $g_j(.)$ characterized by $N(\mu_i, \Sigma_i)$ and $N(\mu_j, \Sigma_j)$, is

$$d(i, j) = \int g_i(x) \ln \frac{g_i(x)}{g_j(x)} dx + \int g_j(x) \ln \frac{g_j(x)}{g_i(x)} dx$$

$$= \sum_k \left[\frac{\sigma_i^2(k) - \sigma_j^2(k) + (\mu_i(k) - \mu_j(k))^2}{\sigma_j^2(k)} + \frac{\sigma_j^2(k) - \sigma_i^2(k) + (\mu_j(k) - \mu_i(k))^2}{\sigma_i^2(k)} \right] \quad (12.9)$$

where $\mu_i(k)$ is the k-th element of mean vector μ_i while $\sigma_i^2(k)$ the k-th diagonal element of the covariance matrix Σ_i for Gaussian $g_i(.)$.

Estimating the centroid of a cluster of Gaussians is another important issue in such a tree structure. The cluster centroid of Gaussian components can be esti-mated using maximum likelihood (ML) criterion. In Shinoda and Lee (2001), it was assumed that the numbers of data samples from each mixture component are equal. However, this may cause some performance degradation because the acoustic space is modeled inappropriately. By taking into account of the mixture weights, the mean and covariance of a node c with a set of nodes, R, as its descendants, are estimated as (Xiang and Berger, 2003)

$$\mu_c(k) = \frac{\sum_{i \in R} w_i \mu_i(k)}{\sum_{i \in R} w_i} \tag{12.10}$$

$$\sigma_c^2(k) = \frac{\sum_{i \in R} w_i (\sigma_i^2(k) + \mu_i^2(k))}{\sum_{i \in R} w_i} - \mu_c^2(k), \tag{12.11}$$

where $\mu_c = \{\mu_c(k)\}^T$ is the mean vector, and $\Sigma_c = Diag\{\sigma_c^2(k)\}$, the covariance matrix. The weight of R is calculated as the sum of all weights w_i for $i \in R$

$$w_c = \sum_{i \in R} w_i \tag{12.12}$$

12.3.2 Tree construction

Before constructing the tree, the number of layers, L, and the number of branches from a node in each upper L-2 layer should be first determined, and then the tree is constructed as follows.

1) The pdf of the root node is calculated using 12.10, 12.11, and 12.12 with all Gaussian mixture components of the UBM. All the Gaussian components belong to the root node. Set the root node as the current node.
2) The pdf for each child of the current node is initiated by the *minimax* method and then interpolated with the parameters of the parent node (Shinoda and Lee, 2001).
3) The K-means algorithm is applied repeatedly to cluster the Gaussian mixture components belonging to the current node into several classes until convergence (Huang et al, 2001).

   a) Assign each Gaussian kernel to the nearest child node.
   b) Update the child node pdf and corresponding weight by using 12.10, 12.11, and 12.12.
   c) Calculate the total distortions from each Gaussian mixture component to the corresponding child node which belongs to.

4) Set each child node to be the current node and go to the Step (2) until the nodes in layer L-1 are generated.

It should be pointed out that the number of branches for those nodes in Layer L-1 varies from node to node and depends on the distribution of the Gaussian mixture components and the approach to tree construction. However the total number of leaf nodes is always equal to M.

12.3.3 Mixture components selection

For each test feature vector, the N Gaussian components with the top scores are selected by searching down the tree structure as follows:

1) Set all child nodes of the root as candidates.
2) Calculate weighted likelihood score at each node in the set of candidates for the test feature vector and sort all candidate nodes in a descending order according to the corresponding likelihood scores.

3) If layer L is reached, select the top N scoring components and stop searching. Otherwise, set all child nodes of the top K nodes as the candidates set and go to the Step (2).

Obviously the N components can not be guaranteed to be the actual top N scoring components in the UBM but just approximately. We propose here to use a new parameter K to define a search width to find the best compromise between efficiency and recognition accuracy. The larger the number K, the more components are scored and the closer the selected N components to the actual top N components. In the extreme case that K is larger than the total number of nodes in layer L-1, all components in the UBM will be scored and the selected N components are the actual top N components.

12.3.4 Tree structure & algorithm efficiency

To investigate the relationship between the structure of the tree and the efficiency of the algorithm, the actual computations and a computational reduction factor are first defined, and tree structures with different layer number L and search width K are then investigated and compared.

12.3.4.1 Measure of computation efficiency

The computational load of a speaker identification system is: computation cost defined as the average number of Gaussian likelihood calculation for each test frame, and a computation reduction factor, which is an indicator of efficiency improvement of a proposed method, is defined as the ratio of the computation costs with/without using the method. For an efficient method, the factor should be high-er than 1, actually, the higher the better.

12.3.4.2 Tree structure & algorithm efficiency

K	L	R_1	R_2	R_3	R_4	M_T	$F_{Selection}$
1	3	32	32			64	16
1	4	8	8	16		32	32
1	4	8	16	8		32	32
1	4	16	8	8		32	32
2	3	32	32			96	11
2	3	64	16			96	11
2	4	16	8	8		48	21
4	3	64	16			128	8
4	4	16	8	8		80	13
4	5	16	4	4	4	64	16

Table 12.1 Theoretic M_T's and $F_{Selection}$'s for different tree structures, given M=1024.

With the above definitions, the computation cost for the N-best components selection is evaluated as

$$M_U, \tag{12.13}$$

where M_U is the number of Gaussian mixtures for the UBM ($M_U = M$), and the reduction factor, denoted by $F_{Selection}$, is defined as

$$\frac{M_U}{M_T}, \tag{12.14}$$

where M_T is the average number of likelihood computation times for a test feature vector when using the tree-based kernel selection method.

Given a tree structure and the search width, M_T can not be determined easily, because the number of branches for those nodes in the lowest non-leaf layer varies from node to node. But if we assume the nodes in the lowest non-leaf layer have the same number of branches, M_T can be determined.

Suppose the number of layers is L and the numbers of branches for upper $L-1$ layers are $R_1, R_2, ..., R_{L-1}$, where $R_1 \times R_2 \times ... \times R_{L-1} = M$, and the search width is K, where K is not larger than any of $R_1, R_2, ..., R_{L-1}$, then the computational cost for the selection is

$$M_T = R_1 + K \times R_2 + ... + K \times R_{L-1}$$
$$\geq (L-1) \times (R_1 \times K \times R_2 \times ... K \times R_{L-1})^{1/(L-1)}$$
$$= (L-1) \times (K^{L-2} \times M)^{1/(L-1)} \tag{12.15}$$

If and only if

$$R_1 = K \times R_2 = ... = K \times R_{L-1} \tag{12.16}$$

M_T reaches the lower limit $(L-1) \times (K^{L-2} \times M)^{\frac{1}{L-1}}$.

Since K and $R_1, R_2, ..., R_{L-1}$ are all integers, M_T cannot reach the lower limit for all tree structures. But the closer $R_1, K \times R_2, ..., K \times R_{L-1}$ are to each other, the lower M_T is. According to this fact, ten tree structures with low M_T's for different K and L were designed, and the structures as well as the corresponding theoretic M_T's and $F_{Selection}$'s are listed in Table 12.1.

Given $K = 1$ or $K = 2$, a tree structure with $L \geq 4$ layers can bring a larger $F_{Selection}$, but the recognition rate of identification will be reduced with a larger $F_{Selection}$, which will be confirmed with the following experiments. Given $K = 4$ and $L \geq 6$, $M_T \geq (6-1) \times (4^4 \times 1024)^{\frac{1}{5}} = 60.6$according to 12.15, and then $F_{Selection} \leq 1024/60.6 = 16.9$, which means a larger L will not virtually bring a larger $F_{Selection}$ compared with the 5-layer tree structure in the last row of Table 12.1. Only ten tree structures listed in Table 12.1 will be tested in this paper.

12.4 Observation reordering based pruning

12.4.1 Beam search

In speaker identification with a large number of speakers, the likelihood calculation for all speaker models is another major computation bottleneck. A beam-search pruning algorithm can be applied to reduce the computational load. For an observation sequence $X = x_1, x_2, ..., x_T$, a threshold at time $\tau (1 \leq \tau \leq T)$ can be defined as follows

$$\Theta_\tau = \{ \max_{s \in S(\tau)} \sum_{t=1}^{\tau} \log(x_t | \lambda_s) \} - B \tag{12.17}$$

where $S(\tau)$ denotes the current set of active models at time τ and B is a constant used to define the user controlled beam-width. During processing, active speaker models whose log-likelihood score falls below Θ_τ are eliminated from the search.

12.4.2 Observation reordering based pruning (ORBP)

In speech processing, the feature vectors are typically extracted from overlap-ping time windows (the so-called *frames*) during which the vocal tract characteristics are assumed quasi-stationary. In general adjacent observation frames are correlated with each other and they provide similar acoustic information. This high degree correlation between neighboring observations hampers the efficiency of the beam-search in a speaker independent system, i.e., many observations must be examined before unlikely speakers can be screened out.

As shown in 12.8, the order of the observation sequence does not affect the final decision of identification. Then an observation reordering based pruning (ORBP) algorithm was proposed to improve the information gained from successive observations for those applications in which the entire observation sequence is known (Pellom and Hansen, 1998). This ORBP algorithm has two advantages: first, only the observation sequence is reordered and all observation vectors are still used for identification; second, there is no virtual computational overhead being required to reorder the observation sequence. The observation reordering algorithm can improve the efficiency of pruning significantly without affecting the recognition rate.

For an observation sequence $X = x_1, x_2, ..., x_T$, the reordered sequence Y is obtained as follows.

1) Initialize $i = 1$ and form a sequence of observations $O^{(i)}$ containing n observations selected from uniformly spaced interval across the vectors contained in XY and initialize Y with $O^{(i)}$.
2) Form a sequence of observations $O^{(i+1)}$ by sampling the observations nearest to the midpoints of elements found in Y (in the sense of index). For example, if x_1 and x_5 are part of Y, then x_3 would be placed in $O^{(i+1)}$.
3) Append $O^{(i+1)}$ to Y and increase the pass count: $i = i + 1$.
4) Repeat Steps (2) and (3) until all observations in X are reordered in X.

For clarity, a sample is illustrated here. For observations $X = x_1, x_2, ..., x_{16}$ and an initial uniform sampling of $(n = 4)$ frames, $O^{(1)} = x_1, x_5, x_9, x_{13}$ will be first formed, and then $O^{(2)} = x_3, x_7, x_{11}, x_{15}$ and $O^{(3)} = x_2, x_4, x_6, x_8, x_{10}, x_{12}, x_{14}, x_{16}$ (Pellom and Hansen, 1998). Finally, the reordered observation sequence is: $Y = x_1, x_5, x_9, x_{13}, x_3, x_7, x_{11}, x_{15}, x_2, x_4, x_6, x_8, x_{10}, x_{12}, x_{14}, x_{16}$.

The reordered observation sequence, Y, is processed by the speaker identification system with the standard beam-search pruning. During processing, speaker models whose log-likelihood score fall below the continuously-updated threshold Θ_τ are eliminated. When there is only one surviving speaker or all observations have been scored and the highest probable speaker is picked, the process is finished.

12.5 Experiments

12.5.1 Experimental setup

12.5.1.1 Database

The evaluation database used in this study is a telephone speech corpus record-ed by 1031 speakers. Each speaker has 30 seconds of speech for training and 1 or 2 utterances for test. There are 1 816 test segments in total and the duration of each test segment varies from 1 to 10 seconds, or 7 seconds averaged over all test segments. The UBM was estimated by using 2 hours of speech from a set of 60 male and 60 female speakers who are not used for evaluations.

12.5.1.2 Front-end processing

The front-end feature analysis consists of: (1) the speech is segmented into 20ms time window shifted every 10ms; (2) silence frames were removed with an energy based speech activity detection algorithm; (3) 16-dimensional mel-frequency cepstral coefficients (MFCC) are extracted from mel-scale filter bank analyzed speech; (4) for bandlimited telephone speech, cepstral analysis is per-formed over the mel-filters from 300 - 3 400 Hz; (5) delta cepstrum is computed using a Least Squares fitted first order difference over a window spanning over 2 frames from the current vector (Soong and Rosenberg, 1988); (6) cepstral mean normalization (CMN) (Atal, 1974) is finally applied to mel-frequency cepstral feature vectors to remove convolutional (linear in the cepstral domain) linear channel effect.

12.5.2 Experimental results

12.5.2.1 Baseline system

A conventional GMM-UBM based system is used as the baseline, where a UMB with $M = 1024$ Gaussian mixture components and the speaker models are derived from the UBM via the MAP adaptation. Only top $N = 4$ mixture components of the UBM are used for computing the speaker model likelihoods. The correct rate for this baseline GMM-UBM system is 95.32%, and the computation cost is $1024 + 4 \times 1031 = 5184$, which is evaluated by

$$M_U + N \times S, \qquad (12.18)$$

where S is the number of speaker models in the system.

12.5.2.2 Tree-based kernel selection

K	L	R_1	R_2	R_3	R_4	$F_{Selection}$	Corr.(%)
1	3	32	32			14.1	94.93
1	4	8	8	16		25.4	94.44
1	4	8	16	8		28.1	93.94
1	4	16	8	8		28.9	94.00
2	3	32	32			10.1	95.21
2	3	64	16			9.9	95.26
2	4	16	8	8		18.7	94.77
4	3	64	16			6.6	95.26
4	4	16	8	8		11.0	95.15
4	5	16	4	4	4	14.7	95.26

Table 12.2 Experimental results for TBKS.

The effectiveness of the kernel selection should be evaluated with not only the $F_{Selection}$ but also the recognition rate of the identification system. The results for the ten tree structures in Table 12.1, including the actual $F_{Selection}$'s and the recognition rates, are listed in Table 12.2. Table 12.2 shows that all the actual $F_{Selection}$'s are lower than the corresponding theoretic $F_{Selection}$'s, which is because the numbers of branches for the nodes in the lowest non-leaf layer are not uniform for any tree structure. But the actual $F_{Selection}$'s are close to the theoretic $F_{Selection}$'s, which means our analysis is reasonable.

For $K = 1$ and $K = 2$, tree structures of layer $L = 4$ yield larger $F_{Selection}$'s, com-pared with tree structures of layer $L = 3$, but with more than 10% relative degradation of performance, i.e., 94.44%, 93.94%, 94.00% and 94.77% vs. 95.32% of the baseline system. These structures do not meet our performance expectation. For $K = 4$, a good tradeoff between $F_{Selection}$ and correct rate, a computation reduction factor of about 14.7 for top components selection with only about 1% of relative reduction of correct rate, is achieved with a 5-layer tree structure. This tree structure is regarded as the best structure in this study and will used together with the observation reordering based pruning algorithm for speaker identification.

The effectiveness of the TBKS method is also evaluated with the computation reduction in the overall system, evaluated as

$$\frac{M_U + N \times S}{M_T + N \times S},$$ (12.19)

With the best 5-layer tree structure, the computation reduction factor for the overall system is 1.24. Though the $F_{Selection}$ for the best structure is very high (14.7), but the improvement of the overall system computation efficiency is not good because the likelihood computation of speaker models still remains the same.

12.5.2.3 Noise robustness of TBKS

Corr.(%)	GMM-UMB	5-layer Tree
Babble	94.83	94.70
Factory	94.17	94.17
Pink	93.58	93.51
White	88.77	88.63

Table 12.3 Experimental results for TBKS in noisy environments.

Four different noises, including: babble, factory, pink, and white noises, from *Noisex* (Varga, 1992) are added to the clean test speech utterances to evaluated the robustness of the TBKS method in noisy environments. For each kind of noise, every clean speech utterance is added with an am-plitude modulated noise segment randomly selected from the corresponding noise database to get a noisy speech utterance, where the amplitude modulation is randomly generated in a predefined range which can make sure that the SNR of the noisy speech is between 15dB and 30dB. Both the baseline GMM-UBM system and the best 5-layer tree structure are evaluated with the four generated noisy speech databases and the results are list in Table 12.3. As shown in the results, the correct rates degrade in all four noisy environments for both the baseline and the 5-layer tree TBKS systems. The latter one yields almost the same correct rates as the former one and the av-erage $F_{Selection}$ for all kinds of noisy speech utterances is about 14.5 which is close to the value for clean utterances. From this it can be seen that the TBKS method improves the computational efficiency for the GMM-UBM based speaker identification system without degrading the speaker identification performance, in not only clean but also noisy environments.

12.5.2.4 *Observation reordering based pruning*

The observation reordering based pruning (ORBP) algorithm was first tested without being used together with TBKS. Each test observation sequence was reor-dered and submitted to the GMM-UBM identification system with the standard beam search. For each test feature vector, all components in the UBM were scored to find the top $N = 4$, and then the scores for each surviving speaker were accumulated In recognition, the number of Gaussian likelihood calculation was accumulated with all active speaker models until only one speaker remains as the sole survivor or all observations are scored and the speaker whose model yields the highest score is found. After the identification decision was made, this number was divided by the number of all observations to calculate the computational cost for the speaker models likelihood calculation, M_S, no matter all observations were processed or not. Finally, the computational reduction factor for speaker models likelihood calculation was evaluated as

$$\frac{N \times S}{M_S}. \tag{12.20}$$

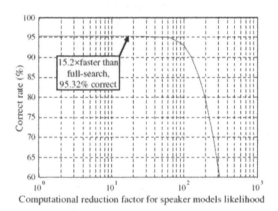

Fig. 12.3 Experimental results for ORBP.

　This experiment was repeated with different beam widths and the results are shown in Figure 12.3. As shown in Figure 12.3, very similar correct rates are obtained with an increase of speed-up factors correspond to reduced beam widths. The observation reordering based pruning (ORBP) algorithm can speed up the baseline system by a factor of 15.2 in speaker model likelihood computation while maintaining the same perfor-mance at 95.32% correct rate. However, the computation reduction factor for the overall system is only 4.00, which is evaluated by

$$\frac{M_U + N \times S}{M_U + M_S}. \tag{12.21}$$

12.5.2.5 *Combing TBKS and ORBP*

Either TBKS or ORBP, does not achieve a high enough computation reduction of the overall computations, the factor is only 1.24 for TBKS and 4.00 for ORBP. A further experiment was performed to investigate the effectiveness of joint TBKS and ORBP, where the computation reduction factor for the overall system is

$$\frac{M_U + N \times S}{M_T + M_S}. \tag{12.22}$$

The result is listed in Table 12.4. Table 12.4 shows when the tree-based kernel selection method and the observation reordering based pruning algorithm are integrated into the GMM-UBM system, a dramatic improvement of 15.8 times in computation and virtually no performance degradation (1% relative error increase), compared with the baseline system.

	$F_{Overall}$	Corr.(%)
Baseline	1	95.32
Integrated	15.8	95.26

Table 12.4 Experimental results for the GMMCUBM system integrated with both TBKS and ORBP.

12.6 Conclusions

In this paper, a tree-based kernel selection method is proposed to efficiently select the N-best Gaussian components in the UBM for GMM-UBM based speaker identification applications. The relationship between the form of tree structure and resultant computational efficiency was evaluated on a 1 031 speaker database, both in clean and noisy conditions. The experiments show that the proposed tree-based kernel selection can speed up the kernel selection of UBM by a factor of 14.7 at a 1% degradation of relative recognition performance, with a 5-layer tree. Additionally, a previously proposed observation reordering based pruning algorithm was tested and speaker model likelihood computation can be reduced by 15.2 times without degrading the recognition rate. When both TBKS and ORBP were integrated into the GMM-UBM based speaker identification system, a speedup factor of 15.8 of the overall system and 1% relative reduction in recognition rate was achieved. We also show that the TBKS search efficiency is robust to additive background noise.

References

1. Atal, B.S., 1974. Effectiveness of Linear Prediction Characteristics of the Speech Wave for Automatic Speaker Identification and Verification. Journal of the Acoustical So-ciety of America 55(6), 1304-1312.

2. Auckenthaler, R., Mason J., 2001. Gaussian selection applied to text-independent speaker verification. Proc. A Speaker Odyssey-Speaker Recognition Workshop.

3. Campbell, J., 1997. Speaker recognition: a tutorial. Proc. IEEE 85, 1437-1462.

4. Dempster, A., Laird, N., Dubin, D., 1977. Maximum likelihood from incomplete data via the EM algorithm. J. R. Statist. Soc. 39, 1-38.

5. Gauvain, J.L., Lee C.H., 1994. Maximum a posteriori estimation for multivariate Gaussian Mixture observations of Markov chains. IEEE Trans. on Speech and Audio Process. 2(2), 291-298.

6. Huang, X., Acero, A., Hon, H., 2001. Spoken Language Processing: A Guide to Theory, Algorithm, and System Development. Prentice Hall.

7. Mclaughlin, J., Reynolds, D.A., Gleason, T., 1999. A study of computation speed-ups of the GMM-UBM speaker recognition system. In: Proc. Eurospeech, 1215-1218.

8. Ney, H., Ortmanns, S., 1999. Dynamic Programming Search for Continuous Speech Recognition. IEEE Signal Processing Magazine, 64-83.

9. Pellom, B.L., Hansen J.H.L., 1998. An efficient scoring algorithm for Gaussian mixture model based speaker identification. IEEE Signal Processing Letter 5(11), 281-284.

10. Ramachandran, R.P., Farrell, K.R., Ramachandran, R.. Mammone, R.J , 2002. Speaker recognition - general classifier approaches and data fusion methods. Pattern Rec-ognition 35, 2801-2821.

11. Reynolds, D.A., 1994. Experimental evaluation of features for robust speaker identification. IEEE Trans. on Speech and Audio Process. 2(4), 639-644.

12. Reynolds, D.A., 1995. Speaker identification and verification using Gaussian mixture speaker models. Speech Communication 17, 91-108.

13. Reynolds, D.A., Rose R.C., 1995. Robust text-independent speaker identification using Gaussian mixture speaker models. IEEE Trans. on Speech and Audio Process. 3(1), 72-83.

14. Reynolds, D.A., 1997. Comparison of background normalization methods for text-independent speaker verification. In: Proc. of Eurospeech, pp. 963-966.

15. Reynolds D.A., Quatieri T., Dunn R., 2000. Speaker verification using adapted Gaussian mixture models. Digital Signal Processing 10, 19-41.

16. Reynolds, D.A. 2002. An overview of automatic speaker recognition technology. In: Proc. IEEE Internat. Conf. on Acoust., Speech and Signal Process. (ICASSP), pp. 472-475.

17. Shinoda, K., Lee, C.H., 2001. A structural bayes approach to speaker adaptation. IEEE Trans. on Speech and Audio Process. 9(3), 276-287.

18. Soong F.K., Rosenberg, A.E., 1988. On the use of instantaneous and transitional spectral information in speaker recognition. IEEE Trans. on Acoust., Speech and Signal Process. 36(6), 871-879.

19. Soong, F.K., Rosenberg A.E., Rabiner L.R., Juang B.H., 1985. A vector quantiza-tion approach to speaker recognition. In: Proc. IEEE Internat. Conf. on Acoust., Speech and Signal Process. (ICASSP), pp. 387-390.

20. Varga, A.P., Steeneken, H.J.M., Tomlinson, M., Jones, D., 1992. The NOISEX-92 study on the effect of additive noise on automatic speech recognition. Technical Report, Speech Research Unit, Defense Research Agency, Malvern, UK.

21. Watanabe, T., Shinoda, K., Takagi, K., Yamada, E., 1994. Speech Recognition using tree-structured probability density function. In: Proc. Internat. Conf. Speech Language Process., pp. 223-226.

22. Xiang, B., Berger, T., 2003. Efficient text-independent speaker verification with structural Gaussian mixture models and Neural Network. IEEE Trans. on Speech and Audio Process.11(5), 447-456.

Chapter 13
Word Graph Based Feature Enhancement for Noisy Speech Recognition*

Zhi-Jie Yan, Frank K. Soong and Ren-Hua Wang

Abstract This paper presents a word graph based feature enhancement method for robust speech recognition in noise. The approach uses signal processing based speech enhancement as a starting point, and then performs Wiener filtering to remove residual noise. During the process, a decoded word graph is used to directly guide the feature enhancement with respect to the HMM for recognition, so that the enhanced feature can match the clean speech model better in the acoustic space. The proposed word graph based feature enhancement method was tested on the Aurora 2 database. Experimental results show that an improved recognition performance can be obtained comparing with conventional signal processing based and GMM based feature enhancement methods. With signal processing based Weighted Noise Estimation and GMM based method, the relative error rate reductions are 35.44% and 42.58%, respectively. The proposed word graph based method improves the performance further, and a relative error rate reduction of 57.89% is obtained.

Key words: Speech recognition, Robustness, Speech enhancement

13.1 Introduction

It has been well-known that the performance of Automatic Speech Recognition (ASR) system degrades dramatically when there is a mismatch between training and testing environments. For the ASR systems deployed in real conditions, this mismatch is usually caused by additive noise and channel distortion. Consequently, robust speech recognition which has the ability to compensate various kinds of noise and channel effect is desired as one of the key techniques for real-world ASR applications.

Previous research which focused on minimizing environmental mismatch can be categorized into the following three groups: (a) *Signal processing based compensation*, which tries to find robust features (e.g., Mel-Frequency Cepstral Coefficients, MFCC) or to compensate noise and channel effect over the representation of speech (e.g., Spectral Subtraction [1], Cepstral Mean Normalization, CMN [2]); (b) *Model based compensation*, which tries to adapt model or to transform feature with respect to the model so that the speech variation in noisy environments can be better handled (e.g., Parallel Model Combination, PMC [3], and Feature-space Maximum Likelihood Linear Regression, fMLLR [4]); (c) *Combination of signal processing based and model*

Zhi-Jie Yan and Ren-Hua Wang
iFlytek Speech Lab, University of Science and Technology of China, Hefei, P. R. China, 230027
e-mail: yanzhijie@ustc.edu, rhw@ustc.edu.cn

Frank K. Soong
Microsoft Research Asia, Beijing China, e-mail: frankkps@microsoft.com

* Source: Proceeding of Acoustics, Speech and Signal Processing, 2007. ICASSP 2007. IEEE International Conference on Volume 4, 15-20 April 2007 Pages:IV-373 - IV-376 Copyright ©2007 IEEE. Reprinted, with permission. DOI:10.1109/ICASSP.2007.366927

based methods, which tries to benefit from both approaches (e.g., model based compensation [5], and Model Based Wiener filter, MBW [6]).

Generally speaking, the methods in the first group are simple and efficient, while the methods in the second group can achieve a better recognition performance at the cost of much more computational load. Compared with the first two groups, the methods in the third group aim to take advantages of both signal processing based and model based approaches, and try to achieve a reasonable recognition performance while maintaining a relatively low computational cost.

In this paper, we present a word graph based feature enhancement method, which belongs to the third group of the compensation approaches. The proposed method is based upon Wiener filtering of the Mel-filter bank energy, given (a) the input noisy speech, (b) a signal processing based estimate of noise, and (c) a clean trained Hidden Markov Model (HMM) which is used for both feature enhancement and speech recognition. In our approach, the input noisy speech is first de-noised and channel-normalized via signal processing based method. The roughly processed signal is then decoded using the clean speech model, and a word graph is obtained to represent the hypothesis space. After that, both static and dynamic features of the model based clean speech are estimated, and the speech parameter sequence for Wiener filtering is synthesized in Maximum Likelihood (ML) sense. Finally, Wiener filtering is performed using the input noisy speech, the estimated noise, and the synthesized model based clean speech. The output of the filter is re-decoded in a word graph constrained second pass decoding, to get the final recognition results.

The main difference compared with previous research [5, 6] is that in our approach, a word graph is constructed to directly guide the feature enhancement process with respect to the clean speech model for recognition. As a result, a same HMM can be used for both enhancement and recognition, and the use of another Gaussian Mixture Model (GMM) in [5, 6] becomes unnecessary. The word graph based approach enables us to exploit the temporal resolution of the HMM, as well as to improve the estimate accuracy of the model based clean speech via imposing the explicit constraint between its static and dynamic features. Therefore, the enhanced speech feature after Wiener filtering can match the clean speech model better in the acoustic space, and thus leads to an improved recognition performance.

The rest of this paper is organized as follows: In Section 13.2, the word graph based feature enhancement method is first described from a global point of view, and then specified in the details of the processing steps. In Section 13.3, experimental results of the proposed method are presented and compared with conventional methods. Finally, we draw our conclusions and future work in Section 13.4.

13.2 Word Graph Based Feature Enhancement

13.2.1 System Overview

The flowchart of the word graph based feature enhancement method can be illustrated by Fig. 13.1. The input noisy speech, X, is first fed into the signal processing based speech enhancement block, in which Weighted Noise Estimation [7] is performed to get a rough estimate of the noise spectrum N, as well as the corresponding clean speech S_1. Then, S_1 is converted to MFCC coefficients, and the cepstral mean $\overline{S_1}$ is subtracted from it to normalize the channel effect. After that, the normalized speech, S_2, is decoded using the clean speech HMM, and a word graph representing the hypothesis space is constructed. By merging the kernel parameters of the clean speech model according to their posterior probabilities, a model based estimate of the clean speech, S_3, can be synthesized. S_3 is then transformed back to Mel-filter bank energy, and Wiener filtering is performed to get the final estimate of the clean speech, S_4. In the last step, S_4 is re-decoded in a constrained search space defined by the word graph, and the final recognition output is obtained.

In the following subsections, the processing steps of the method will be specified in details:

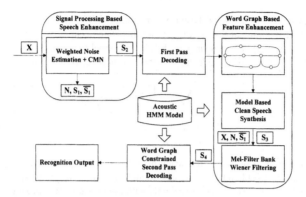

Fig. 13.1 Flowchart of the word graph based feature enhancement.

13.2.2 Signal Processing Based Speech Enhancement

The input noisy speech X is first fed into the speech enhancement block, where it is converted to the linear spectral domain, and signal processing based speech enhancement is performed. The purpose of this step is to get a rough estimate of the noise and clean speech with relatively low computational cost. Because the accuracy of the word graph decoding relies greatly on the Signal-to-Noise Ratio (SNR) of the input speech, it is then necessary to remove the noise effect via signal processing based enhancement before a clean trained speech model can be applied.

In our approach, Weighted Noise Estimation [7] is performed to estimate the noise spectrum. This method continuously updates the noise estimate N, using weighted noisy speech according to the estimated SNR. Consequently, the corresponding clean speech S_1 can be obtained by using conventional spectral subtraction.

Besides additive noise, channel effect should also be considered. In our approach, CMN is performed on S_1 to get the channel-normalized MFCC coefficients, S_2. Meanwhile, the cepstral mean $\overline{S}_1$ is also stored for latter process.

13.2.3 First Pass Decoding and Word Graph Construction

S_2 is decoded using the clean trained HMM to construct a word graph which compactly represents the hypothesis space. Even after signal processing based speech enhancement, S_2 may still have some residual noise which can lead to incorrect decoding. But the word graph based approach would have more chance that the correct hypotheses exist in the graph with relatively lower posterior probabilities (or likelihoods) than the incorrect first best hypothesis. Therefore, they can still be recovered in the latter Wiener filtering process with the help of the clean speech model.

Once the word graph has been decoded, kernel posterior probabilities for each Gaussian component of the model can be calculated. These posterior probabilities will serve as the weighting coefficients for synthesizing the model based clean speech for Wiener filtering. Using the word graph, the posterior probability of kernel k at time t, given the entire observation sequence o_1^T can be formulated as:

$$p([k;t] \mid o_1^T) = \sum_{\substack{\forall [w;s,e] \\ s \leq t \leq e \\ j \in w, k \in j}} p([w;s,e] \mid o_1^T) \cdot p([j;t] \mid w) \cdot p([k;t] \mid j)$$

$$(13.1)$$

in which $p([w;s,e] \mid o_1^T)$ is the Word Posterior Probability (WPP) of word w in the word graph, starting at time s and ending at time e; $p([j;t] \mid w)$, the state occupancy probability of state j at time t, given w; $p([k;t] \mid j)$, the occupancy probability of kernel k in state j at time t.

In Eq. (13.1), $p([w;s,e] \mid o_1^T)$ is calculated as the conventional WPP [8] defined as:

$$p([w;s,e] \mid o_1^T) = \sum_{\substack{\forall M,[w;s,e]_1^M \\ \exists n, 1 \le n \le M \\ w=w_n, s=s_n, e=e_n}} \frac{\prod_{m=1}^M p(o_{s_m}^{e_m} \mid w_m) \cdot p(w_m \mid w_1^M)}{p(o_1^T)} \tag{13.2}$$

in which M is the number of words in a string hypothesis; $p(o_{s_m}^{e_m} \mid w_m)$ and $p(w_m \mid w_1^M)$ are the scaled acoustic model likelihood and language model likelihood, respectively. Within the word graph, $p([w;s,e] \mid o_1^T)$ can be calculated efficiently with the forward-backward algorithm.

In our approach, state occupancy probability $p([j;t] \mid w)$ is calculated using Viterbi approximation, so it equals one for the states of the best alignment path $J([w;s,e],o_s^e)$ and zero otherwise:

$$p([j;t] \mid w) \overset{\text{Viterbi}}{\approx} \delta(j, J_t([w;s,e],o_s^e)) \tag{13.3}$$

Finally, $p([k;t] \mid j)$ is calculated as the kernel output probability normalized by the state output probability:

$$p([k;t] \mid j) = \frac{c_{jk} \cdot p(o_t \mid \mu_k, \Sigma_k)}{\sum_{l=1}^L c_{jl} \cdot p(o_t \mid \mu_l, \Sigma_l)} \tag{13.4}$$

in which L is the number of Gaussian components of state j; c_{jk} is the component weight of kernel k; μ_k and Σ_k are the mean vector and covariance matrix of that kernel, respectively.

13.2.4 Model Based Clean Speech Synthesis

The model based clean speech estimate for Wiener filtering is constructed in two steps. In the first step, for each time frame t, the expected values of the mean and covariance of the clean speech feature are calculated using the kernel posterior probabilities along with the kernel parameters (diagonal covariance matrix is used in our experiments):

$$\hat{\mu}(t) = E\{\mu \mid \mu_k, p([k;t] \mid o_1^T)\}$$
$$= \sum_{k=1}^K p([k;t] \mid o_1^T) \cdot \mu_k \tag{13.5}$$

and

$$\hat{\Sigma}(t) = E\{[\mu - \hat{\mu}][\mu - \hat{\mu}]^\top \mid \mu_k, \Sigma_k, p([k;t] \mid o_1^T)\}$$
$$= \sum_{k=1}^K p([k;t] \mid o_1^T) \cdot (\Sigma_k + \mu_k \mu_k^\top) - \hat{\mu}(t)\hat{\mu}(t)^\top \tag{13.6}$$

In contrast to former approaches that only use static means of the speech feature, in Eqs. (13.5) and (13.6), we calculate the expected values using both static and dynamic (first- and second-order delta) features of the kernels. As a result, in the second step, the model based estimate of the clean speech S_3 can be synthesized in ML sense by imposing the explicit constraint between its static and dynamic features. Following this way, the accuracy of the model based clean speech for Wiener filtering can be improved by considering not only its static "level", but also its dynamic "trend".

It can be seen from [9] that, the ML solution of S_3 can be obtained by solving the weighted normal equation:

$$\mathbf{W}^\top \mathbf{U}^{-1} \mathbf{W} C = \mathbf{W}^\top \mathbf{U}^{-1} M \tag{13.7}$$

where $\mathbf{W}$ is the weighting matrix for computing the dynamic features, via $\mathbf{W}$ which imposes the static-dynamic constraint [9], and

$$C = [c(1)^\top, c(2)^\top, \dots, c(T)^\top]^\top \tag{13.8}$$

is the synthesized clean speech S_3 in terms of its MFCC parameter sequence;

$$\mathbf{U}^{-1} = \mathrm{diag}[\hat{\Sigma}^{-1}(1), \hat{\Sigma}^{-1}(2), \dots, \hat{\Sigma}^{-1}(T)]$$
$$M = [\hat{\mu}(1)^\top, \hat{\mu}(2)^\top, \dots, \hat{\mu}(T)^\top]^\top \tag{13.9}$$

are the matrices composed by the expected mean and covariance values calculated by Eqs. (13.5) and (13.6). Because of the band diagonal structure of $\mathbf{W}^\top \mathbf{U}^{-1} \mathbf{W}$, Eq. (13.7) can be solved efficiently in a time-recursive manner by the QR decomposition.

13.2.5 Wiener Filtering and Constrained Second Pass Decoding

Wiener filtering of the Mel-filter bank energy is performed in the linear spectral domain, so the estimated cepstral mean $\overline{S_1}$ is first added back to S_3 (i.e., $c(t)$ in the cepstral domain), and an Inverse Discrete Cosine Transform (IDCT) followed by an exponential transform is performed:

$$S_3^{\mathrm{FBE}}(t) = \exp\left\{\mathrm{IDCT}[c(t) + \overline{S_1}]\right\} \tag{13.10}$$

where the superscript "FBE" stands for Mel-filter bank energy.

Meanwhile, the input noisy speech X and the estimated noise N can also be converted to Mel-filter bank energies. Wiener filtering can then be performed to get the final estimate of the clean speech, S_4:

$$S_4^{\mathrm{FBE}}(t) = \frac{S_3^{\mathrm{FBE}}(t)}{S_3^{\mathrm{FBE}}(t) + N^{\mathrm{FBE}}(t)} \cdot X^{\mathrm{FBE}}(t) \tag{13.11}$$

In the last step, S_4^{FBE} is converted to the cepstral domain, where its cepstral mean is removed so that a second pass decoding can be performed. As we have already got a word graph after the first pass decoding, it is then possible to re-score the word graph or to re-decode S_4 within the constrained search space defined by the word graph. Because in most cases, the Word Graph Error Rate (GER, computed by determining the sentence through the word graph that best matches the reference in terms of word errors) is considerably lower than the Word Error Rate (WER) of the first best hypothesis, the word graph constrained second pass decoding can achieve a reasonably low WER while significantly reducing the computational cost of another pass of completely free decoding.

Aurora 2 Reference Word Error Rate			
Testing Set	Set A	Set B	Set C	Overall
WER (%)	38.42	42.59	30.57	38.52

Table 13.1 Aurora 2 reference Word Error Rate using MFCC_0DA.

Signal Processing Based Speech Enhancement			
Testing Set	Set A	Set B	Set C	Overall
WER (%)	25.27	25.47	22.87	24.87
Relative	34.23%	40.21%	25.18%	35.44%
GER (%)	5.59	6.07	4.58	5.58

Table 13.2 Performance of signal processing based speech enhancement (absolute, relative to the reference, and graph error rate).

13.3 Experiments

13.3.1 Experimental Setup

The word graph based feature enhancement method has been tested on the Aurora 2 database. Because transforms between spectral domain and cepstral domain are needed, a 39-dimensional MFCC feature vector, including c_0 to c_{12} and their first and second order dynamic coefficients, was used in our system. An HMM used for both enhancement and recognition was trained with ETSI provided scripts [10] using HTK. As a result, 11 whole word digit models were trained, each with 16 emitting states and 3 Gaussian components per state. A three-state silence model was also constructed with 6 Gaussian components per state, while a one-state short pause model, tied with the central state of the silence model, was used.

Because our approach uses the same clean trained HMM for both enhancement and recognition, the Aurora 2 clean-condition training scenario is just suitable to evaluate the performance of our algorithm. Besides the baseline system, three feature enhancement methods have been compared in our experiments: (a) Signal processing based speech enhancement using Weighted Noise Estimation and CMN; (b) The GMM based feature enhancement method similar to that of in [5, 6], and (c) The proposed word graph based feature enhancement method. Note that method (a) actually serves as a starting point for the latter two feature enhancement methods (b) and (c) (reference to Fig. 13.1).

13.3.2 Signal Processing Based Speech Enhancement

The reference word error rate of Mel-cepstrum on the Aurora 2 database is given in Table 13.1 (slightly better than [10] because we use c_0 instead of log-energy). After signal processing based speech enhancement, the word error rate and word graph error rate are shown in Table 13.2. It is shown from the table that, signal processing based feature enhancement consistently improves the recognition performance, and the overall relative error rate reduction is 35.44%. Moreover, the GER of the decoded word graph is significantly lower than the WER of the first best hypothesis (only about $1/4 \sim 1/5$). So the word graph constructed in the first pass decoding can be used not only to guide the feature enhancement process, but also to narrow the search space in the second pass decoding.

13.3.3 GMM Based Feature Enhancement

Conventional GMM based feature enhancement method was performed in our experiments for comparison purpose, and its performance is given in Table 13.3. In this case, the acoustic model in Fig. 13.1 is replaced by a GMM with 128 Gaussian components, and the word graph is a single path of the GMM states. As shown in the table, GMM based feature enhancement reduces the word error rate further, and the overall relative error rate reduction is improved to 42.58%.

GMM Based Feature Enhancement			
Testing Set	Set A	Set B	Set C	Overall
WER (%)	22.85	21.45	21.99	22.12
Relative	40.52%	49.64%	28.05%	42.58%

Table 13.3 Performance of the GMM based feature enhancement.

Word Graph Based Feature Enhancement			
Testing Set	Set A	Set B	Set C	Overall
WER (%)	16.79	15.92	15.68	16.22
Relative	56.31%	62.62%	48.70%	57.89%
Word Graph Based Feature Enhancement (UD)			
Testing Set	Set A	Set B	Set C	Overall
WER (%)	16.58	15.87	15.70	16.12
Relative	56.85%	62.73%	48.66%	58.15%

Table 13.4 Performance of the word graph based feature enhancement (UD = unconstrained second pass decoding).

13.3.4 Word Graph Based Feature Enhancement

The performance of the proposed word graph based feature enhancement method is shown in Table 13.4. The results show that the performance is further improved over the GMM based method, and an overall relative error rate reduction of 57.89% is obtained. As we were using word graph constrained second pass decoding, this result is obtained with a minor increase of the computational cost. We also compared the WER if we perform an unconstrained free decoding in the second pass, and the result is given in the "UD" part of Table 13.4. The experimental results suggest that the difference between the two decoding scenarios is minimal, and the costly unconstrained second pass decoding is not necessary. This is true especially when the GER of the word graph is sufficiently low.

Fig. 13.2 shows the recognition results of the three enhancement methods as a function of SNR. The word graph based feature enhancement method consistently achieves the best performance at different SNRs. It outperforms the other two methods especially when SNR is low.

13.4 Conclusions

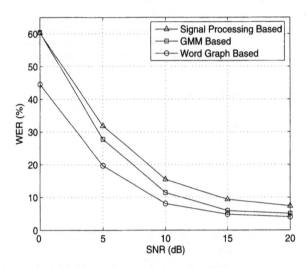

Fig. 13.2 Performance of the enhancement methods against SNR.

In this paper we presented a word graph based feature enhancement method for robust speech recognition in noise. This method performs signal processing based speech enhancement as a foundation, and then using it to construct the word graph. After that, a maximum likelihood estimate of the model based clean speech is synthesized using the word graph and clean trained speech model, so Wiener filtering can be carried out to get the output speech feature for recognition. The word graph based method enables us to directly guide the feature enhancement process with respect to the model for recognition, and the temporal resolution as well as the dynamic feature of the HMM can also be exploited. Experimental results suggest that the word graph based feature enhancement method outperforms conventional signal processing based and GMM based methods under different SNRs. In future work, we are planning to adapt the method to achieve an improved performance when not only the clean speech, but also the noise statistical information, can be observed.

References

1. P. Lockwood and J. Boudy, *Experiments with a Nonlinear Spectral Subtractor (NSS), Hidden Markov Models and the projection, for robust speech recognition in cars*, Speech Communication, vol. 11, no. 2-3, pp. 215-228, 1992.
2. F. Liu, R. Stern, X. Huang, and A. Acero, *Efficient cepstral normalization for robust speech recognition*,in Proc. ARPA Human Language Technology Workshop, 1993, pp. 69-73.
3. M. J. F. Gales and S. J. Young, *Robust continuous speech recognition using parallel model combination*,IEEE Trans. on Speech and Audio Processing, vol. 4, pp. 352-359, 1996.
4. M. J. F. Gales, *Maximum likelihood linear transformations for hmm-based speech recognition*,Tech. Rep., CUED/FINFENG/ TR 291, Cambridge University, 1997.
5. J. C. Segura, A. de la Torre, M. C. Benitez, and A. M. Peinado, *Model-based compensation of the additive noise for continuous speech recognition. Experiments using the AURORA II database and tasks*, in Proc. Eurospeech2001, 2001, vol. 1, pp. 217-220.

6. T. Arakawa, M. Tsujikawa, and R. Isotani, *Model-based Wiener ..lter for noise robust speech recognition*,in Proc. ICASSP2006, 2006, vol. 1, pp. 537-540.

7. [7] M. Kato, A. Sugiyama, and M. Serizawa, *Noise suppression with high speech quality based on weighted noise estimation and MMSE STSA*,Electronics and Communications in Japan, vol. 89, no. 2, pp. 43-53, 2006.

8. W. K. Lo and F. K. Soong, *Generalized posterior probability for minimum error veri..cation of recognized sentences*,in Proc. ICASSP2005, 2005, pp. 85-88.

9. K. Tokuda, T. Yoshimura, T. Masuko, T. Kobayashi, and T. Kitamura, *Speech parameter generation algorithms for HMMbased speech synthesis*,in Proc. ICASSP2000, 2000, pp. 1315-1318.

10. H. G. Hirsch and D. Pearce, *The Aurora experimental framework for the performance evaluation of speech recognition under noisy conditions*,in Proc. ISCA ITRW ASR2000, 2000, pp. 181-188.

Part IV
Search and Mining

Chapter 14
Building Bridges for Web Query Classification*

Dou Shen, Jian-Tao Sun, Qiang Yang and Zheng Chen

Abstract Web query classification (QC) aims to classify Web users' queries, which are often short and ambiguous, into a set of target categories. QC has many applications including page ranking in Web search, targeted advertisement in response to queries, and personalization. In this paper, we present a novel approach for QC that outperforms the winning solution of the ACM KDDCUP 2005 competition, whose objective is to classify 800,000 real user queries. In our approach, we first build a bridging classifier on an intermediate taxonomy in an offline mode. This classifier is then used in an online mode to map user queries to the target categories via the above intermediate taxonomy. A major innovation is that by leveraging the similarity distribution over the intermediate taxonomy, we do not need to retrain a new classifier for each new set of target categories, and therefore the bridging classifier needs to be trained only once. In addition, we introduce category selection as a new method for narrowing down the scope of the intermediate taxonomy based on which we classify the queries. Category selection can improve both efficiency and effectiveness of the online classification. By combining our algorithm with the winning solution of KDDCUP 2005, we made an improvement by 9.7% and 3.8% in terms of precision and F1 respectively compared with the best results of KDDCUP 2005.

Key words: Web Query Classification, Bridging Classifier, Category Selection, KDDCUP 2005

14.1 Introduction

With exponentially increasing information becoming available on the Internet, Web search has become an indispensable tool for Web users to gain desired information. Typically, Web users submit a short Web query consisting of a few words to search engines. Because these queries are short and ambiguous, how to interpret the queries in terms of a set of target categories has become a major research issue. In this paper, we call the problem of generating a ranked list of target categories from user queries the query classification problem, or QC for short.

The importance of QC is underscored by many services provided by Web search. A direct application is to provide better search result pages for users with interests of different categories. For example, the users issuing a Web query "apple" might expect to see Web pages related to the fruit

---

Dou Shen and Qiang Yang
Department of Computer Science and Engineering, Hong Kong University of Science and Technology, e-mail: {dshen,qyang}@cs.ust.hk

Jian-Tao Sun and Zheng Chen
Microsoft Research Asia, Beijing, P.R.China, e-mail: {jtsun, zhengc}@microsoft.com

* Source: Proceedings of the 29th ACM International Conference on Research and Development in Information Retrieval (SIGIR 06) Pages 131-138 Copyright ©2006 Association for Computing Machinery, Inc. Reprinted by permission. DOI Bookmark: http://doi.acm.org/10.1145/1148170.1148196

apple, or they may prefer to see products or news related to the computer company. Online advertisement services can rely on the QC results to promote different products more accurately. Search result pages can be grouped according to the categories predicted by a QC algorithm. However, the computation of QC is non-trivial, since the queries are usually short in length, ambiguous and noisy (e.g., wrong spelling). Direct matching between queries and target categories often produces no result. In addition, the target categories can often change, depending on the new Web contents as the Web evolves, and as the intended services change as well.

KDDCUP 2005 (http://www.acm.org/sigkdd/kddcup) highlighted the interests in QC, where 800,000 real Web queries are to be classified into 67 target categories. Each query can belong to more than one target category. For this task, there is no training data provided. As an example of a QC task, given the query "apple", it should be classified into "Computers\Hardware; Living\Food&Cooking".

The winning solution in the KDDCUP 2005 competition, which won on all three evaluation metrics (precision, F1 and creativity), relied on an innovative method to map queries to target categories. By this method, an input query is first mapped to an intermediate category, and then a second mapping is applied to map the query from the intermediate category to the target category. However, we note that this method suffers from two potential problems. First, the classifier for the second mapping function needs to be trained whenever the target category structure changes. Since in real applications, the target categories can change depending on the needs of the service providers, as well as the distribution of the Web contents, this solution is not flexible enough. What would be better is to train the classifiers once and then use them in future QC tasks, even when the target categories are different. Second, the winners used the Open Directory Project (ODP) taxonomy as the intermediate taxonomy. Since the ODP contains more than 590,000 different categories, it is costly to handle all mapping functions. It is better to select a portion of the most relevant parts of the intermediate categories.

In this paper, we introduce a novel QC algorithm that solves the above two problems. In particular, we first build a bridging classifier on an intermediate taxonomy in an offline mode. This classifier is then used in online mode to map users' queries to the target categories via the above intermediate taxonomy. Therefore, we do not have to build the classifier each time the target categories change. In addition, we propose a category-selection method to select the categories in the intermediate taxonomy so that the effectiveness and efficiency of the online classification can be improved.

The KDDCUP 2005 winning solution included two kinds of base classifiers and two ensemble classifiers of them. By comparing our new method with any base classifier in the winner's solution for the KDDCUP 2005 competition, we found that our new method can improve the performance by more than 10.4% and 7.1% in terms of precision and F1 respectively, while our method does not require the extra resource such as WordNet [8]. The proposed method can even achieve a similar performance to the winner's ensemble classifiers that achieved the best performance in the KDDCUP 2005 competition. Furthermore, by combining the our method with the base classifiers in the winner's solution, we can improve the classification results by 9.7% in terms of precision and 3.8% in terms of F1 as compared to the winner's results.

This rest of the paper is organized as follows. We define the query classification problem in Section 14.2. Section 14.3 presents the methods of enriching queries and target categories. In Section 14.4, we briefly introduce the previous methods and put forward a new method. In Section 14.5, we compare the approaches empirically on the tasks of KDDCUP 2005 competition. We list some related works in Section 14.6. Section 14.7 gives the conclusion of the paper and some possible future research issues.

14.2 Problem Definition

The query classification problem is not as well-formed as other classification problems such as text classification. The difficulties include short and ambiguous queries and the lack of training data. In this section, inspired by KDDCUP 2005, we give a stringent definition of the QC problem.

Query Classification:

* *The aim of query classification is to classify a user query Q_i into a ranked list of n categories $C_{i1}, C_{i2}, ..., C_{in}$, among a set of N categories $\{C_1, C_2, ..., C_N\}$. Among the output, C_{i1} is ranked higher than C_{i2}, and C_{i2} is higher than C_{i3}, and so on.*
* *The queries are collected from real search engines submitted by Web users. The meaning and intension of the queries are subjective.*
* *The target categories are a tree with each node representing a category. The semantic meaning of each category is defined by the labels along the path from the root to the corresponding node.*

In addition, the training data must be found online because, in general, labeled training data for query classification are very difficult to obtain.

Figure 14.1 illustrates the target taxonomy of the KDDCUP 2005 competition. Because there are no data provided to define the content and the semantics of a category, as in conventional classification problems, a new solution needs be found. As mentioned above, an added difficulty is that the target taxonomy may change frequently. The queries in this problem are from the MSN search engine (http://search.msn.com). Several examples of the queries are shown in Table 14.1. Since a query usually contains very few words, the sparseness of queries becomes a serious problem as compared to other text classification problems.

1967 shelby mustang
actress hildegarde
a & r management" property management Maryland
netconfig.exe

Table 14.1 Examples of queries.

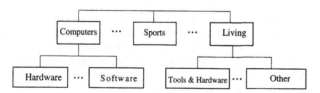

Fig. 14.1 An Example of the Target Taxonomy.

14.3 Query and Category Enrichment

In this section, we discuss the approaches for enriching queries and categories, which are critical for the query classification task.

14.3.1 Enrichment through Search Engines

Since queries and categories usually contain only a few words in the QC problem, we need to expand them to obtain richer representations. One straightforward method is to submit them to search engines to get the related pages (for categories, we can take their labels as the queries and submit them to search engines, such as "Computers\Hardware" in Figure 14.1). The returned Web pages from search engines provide the context of the queries and the target categories, which can help determine the meanings/semantics of the queries and categories.

Given the search results for a query or category, we need to decide what features should be extracted from the pages to construct the representation. Three kinds of features are considered in this paper: the title of a page, the snippet generated by the search engines, and the full plain text of a page. The snippet is in fact a short query-based summary of a Web page in which the query words occur frequently. The full plain text is all the text in a page with the html tags removed. Since the title of a page is usually very short (5.2 words on average for our data set), we combine it with other kinds of features together. These features are studied in our experiments.

Besides the above textual features, we can also obtain the category information of a Web page through the directory information from search engines. For example, Google's "Directory Search" can provide the labels of the returned Web pages. Such labels will be leveraged to classify a query, as stated in Section 14.4.1.

14.3.2 Word Matching Between Categories

The query classification problem can be converted to a traditional text classification problem by finding some training data online for each category in the target taxonomy. Our method of collecting the training data is by finding documents in certain intermediate taxonomies that are found online. To do so, we need to construct mapping functions between the intermediate categories and the target categories. Given a certain category in an intermediate taxonomy, we say that it is directly mapped to a target category if and only if the following condition is satisfied: one or more terms in each node along the path in the target category appear along the path corresponding to the matched intermediate category. For example, the intermediate category "Computers\Hardware \Storage" is directly mapped to the target category "Computers\Hardware" since the words "Computers" and "Hardware" both appear along the path *Computers → Hardware → Storage* as shown in Figure 14.2. We call this matching method *direct matching*.

After constructing the above mapping functions by exact word matching, we may still miss a large number of mappings. To obtain a more complete mapping function, we expand the words in the labels of the target taxonomy through a thesaurus such as the WordNet [8]. For example, the keyword "Hardware" is extended to "Hardware & Devices & Equipments". Then an intermediate category such as "Computers\Devices" can now be mapped to "Computers\Hardware". This matching method is called *extended matching* in this paper.

14.4 Classification Approaches

In this section, we first describe the state-of-the-art query classification methods. Then we describe our new bridging classifier to address the disadvantages of the existing methods.

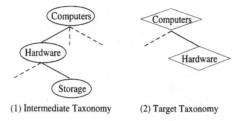

(1) Intermediate Taxonomy   (2) Target Taxonomy

Fig. 14.2 Illustration of the matching between taxonomies.

14.4.1 Classification by Exact Matching

As described in Section 14.3.1, a query can be expanded through search engines which results in a list of related Web pages together with their categories from an intermediate taxonomy. A straightforward approach to QC is to leverage the categories by exact matching. We denote the categories in the intermediate taxonomy and the target taxonomy as C^I and C^T respectively. For each category in C^I, we can detect whether it is mapped to any category in C^T according to the matching approaches given in Section 14.3.2. After that, the most frequent target categories to which the returned intermediate categories have been successfully mapped are regarded as the classification result. That is:

$$c^* = \arg\max_{C_j^T} \left(\sum_{i=1}^{n} I(C^I(i) \text{ is mapped to } C_j^T) \right) \qquad (14.1)$$

In Equation (14.1), $I(\cdot)$ is the indicator function whose value is 1 when its parameter is true and 0 otherwise. $C^I(i)$ is the category in the intermediate taxonomy for the ith page returned by the search engine. n result pages are used for query classification and the parameter n is studied in our experiments.

It is not hard to imagine that the exact matching approach tends to produce classification results with high precision but low recall. It produces high precision because this approach relies on the Web pages which are associated with the manually annotated category information. It produces low recall because many search result pages have no intermediate categories. Moreover, the exact matching approach cannot find all the mappings from the existing intermediate taxonomy to the target taxonomy which also results in low recall.

14.4.2 Classification by SVM

To alleviate the low-recall problem of the exact matching method, some statistical classifiers can be used for QC. In the KDDCUP 2005 winning solution, Support Vector Machine (SVM) was used as a base classifier. Query classification with SVM consists of the following steps: 1) construct the training data for the target categories based on mapping functions between categories, as discussed in Section 14.3.2. If an intermediate category C^I is mapped to a target category C^T, then the Web pages in C^I are mapped into C^T; 2) train SVM classifiers for the target categories; 3) for each Web query to be classified, use search engines to get its enriched features as discussed in Section 14.3.1 and classify the query using the SVM classifiers. The advantage of this QC method is that it can improve the recall of the classification result. For example, assume two intermediate categories, C_1^I and C_2^I, are semantically related with a target category C_1^T. C_1^I can be matched with C_1^T through word matching but C_2^I cannot. For a query to be classified, if a search engine only returns pages of C_2^I, this query cannot be classified into the target category if the exact matching classification method is used. However, if the query is classified by a statistical classifier, it can also be assigned the target category C_1^T, as the classifier is trained using pages of C_1^I, which may also contain terms of C_2^I because the two intermediate categories are similar in topic.

Although statistical classifiers can help increase the recall of the exact matching approach, they still need the exact matching for collecting the training data. What is more, if the target taxonomy changes, we need to collect the training data by exact matching and train statistical classifiers again. In the following sections, we develop a new method to solve the above problems.

14.4.3 Our New Method: Classifiers by Bridges

14.4.3.1 Taxonomy-Bridging Algorithm

We now describe our new QC approach called taxonomy-bridging classifier, or bridging classifier in short, by which we connect the target taxonomy and queries by taking an intermediate taxonomy as a bridge. The idea is illustrated in Figure 14.3, where two vertical lines separate the space into three parts. The square in the left part denotes the queries to be classified; the tree in the right part represents the target taxonomy; the tree in the middle part is an existing intermediate taxonomy. The thickness of the dotted lines reflects the similarly relationship between two nodes. For example, we can see that the relationship between C_i^T and C_j^I is much stronger than that between C_i^T and C_k^I. Given a category C_i^T in the target taxonomy and a query to be classified q_k, we can judge the similarity between them by the distributions of their relationship to the categories in the intermediate taxonomy. By defining the relationship and similarity under the probabilistic framework, the above idea can be explained by Equation (14.2).

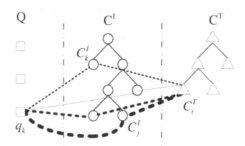

Fig. 14.3 Illustration of the Bridging Classifier.

$$p(C_i^T|q) = \sum_{C_j^I} p(C_i^T, C_j^I|q)$$

$$= \sum_{C_j^I} p(C_i^T|C_j^I, q) p(C_j^I|q)$$

$$\approx \sum_{C_j^I} p(C_i^T|C_j^I) p(C_j^I|q) \qquad (14.2)$$

$$= \sum_{C_j^I} p(C_i^T|C_j^I) \frac{p(q|C_j^I)p(C_j^I)}{p(q)}$$

$$\propto \sum_{C_j^I} p(C_i^T|C_j^I) p(q|C_j^I) p(C_j^I)$$

In Equation (14.2), $p(C_i^T|q)$ denotes the conditional probability of C_i^T given q. Similarly, $p(C_i^T|C_j^I)$ and $p(q|C_j^I)$ denotes the probability of C_i^T and q given C_j^I respectively. $p(C_j^I)$ is the prior probability of C_j^I which can be estimated from the Web pages in C^I. If C_i^T is represented by a set of words $(w_1, w_2, \ldots, w_n)$ where each word w_k appears n_k times, $p(C_i^T|C_j^I)$ can be calculated through Equation (14.3)

$$p(C_i^T|C_j^I) = \prod_{k=1}^n p(w_k|C_j^I)^{n_k} \qquad (14.3)$$

where $p(w_k|C_j^I)$ stands for the probability that the word w_k occurs in class C_j^I, which can be estimated by the principle of maximal likelihood. $p(q|C_j^I)$ can be calculated in the same way as $p(C_i^T|C_j^I)$.

A query q can be classified according to Equation (14.4):

$$c^* = \arg\max_{C_i^T} p(C_i^T|q) \qquad (14.4)$$

To make our bridging classifier easier to understand, we can explain it in another way by rewriting Equation (14.2) as Equation (14.5),

$$p(C_i^T|q) = \sum_{C_j^I} p(C_i^T, C_j^I|q)$$

$$= \sum_{C_j^I} p(C_i^T|C_j^I, q) p(C_j^I|q)$$

$$\approx \sum_{C_j^I} p(C_i^T|C_j^I) p(C_j^I|q) \qquad (14.5)$$

$$= \sum_{C_j^I} \frac{p(C_j^I|C_i^T)p(C_i^T)}{p(C_j^I)} p(C_j^I|q)$$

$$= p(C_i^T) \sum_{C_j^I} \frac{p(C_j^I|C_i^T)p(C_j^I|q)}{p(C_j^I)}$$

Let us consider the numerator on the right side of the Equation (14.5). Given a query q and C_i^T, $p(C_j^I|C_i^T)$ and $p(C_j^I|q)$ are fixed and $\sum_{C_j^I} p(C_j^I|C_i^T) = 1$, $\sum_{C_j^I} p(C_j^I|q) = 1$. $p(C_j^I|C_i^T)$ and $p(C_j^I|q)$ represent the probability that C_i^T and q belong to C_j^I. It is easy to prove that $p(C_i^T|q)$ tends to be larger when q and C_i^T tends to belong to the same category in the intermediate taxonomy. The denominator $p(C_j^I)$ reflects the size of category C_j^I which acts as a weighting factor. It guarantees that the higher the probability that q and C_i^T belong to the smaller sized category (where size refers to the number of nodes underneath the category in the tree) in the intermediate taxonomy, the higher the probability that q belongs to C_i^T. Such an observation agrees with our intuition, since a larger category tends to contain more sub-topics while a smaller category contains fewer sub-topics. Thus we can say with higher confidence that q and C_i^T are related to the same sub-topic when they belong to the same smaller category.

14.4.3.2 Category Selection

The intermediate taxonomy may contain enormous categories and some of them are irrelevant to the query classification task corresponding with the predefined target taxonomy. Therefore, to reduce the computation complexity, we should perform "Category Selection" in a similar sense of "Feature Selection" in text classification [15]. Two approaches are employed in this paper to evaluate the goodness of a category in the intermediate taxonomy. After sorting the categories according to the scores calculated by the following two approaches, category selection can be fulfilled by selecting the top n categories.

Total Probability (TP): this method gives a score to each category in the intermediate taxonomy according to its probability of generating the categories in the target taxonomy, as shown in Equation (6).

$$Score(C_j^I) = \sum_{C_i^T} P(C_i^T | C_j^I) \qquad (14.6)$$

Mutual Information (MI): MI is a criterion commonly used in statistical language modeling of word associations and other related applications [15]. Given a word t and a category c, the mutual information between t and c is defined as:

$$MI(t,c) = \log \frac{P(t \wedge c)}{P(t) \times P(c)} \qquad (14.7)$$

By considering the two-way contingency table for t and c, where A is the number of times t and c co-occur, B is the number of times that t occurs without c, C is number of times c occurs without t and N is the total number of documents, then the mutual information between t and c can be estimated using:

$$MI(t,c) \approx \log \frac{A \times N}{(A+C) \times (A+B)} \qquad (14.8)$$

Since the name of a category in the target taxonomy usually contains more than one term, we define the "mutual information" between a category in the intermediate taxonomy C_j^I and a category in the target taxonomy C_i^T as:

$$MI(C_i^T, C_j^I) = \frac{1}{|C_i^T|} \sum_{t \in C_i^T} MI(t, C_j^I) \qquad (14.9)$$

where $|C_i^T|$ is the number of terms in the name of C_i^T.

To measure the goodness of C_j^I in a global category selection, we combine the category-specific scores of C_j^I by:

$$MI_{avg}(C_j^I) = \sum_{C_j^T} MI(C_i^T, C_j^I) \qquad (14.10)$$

14.4.3.3 Discussions

As we can see, in the bridging classifier, we do not need to train a classifier function between an intermediate taxonomy and the target taxonomy. We only need to build the classifiers on the intermediate taxonomy once and it can be applied to any target taxonomy. The framework can be extended in two directions. One is to include some training data for each target category. With the training data, we do not have to treat the labels of the target categories as queries and retrieve related Web pages through search engines to represent the categories. We can extract features from the training data directly. The second extension is to use other sophisticated models such as the n-gram model [9] or SVM [10] for computing $p(C_i^T | C_j^I)$ and $p(q | C_j^I)$.

14.5 Experiments

In this section, we first introduce the data set and the evaluation metrics. Then we present the experiment results and give some discussions.

14.5.1 Data Set and Evaluation Metrics

14.5.1.1 Data sets

In this paper, we use the data sets from the KDDCUP 2005 competition which is available on the Web[1] . One of the data sets contains 111 sample queries together with the category information. These samples are used to exemplify the format of the queries by the organizer. However, since the category information of these queries is truthful, they can serve as the validation data. Another data set contains 800 queries with category information labeled by three human labelers. In fact, the organizers provided 800,000 queries in total which are selected from the MSN search logs for testing the submitted solutions. Since manually labeling all the 800,000 queries is too expensive and time consuming, the organizers randomly selected 800 queries for evaluation.

We denote the three human query-labelers (and sometimes the dataset labeled by them if no confusion is caused) as L1, L2 and L3, respectively. Each query has at most five labels in ranked order. Table 14.2 shows the average precision and F1 score values of each labeler when evaluated against the other two labelers. The average values among the three labelers are around 0.50 which indicates that the query classification problem is not an easy task even for human labelers. In this paper, all the experiments use only the 800 queries, except in the ensemble classifiers, where we use the 111 sample queries to tune the weight of each single classifier.

	L1	L2	L3	Average
F1	0.538	0.477	0.512	0.509
Pre	0.501	0.613	0.463	0.526

Table 14.2 The Average Scores of Each Labeler When Evaluated Against the Other Two Labelers

The existing intermediate taxonomy used in the paper is from Open Directory Project (ODP, http://dmoz.org/). We crawled 1,546,441 Web pages from ODP which spanned over 172,565 categories. The categories have a hierarchical structure as shown in Figure 2(1). We can consider the hierarchy at different levels. Table 14.3 shows the number of categories on different levels. The first row counts all the categories while the second row counts only the categories containing more than 10 Web pages. Table 14.4 summarizes the statistics of Web page numbers in the categories with more than 10 documents on different levels. As we can see, when we move down to the lower levels along the hierarchy, more categories appear while each category contains fewer Web pages. In order to remove noise, we consider the categories with more than 10 pages in this paper.

	Top 2	Top 3	Top 4	Top 5	Top All
#doc > 0	435	5,300	24,315	56,228	172,565
#doc > 10	399	4,011	13,541	23,989	39,250

Table 14.3 Number of Categories on Different Levels

---

[1] http://www.acm.org/sigs/sigkdd/kdd2005/kddcup.html

	Top 2	Top 3	Top 4	Top 5	Top All
Largest	211,192	153,382	84,455	25,053	920
Smallest	11	11	11	11	11
Mean	4,044.0	400.8	115.6	61.6	29.1

Table 14.4 Statistics of the Numbers of Documents in the Categories on Different Levels

14.5.1.2 Evaluation Measurements

In KDDCUP 2005, precision, performance and creativity are the three measures to evaluate the submitted solutions. "creativity" refers to the novelty of the solutions judged by experts. The other two measures are defined according to the standard measures to evaluate the performance of classification, that is, precision, recall and F1-measure [12]. Precision (P) is the proportion of actual positive class members returned by the system among all predicted positive class members returned by the system. Recall (R) is the proportion of predicted positive members among all actual positive class members in the data. F1 is the harmonic mean of precision and recall as shown below:

$$F1 = 2 \times P \times R/(P+R) \tag{14.11}$$

"performance" adopted by KDDCUP 2005 is in fact F1. Therefore, we denote it by F1 instead of "performance" for simplicity.

As 3 labelers were asked to label the queries, the results reported are averaged over the values evaluated on each of them.

14.5.2 Results and Analysis

14.5.2.1 Performance of Exact matching and SVM

In this section, we study the performance of the two methods which tightly depend on word matching: exact matching and SVM, as well as the effect of query and category expansion. Table 14.5 shows the results of the category expansion through intermediate taxonomy by word matching, that is the results of collecting training data for the target taxonomy. Each element in the table represents the number of documents collected for the target categories. The first row contains the results by direct matching while the second row contains the results after expanding the category names through extended matching. We can see that after extending the names of the target categories, the number of documents collected for the target categories increases. We expect that the expansion with the help of WordNet should provide more documents to reflect the semantics of the target categories which is verified by Table 14.6.

	Min	Max	Median	Mean
Direct Matching	4	126,397	2,389	14,646
Extended Matching	22	227,690	6,815	21,295

Table 14.5 Number of Pages Collected for Training under Different Category Expansion Methods

Table 14.6 presents the result comparisons of the exact matching method and SVM. We enrich the query by retrieving the relevant pages through Google (http://www.google.com). The top n

returned pages are used to represent the query where n varies from 20 to 80, with the step size of 20. Two approaches are used to extract features from the returned pages. One is to extract the snippet of the returned pages and the other is to extract all the text in the Web pages except the HTML tags. The Web pages' titles will be added to both of these two kinds of features. The column "0" means that we use only the terms in the query without enrichment.

(1)Measured by F1

n		0	20	40	60	80
Exact-D		Null	**0.251**	0.249	0.247	0.246
Exact-E		Null	0.385	**0.396**	0.386	0.384
SVM-D	snippet	0.205	0.288	**0.292**	0.291	0.289
	full text		0.254	**0.276**	0.267	0.273
SVM-E	snippet	0.256	0.378	**0.383**	0.379	0.379
	full text		0.316	**0.340**	0.327	0.336

(2) Measured by Precision

n		0	20	40	60	80
Exact-D		Null	**0.300**	0.279	0.272	0.268
Exact-E		Null	0.403	**0.405**	0.389	0.383
SVM-D	snippet	0.178	**0.248**	**0.248**	0.244	0.246
	full text		0.227	0.234	**0.242**	0.240
SVM-E	snippet	0.212	**0.335**	0.321	0.312	0.311
	full text		0.288	**0.309**	0.305	0.296

Table 14.6 Performance of Exact Matching and SVM

In our experiments, we expand the target categories through the ODP taxonomy; that is, we collect the training data for the target categories from ODP. When constructing the mapping relationship as shown in Section 14.3.2, if we use direct matching, we denote SVM and the exact matching method with "SVM-D" and "Extact-D" respectively. Otherwise,if we use the extended matching method, we denote SVM and the exact matching method with "SVM-E" and "Extact-E" respectively. The exact matching method needs the category list of the retrieved Web pages for each query. The category information is obtained through Google's "Directory Search" service (http://www.google.com/dirhp).

From Table 14.6 we can see that "Exact-E" is much better than "Exact-D", and "SVM-E" is much better than "SVM-D". This indicates that the extended matching with the help of WordNet can achieve a more proper representation of the target category. We can also observe that "Exact-E" performs better than "SVM-E". Another observation is that the "snippet" representation outperforms "full text" consistently. The reason is that the "snippet" provides a more concise context of the query than the "full text" which tends to introduce noise. We can also see that most of the classifiers achieve the highest performance when the queries are represented by the top 40 search result pages. Therefore, in the later experiments, we use snippets of the top 40 pages to represent queries.

14.5.2.2 Performance of the Bridging Classifier

As we can see in the above experiments, the thesaurus WordNet plays an important role in both the exact matching method and SVM since it can help expand the words in the labels of the target categories, which can further improve the mapping functions. However, the effect of a thesaurus may be limited due to the following reasons: 1) there may be no thesaurus in some fields; 2) it is hard to determine the precise expansion of the words even with a high-quality thesaurus, especially with the rapidly changing usage of words on the Web. Therefore, we put forward the bridging classifier which only relies on the intermediate taxonomies.

In order to expand a target category, we can treat its name as a query and submit it to search engines. We use the snippet of the top n returned pages to represent a category since we learned from the query expansion that snippet performs better than "full text". The parameter n varies from 20 to 100. Table 14.7 shows the results when "top all" categories in the ODP taxonomy are used for bridging the queries and the target taxonomy. The effect of different levels of the intermediate taxonomy will be studied later. From Table 14.7, we can see that the bridging classifier achieves the best performance when n equals 60. The best F1 and precision achieved by the bridging classifier is higher than those achieved either by the exact matching method or SVM. The relative improvement is more than 10.4% and 7.1% in terms of precision and F1 respectively. The main reason for the improvement is that the bridging classifier can make thorough use of the finer grained intermediate taxonomy in a probabilistic way. While the previous methods including the exact matching method and SVM exploit the intermediate taxonomy in a hard way when constructing the mapping function as shown in Section 14.3.2.

n	20	40	60	80	100
F1	0.414	0.420	**0.424**	0.421	0.416
Precision	0.437	0.443	**0.447**	0.444	0.439

Table 14.7 Performances of the Bridging Classifier with Different Representations of Target Categories

	Top 2	Top 3	Top 4	Top 5	Top All
F1	0.267	0.285	0.312	0.352	**0.424**
Precision	0.270	0.291	0.339	0.368	**0.447**

Table 14.8 Performances of the Bridging Classifier with Different Granularity

Table 14.8 shows the performance of the bridging classifier when we change the granularity of the categories in the intermediate taxonomy. To change the granularity of the categories, we use the categories on the top L level by varying L. It is clear that the categories have larger granularity when L is smaller. From Table 14.8, we can see that the performance of the bridging classifier improves steadily by reducing the granularity of categories. The reason is that categories with large granularity may be a mixture of several target categories which prohibit distinguishing the target categories.

However, reducing the granularity of categories in the intermediate taxonomy will certainly increase the number of the intermediate categories which will thus increase the computation cost. One way to solve this problem is to do category selection. Figure 14.4 shows the performance of the bridging classifier when we select the categories from all the ODP taxonomy through the two category selection approaches proposed in Section 14.4.3.2. We can see that when the category number is around 18,000, the performance of the bridging classifier is comparable to, if not better than, the previous approaches, including the exact matching method and SVM. MI works better than TP in that MI can not only measure the relevance between the categories in the target taxonomy and those in the intermediate taxonomy, but also favors the categories which are more powerful to distinguish the categories in the target taxonomy. However, TP only cares about the merit of relevance.

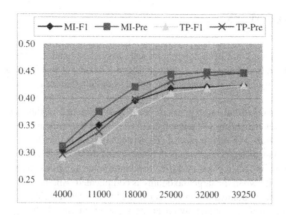

Fig. 14.4 Effect of category selection.

14.5.2.3 Ensemble of Classifiers

The winner of the KDDCUP 2005 competition found that the best result was achieved by combining the exact matching method and SVM. In the winning solution, besides the exact matching method on Google's directory search, two other exact matching methods are developed using LookSmart (http://www.looksmart.com) and a search engine based on Lemur (http://www.lemurproject.org) and their crawled Web pages from ODP [11]. Two classifier-combination strategies are used, with one aiming at higher precision (denoted by EV, where 111 samples are used as the validation data to tune the weight of each base classifier) and the other aiming at higher F1 (denoted by EN in which the validation data set is ignored). EV assigns a weight to a classifier proportional to the classifier's precision while EN gives equal weights to all classifiers. We follow the same strategy to combine our new method with the winner's methods, which is denoted as *"Exact-E"+"SVM-E"+Bridging* as shown in Table 14.9. The numbers in the parentheses are the relative improvement. Note that the bridging classifier alone achieves similar F1 measurement as the KDDCU 2005 winning solution ("Exact-E"+"SVM-E" with the EV combination strategy) but improves the precision by 5.4%. From Table 14.9 we can also find that the combination of the bridging classifier and the KDDCUP 2005 winning solution can improve the performance by 9.7% and 3.8% in terms of precision and F1, respectively, when compared with the winning solution. This indicates that the bridging classifier works in a different way as the exact matching method and SVM, and they are complimentary to each other.

		"Exact-E" + "SVM-E"	"Exact-E" + "SVM-E" +Bridging
EV	F1	0.426	0.429(+0.007)
	Precision	0.424	0.465(+0.097)
EN	F1	0.444	0.461(+0.038)
	Precision	0.414	0.430(+0.039)

Table 14.9 Performances of Ensemble Classifiers

14.6 Related Work

Though not much work has been done on topical query classification, some work has been conducted on other kinds of query classification problems. Gravano et al. classified the Web queries by geographical locality [3] while Kang et al. proposed to classify queries according to their functional types [4].

Beitzel et al. studied the same problem in [2] as we pursued in this paper, with the goal to classify the queries according to their topic(s). They used two primary data sets containing the queries from the AOL web search service. These queries were manually classified into a set of 18 categories. The main difference between our problem and that of [2] is that we did not have training data as given input. In fact, it is a very difficult and time consuming task to provide enough training examples, especially when the target taxonomy is complicated. Another potential problem related to the training data, as pointed out in [2], is caused by the ongoing changes in the query stream, which makes it hard to systematically cover the space of queries. In this paper, we just rely on the structure and category names of the target taxonomy without training data, which is consistent with the task of KDDCUP 2005.

KDDCUP 2005 provides a test bed for the Web query classification problem. There are a total of 37 solutions from 32 teams attending the competition. As summarized by the organizers [6], most solutions expanded the queries through search engines or WordNet and expanded the category by mapping between some pre-defined/existing taxonomy to the target taxonomy. Some solutions require human intervention in the mapping process [5, 13].

Besides classifying the queries into target taxonomy, we can also cluster the queries to discover some hidden taxonomies through unsupervised methods. Both Beeferman [1] and Wen [14] used search engines' clickthrough data to cluster the queries. The former makes no use of the actual content of the queries and URLs, but only how they co-occur within the clickthrough data, while the latter exploits the usage of the content. Although the work in [1] and [14] proved the effectiveness of the clickthrough data for query clustering, we did not utilize them in our solution due to the following two reasons: 1) the clickthorugh data can be quite noisy and is search engine dependent; 2) it is difficult to obtain the clickthrough data due to privacy and legal issues.

14.7 Conclusion and Future Work

This paper presented a novel solution for classifying Web queries into a set of target categories, where the queries are very short and there are no training data. In our solution, an intermediate taxonomy is used to train classifiers bridging the queries and target categories so that there is no need to collect the training data. Experiments on the KDDCUP 2005 data set show that the bridging classifier approach is promising. By combining the bridging classifier with the winning solution of KDDCUP 2005, we made a further improvement by 9.7% and 3.8% in terms of precision and F1 respectively compared with the best results of KDDCUP 2005. In the future, we plan to extend the bridging classifier idea to other types of query processing tasks, including query clustering. We will also conduct research on how to leverage a group of intermediate taxonomies for query classification.

Acknowlegements

Dou Shen and Qiang Yang are supported by a grant from NEC (NECLC05/06.EG01). We thank the anonymous reviewers for their useful comments.

References

1. D. Beeferman and A. Berger. Agglomerative clustering of a search engine query log. In *KDD '00: Proceedings of the sixth ACM SIGKDD international conference on Knowledge discovery and data mining*, pages 407–416, 2000.
2. S. M. Beitzel, E. C. Jensen, O. Frieder, D. Grossman, D. D. Lewis, A. Chowdhury, and A. Kolcz. Automatic web query classification using labeled and unlabeled training data. In *SIGIR '05: Proceedings of the 28th annual international ACM SIGIR conference on Research and development in information retrieval*, pages 581–582, 2005.
3. L. Gravano, V. Hatzivassiloglou, and R. Lichtenstein. Categorizing web queries according to geographical locality. In *CIKM '03: Proceedings of the twelfth international conference on Information and knowledge management*, pages 325–333, 2003.
4. I.-H. Kang and G. Kim. Query type classification for web document retrieval. In *SIGIR '03: Proceedings of the 26th annual international ACM SIGIR conference on Research and development in informaion retrieval*, pages 64–71, 2003.
5. Z. T. Kardkovács, D. Tikk, and Z. Bánsághi. The ferrety algorithm for the kdd cup 2005 problem. *SIGKDD Explor. Newsl.*, 7(2):111–116, 2005.
6. Y. Li, Z. Zheng, and H. K. Dai. Kdd cup-2005 report: facing a great challenge. *SIGKDD Explor. Newsl.*, 7(2):91–99, 2005.
7. A. McCallum and K. Nigam. A comparison of event models for naive bayes text classication. In *AAAI-98 Workshop on Learning for Text Categorization*, 1998.
8. G. Miller, R. Beckwith, C. Fellbaum, D. Gross, and K. Miller. Introduction to wordnet: an on-line lexical database. *International Journal of Lexicography*, 3(4):23–244, 1990.
9. F. Peng, D. Schuurmans, and S. Wang. Augmenting naive bayes classifiers with statistical language models. *Inf. Retr.*, 7(3-4):317–345, 2004.
10. J. Platt. Probabilistic outputs for support vector machines and comparisons to regularized likelihood methods. In A. Smola, P. Bartlett, B. Scholkopf, and D. Schuurmans, editors, *Advances in Large Margin Classifiers*. MIT Press, 1999.
11. D. Shen, R. Pan, J.-T. Sun, J. J. Pan, K. Wu, J. Yin, and Q. Yang. Q2c@ust: our winning solution to query classification in kddcup 2005. *SIGKDD Explor. Newsl.*, 7(2):100–110, 2005.
12. R. C. van. *Information Retrieval*. Butterworths, London, second edition edition, 1979.
13. D. Vogel, S. Bickel, P. Haider, R. Schimpfky, P. Siemen, S. Bridges, and T. Scheffer. Classifying search engine queries using the web as background knowledge. *SIGKDD Explor. Newsl.*, 7(2):117–122, 2005.
14. J.-R. Wen, J.-Y. Nie, and H.-J. Zhang. Query clustering using content words and user feedback. In *SIGIR '01: Proceedings of the 24th annual international ACM SIGIR conference on Research and development in information retrieval*, pages 442–443, 2001.
15. Y. Yang and J. O. Pedersen. A comparative study on feature selection in text categorization. In *ICML '97: Proceedings of the Fourteenth International Conference on Machine Learning*, pages 412–420, 1997.

Chapter 15
Spectral Domain-Transfer Learning

Xiao Ling, Wenyuan Dai, Gui-Rong Xue, Qiang Yang and Yong Yu*

Abstract Traditional spectral classification has been proved to be effective in dealing with both labeled and unlabeled data when these data are from the same domain. In many real world applications, however, we wish to make use of the labeled data from one domain (called *in-domain*) to classify the unlabeled data in a different domain (*out-of-domain*). This problem often happens when obtaining labeled data in one domain is difficult while there are plenty of labeled data from a related but different domain. In general, this is a *transfer learning* problem where we wish to classify the unlabeled data through the labeled data even though these data are not from the same domain. In this paper, we formulate this cross-domain learning problem under a novel spectral classification framework, where the objective function is introduced to seek consistency between the in-domain supervision and the out-of-domain intrinsic structure. Through optimization of the cost function, the label information from the in-domain data is effectively transferred to help classify the unlabeled data from the out-of-domain. We conduct extensive experiments to evaluate our method and show that our algorithm achieves significant improvements on classification performance over many state-of-the-art algorithms.

Key words: Spectral Classification, Cross-domain Learning

15.1 Introduction

Spectral learning methods such as normalized cut [28] are increasingly being applied to many learning tasks such as document clustering and image segmentation. Exploiting the information in the eigenvectors of a data similarity matrix to find the intrinsic structure, spectral methods have been extended from unsupervised learning to supervised/semi-supervised learning [22, 19], where a unified framework is used for spectral classification (SC). The SC algorithm has been shown to be effective when the data consist of both labeled and unlabeled data. Compared with many other semi-supervised classifiers, the key advantage of SC is its global optimization of objective function.

However, a limitation of these traditional SC methods is that they only focus on the scenario that the labeled and unlabeled data are drawn from the same domain, i.e., with the same bias or

Xiao Ling, Wenyuan Dai, Gui-Rong Xue and Yong Yu
Shanghai Jiao Tong University, 800 Dongchuan Road, Shanghai 200240, China
e-mail: {shawnling, dwyak, grxue, yyu}@apex.sjtu.edu.cn

Qiang Yang
Hong Kong University of Science and Technology, Hong Kong, China
e-mail: qyang@cse.ust.hk

* Source: Conference on Knowledge Discovery in Data, Proceeding of the Fourteenth ACM SIGKDD International Conference on Knowledge Discovery and Data Mining, Las Vegas, Nevada, USA, August 24-27, 2008, Pages 488-496. Copyright©2008 Association for Computing Machinery, Inc. Reprinted by permission. DOI Bookmark: http://doi.acm.org/10.1145/1401890.1401951

feature space. Unfortunately, many scenarios in the real world do not follow this requirement. In contrast to these methods, in this paper, we aim at extending traditional spectral methods to tackle the classification problem when labeled and unlabeled data come from different domains. There are several reasons for why it is important to consider this *cross-domain classification* problem, which is an instance of *transfer learning* [27, 30, 7]. First, the labeled information is often scarce in a target domain, while a lot of available labeled data may exist from a different but related domain. In this case, it would be desired to make maximal use of the labeled information, though their domains are different. For example, suppose that our task is to categorize some text articles, where the labeled data are Web pages and the unlabeled data are Blog entries. This task is important in practice, since there are much fewer labeled Blog articles than Web pages. These two kinds of articles may share many common terms, but the statistical observations of words may be quite different, as blog articles tend to use informal words. Second, the data distribution in many domains changes with time. Thus, classifiers trained during one time period may not be applicable to another time period again. Take spam email filtering for an example. The topics of spam/ham emails often evolve with time. Therefore the labeled data may fall into one set of topics whereas the unlabeled data other topics. Because traditional SC algorithms often fail to generalize across different domains, we must design new ways to deal with the cross-domain classification problem.

This paper focuses on transferring spectral classification models across different domains. Formally speaking, the training data are from a domain $\mathscr{D}_{in}$ and the test data are from another domain $\mathscr{D}_{out}$. $\mathscr{D}_{in}$ is called *in-domain* and $\mathscr{D}_{out}$ *out-of-domain* in order to highlight the crossing of the domains where the label set is the same. In addition, it is assumed that in-domain $\mathscr{D}_{in}$ and out-of-domain $\mathscr{D}_{out}$ are related to make the cross-domain learning feasible. Our objective is to classify the test data from out-of-domain $\mathscr{D}_{out}$ as accurately as possible using the training data from in-domain $\mathscr{D}_{in}$.

Although several cross-domain classification algorithms have been proposed, e.g., [10, 14], they are all based on local optimization. When the labeled and unlabeled data are not sufficiently large, their optimization function may have a lot of local minima and bring much difficulty for classification. In this paper, a cross-domain spectral classification method is proposed, where we design a novel cost function from normalized cut, so that the in-domain supervision is regularized by out-of-domain structural constraints. By *globally* optimizing this cost function, two objectives are simultaneously being followed. On one hand, we seek an optimal partition of the data that respect the label information, where the labels are considered in the form of must-link constraints [31]; that is, the corresponding data points with respect to each constraint must be with the same label. On the other hand, the test data are split as separately as possible in terms of the cut size within the test set, which will facilitate the classification process. To sum up, the supervisory knowledge is used to ensure the correctness when searching for the optimal cut of all data points. At the same time, the data points in the test set are also separated with small cut sizes. To achieve this aim, a regularization form is introduced to combine both considerations, resulting in an effective transferring of the labeled knowledge towards out-of-domain $\mathscr{D}_{out}$.

We set out to test our proposed SC algorithm for cross-domain learning empirically, where our algorithm is referred as the Cross-Domain Spectral Classifier (abbreviated by CDSC). In our experiments, we set up eleven cross-domain problems to evaluate our method. Compared against several state-of-the-art algorithms, our method achieves great improvements on the competent methods.

The rest of this paper is organized as follows. Spectral methods are reviewed in Section 15.2. Section 15.3 dives into details of our method. In Section 15.4, our method is evaluated compared with other classifiers. Following related work discussed in Section 15.5, Section 15.6 concludes this paper with some future work discussion.

15.2 Preliminaries on Spectral Methods

Spectral clustering is aimed at minimizing the inter-cluster similarity and maximizing the intra-cluster connection. Several criteria were proposed to quantify the objective function, such as Ratio Cut [8], Normalized Cut (NCut) [28], Min-Max Cut (MCut) [15]. Using graph theory terminology, the data are modeled as vertices and the edges are valued using the similarity of the endpoints. We denote V as the universe of all examples and $V = A \cup B$ where $\{A, B\}$ is a partition of V. The goal is to find a partition that optimizes the cost function as follows:

$$F_{\text{RatioCut}} = \frac{\text{cut}(A, B)}{|A|} + \frac{\text{cut}(A, B)}{|B|},$$

$$F_{\text{NCut}} = \frac{\text{cut}(A, B)}{\text{assoc}(A, V)} + \frac{\text{cut}(A, B)}{\text{assoc}(B, V)},$$

$$F_{\text{MCut}} = \frac{\text{cut}(A, B)}{\text{assoc}(A)} + \frac{\text{cut}(A, B)}{\text{assoc}(B)}.$$

Here, $\text{assoc}(A, V) = \sum_{i \in A, j \in V} w_{ij}$, $\text{assoc}(A) = \text{assoc}(A, A)$, $\text{cut}(A, B) = \sum_{i \in A, j \in B, A \cap B = \emptyset} w_{ij}$, where w_{ij} represents the similarity between data points i and j. Take normalized cut as an example. The numerator $\text{cut}(A, B)$ measures how loosely the set A and B are connected, while the denominator $\text{assoc}(A, V)$ measures how compact the entire data set is. [28] presents its equivalent objective in matrix representation as

$$F_{\text{NCut}} = \frac{y^T(D - W)y}{y^T D y},$$

where W is the similarity matrix, $D = diag(We)$ (e is a vector with all coordinates 1) and y is the indicator vector of the partition. Since solving the discrete-valued problem is NP-hard, y is relaxed to be continuous. Minimization of this cost function can be done via *Rayleigh quotient* [16]. Given a Laplacian ($L = D - W$) of a graph, the second smallest eigenvector y_1 meets the optimization constraint [9].

15.3 Cross-Domain Spectral Classification

15.3.1 Problem Definition

For conciseness and clarity, in this paper we mainly focus on binary classification on textual data across different domains. Extensions can be easily done for more classes and other domains. Two document sets S_{in} and S_{out} are collected from domains $\mathcal{D}_{in}$ and $\mathcal{D}_{out}$, respectively. We also denote $S = S_{in} \cup S_{out}$. In the binary classification setting, the label set is $\{+1, -1\}$, meaning that $c(\mathbf{d}_i)$ equals $+1$ (positive) or -1 (negative) where $c(\mathbf{d}_i)$ is $\mathbf{d}_i$'s true class label. The objective is to find the hypothesis h which satisfies $h(\mathbf{d}_i) = c(\mathbf{d}_i)$ for as many $\mathbf{d}_i \in S_{out}$ as possible.

15.3.2 Objective Function

In our approach, the main idea is to regularize two objectives, namely, minimizing the cut size on all the data with the least inconsistency of the in-domain data, and at the same time maximizing the separation of the out-of-domain data. Intuitively, the regularization is regarded as the balance between the in-domain supervision and the out-of-domain structure.

15.3.2.1 Supervision from In-domain

Let $n = |S|$ be the size of the whole sample. A similarity matrix $W_{n \times n}$ is calculated according to a certain similarity measure. Then, the supervisory information is incorporated in the form of must-link constraints by building a constraint matrix U, described in more details in the next subsection. In order to measure the quality of a partition, the cost function for all the data is defined as

$$F_1 = \frac{x^T(D-W)x}{x^T Dx} + \beta ||U^T x||^2, \tag{15.1}$$

where $D = diag(We)$ is defined as previously mentioned and x is the indicator vector of the partition. In Equation (15.1), the normalized cut is adopted for the first term and a penalty term $\beta ||U^T x||^2$ is used to guarantee a good partition on the training data. The first term represents the association between two classes. The second term $\beta ||U^T x||^2$ will constrain the partition of training data since any violation of constraints results in penalty regarding F_1 in Equation (15.1). The parameter β controls the enforcement of constraints. This cost function is similar to that proposed in [19].

15.3.2.2 Structure of Out-of-domain Data

In Equation (15.1), F_1 mainly focuses on the labeled data. However, we wish to classify the out-of-domain test data correctly. Thus, it is important to find the optimal partition for the test data as well. The cost function for the test data alone is defined as

$$F_2 = \frac{x^T(D_s - W_s)x}{x^T D_s x}, \tag{15.2}$$

where $D_s = diag(W_s e)$, and W_s is the similarity matrix for test data only. Note that the dimension of W_s is n, similarity entries only within test data are kept, i.e. if node i and j are both in the test data then $W_{s(ij)} = W_{(ij)}$; other entries are set to zero.

15.3.2.3 Integrating In-domain and Out-of-domain via Regularization

Now a regularization parameter is introduced, incorporating Equation (15.1) and Equation (15.2) to get the unified cost function for cross-domain classification:

$$F_{CDSC} = F_1 + \lambda F_2 \tag{15.3}$$
$$= \frac{x^T(D-W)x}{x^T Dx} + \beta ||U^T x||^2 + \lambda \frac{x^T(D_s - W_s)x}{x^T D_s x},$$

where λ is a tradeoff parameter for balancing the supervisory information (Equation (15.1)) and the cut size of the test data (Equation (15.2)). The first term F_1 ensures a good classification model should maximize the correctness of labeled data. In the cross-domain setting, we cannot completely rely on the in-domain data. The second term F_2 can be understood as the cross-domain fitting constraint, which means a good classification model should also keep the test data with adequately good separation. The trade-off between these competing conditions is captured by the parameter

λ, which interestingly, allows the classification model to be balanced between in-domain $\mathscr{D}_{in}$ and out-of-domain $\mathscr{D}_{out}$. In Equation (15.3), when $\lambda = 0$, the overall cost function degenerates into a spectral cost function over all the data in a semi-supervised manner; when λ is large enough, the overall objective is biased towards optimizing only the spectral cost function for the test data without any supervisory knowledge.

15.3.3 Incorporating Constraints

In Equation (15.3), a penalty for violations [31] of the supervisory constraints is introduced. In the binary classification setting, assume there are n_1 positive data and n_2 negative data in the training set. The constraint matrix U is constructed as follows:

$$U = [\mathbf{u}_1, \mathbf{u}_2, \ldots, \mathbf{u}_m],\tag{15.4}$$

where each $\mathbf{u}_i$ is an n-dimensional vector (same row index as W) with two non-zero entries. Each column $\mathbf{u}_k$ has an entry of $+1$ in the ith row, -1 in the jth row and the rest are all zero, which represents a pairwise constraint (data i and data j must be with the same label). Therefore U has $m = n_1 \times (n_1 - 1)/2 + n_2 \times (n_2 - 1)/2$ columns (constraints).

Algorithm 1 FormConstraintMatrix

Input : the size of positive data n_1, the size of negative data n_2 and $n = n_1 + n_2$; here, without loss of generality, we assume the first n_1 examples are positive, and the next n_2 examples are negative.
Output : Constraint Matrix U
Let U be a $n \times \frac{n_1(n_1-1)+n_2(n_2-1)}{2}$ matrix.
Let $colNum = 1$.
Construct the matrix column by column.
for $i \leftarrow 1$ to n_1 **do**
    for $j \leftarrow i+1$ to n_1 **do**
        $U(i, colNum) = 1$
        $U(j, colNum) = -1$
        $colNum = colNum + 1$
    end for
end for
for $i \leftarrow n_1 + 1$ to $n_1 + n_2$ **do**
    for $j \leftarrow i+1$ to $n_1 + n_2$ **do**
        $U(i, colNum) = 1$
        $U(j, colNum) = -1$
        $colNum = colNum + 1$
    end for
end for
return U

The detailed construction of the constraint matrix U is presented in Algorithm 1. It is easily seen with the indicator vector x that

$$U^T x = 0,\tag{15.5}$$

when x satisfies all the constraints. Adding this constraint component into the Normalized Cut criterion [28], the cost function becomes Equation (15.1).

One problem of the constraint matrix U is that the matrix U (with m rows) is greatly over-sized, which makes it hard to compute $U' = UU^T$ in Equation (15.3) ($||U^Tx||^2 = x^TUU^Tx$). To alleviate this oversize problem, U' can be directly built by considering the pairwise property of the constraints. Notice that U'_{ij} is the inner product of ith row and jth row of U. Then U'_{ij} has four cases:

$$U'_{ij} = \begin{cases} n_1 - 1, & i = j \text{ and they are both in positive class;} \\ n_2 - 1, & i = j \text{ and they are both in negative class;} \\ -1, & i \neq j \text{ and } i, j \text{ are in the same class;} \\ 0, & \text{otherwise.} \end{cases}$$

where n_1 is the size of positive data and n_2 is the size of negative data.

15.3.4 Optimization

In this section, the optimization of the overall function (Equation (15.3)) is addressed.

Since Equation (15.3) is difficult to optimize, we have to seek an approximation. In this work, we use $\frac{x^T(D_s - W_s)x}{x^T Dx}$ instead of $\frac{x^T(D_s - W_s)x}{x^T D_s x}$ in F_{CDSC}. Usually, $\frac{x^T(D_s - W_s)x}{x^T Dx}$ might mislead the normalized cut on S_{out}. However, in F_{CDSC}, when F_1 is sufficiently optimized, the partition of in-domain training data will be more or less balanced due to the constraint $\beta||U^Tx||^2$, and thus the balancing functionality of the denominator $x^T Dx$ is reduced on only out-of-domain test data (refer to $x^T D_s x$). Then, we have

$$\begin{aligned} F_{CDSC} &\approx \frac{x^T(D - W)x}{x^T Dx} + \beta||U^Tx||^2 + \lambda \frac{x^T(D_s - W_s)x}{x^T Dx} \\ &= \frac{x^T[(D - W) + \lambda(D_s - W_s)]x}{x^T Dx} + \beta||U^Tx||^2. \end{aligned} \qquad (15.6)$$

The similarity matrix is thus modified by amplifying the similarity inside the test data submatrix. In the interpretation through random walk [24], this modification can be seen as increasing the transition probability inside the test data.

Replacing $y^T = x^T D^{1/2}/||x^T D^{1/2}||$,

$$\frac{x^T(D - W)x}{x^T Dx} = y^T D^{-1/2}(D - W)D^{-1/2}y. \qquad (15.7)$$

Similarly,

$$\frac{x^T(D_s - W_s)x}{x^T Dx} = y^T D^{-1/2}(D_s - W_s)D^{-1/2}y. \qquad (15.8)$$

With Equation (15.5),

$$U^T D^{-1/2}y = 0. \qquad (15.9)$$

Combining Equations (15.7), (15.8) and (15.9), we obtain

F_{CDSC}

$$= \frac{x^T[(D-W)+\lambda(D_s-W_s)]x}{x^T Dx} + \beta||U^T x||^2$$

$$= y^T D^{-1/2}[(D-W+\lambda(D_s-W_s)]D^{-1/2}y$$

$$+ \beta||U^T D^{-1/2}y||^2$$

$$= y^T D^{-1/2}[(D-W)+\beta UU^T + \lambda(D_s-W_s)]D^{-1/2}y$$

$$= \frac{x^T[(D-W)+\beta UU^T + \lambda(D_s-W_s)]x}{x^T Dx}$$

$$= \frac{x^T Tx}{x^T Dx}, \tag{15.10}$$

where $T = (D-W)+\beta UU^T + \lambda(D_s-W_s)$. Then, F_{CDSC} can be minimized by solving an eigensystem:

$$Tx = dDx, \tag{15.11}$$

where d is the eigenvalue. Moreover, Equation (15.11) can also be rewritten into

$$D^{-1/2}TD^{-1/2}y = dy. \tag{15.12}$$

Similar to other spectral methods, y is relaxed to be a real-valued vector. To this end, our problem has been transformed into the minimization of $\frac{x^T(D^{-1/2}TD^{-1/2})x}{x^T x}$, which is called *Rayleigh Quotient*. In [16], we have

Lemma 15.1 (Rayleigh Quotient). *Let A be a real symmetric matrix. Under the constraint that x is orthogonal to the $j-1$ smallest eigenvectors $x_1,\ldots,x_{j-1}$, the quotient $\frac{x^T Ax}{x^T x}$ is minimized by the next smallest eigenvector x_j and its minimum value is the corresponding eigenvalue d_j.*

Furthermore, we can prove

Lemma 15.2. $T' = D^{-1/2}TD^{-1/2}$ *is symmetric and its eigenvectors are orthogonal.*

Proof. Since $D-W, D_s-W_s$ and UU^T are all symmetric, $T = (D-W)+\beta UU^T + \lambda(D_s-W_s)$ is therefore symmetric. With the diagonal matrix $D^{-1/2}$, T' is also symmetric.

Specifically, let $\mathbf{v}, \mathbf{w}$ be arbitrarily two different eigenvectors of T and d_v, d_w be corresponding eigenvalues which are thus different.

$$d_v \mathbf{v}^T \mathbf{w} = (T'\mathbf{v})^T \mathbf{w} = \mathbf{v}^T(T'\mathbf{w}) = d_w \mathbf{v}^T \mathbf{w}.$$

Since $d_v \neq d_w$, $\mathbf{v}^T \mathbf{w}$ should be equal to 0. This implies that $\mathbf{v}$ and $\mathbf{w}$ are orthogonal.

By Lemma 15.1 and Lemma 15.2, the k smallest orthogonal eigenvectors of $T' = D^{-1/2}TD^{-1/2}$ are used after row normalization. Each data point is represented by the corresponding row.

In Algorithm 2, we firstly prepare the data matrix and constraint matrix. Then the cost function is optimized by solving an eigen-system (Equation (15.11)). Finally, we use a traditional classifier for the final prediction, which is similar to the procedure in [22].Empirically, our algorithm improves several other state-of-the-art classifiers as will be shown in the experiment part (Section 15.4).

The major computational cost of the above algorithm is for computing the eigenvectors. The eigenvectors can be obtained by Lanczos method, whose computational cost is proportional to the number of nonzero elements of the target matrix. Thus the cost of our algorithm is $O(kN_L nnz(T'))$, where k denotes the number of eigenvectors desired, N_L is the number of Lanczos iteration steps and $nnz(T')$ is the number of non-zero entries in T'.

Algorithm 2 Cross-Domain Spectral Classification

Input : training data (n_1 positive instances, n_2 negative instances and $n = n_1 + n_2$) and test data, parameters $\{\lambda, \beta, k\}$ and a reasonable classifier $\mathscr{F}$.

Output : class predictions for test data

1: Construct the similarity matrix $W_{n \times n}$ given both training and test data and W_s for only test data, where n to be the number of all the data.

2: Let $D = diag(We)$, $D_s = diag(W_se)$ and
   $U = \textbf{FormConstraintMatrix}(n_1, n_2, n)$.

3: Find the k smallest eigenvectors $\mathbf{x}_1, \mathbf{x}_2, \cdots, \mathbf{x}_k$ of $T' = D^{-1/2}(D - W + \beta UU^T + \lambda(D_s - W_s))D^{-1/2}$ and construct a matrix $X = D^{-1/2}(\mathbf{x}_1, \mathbf{x}_2, \cdots, \mathbf{x}_k)$.

4: Normalize X by row into Y where $Y_{ij} = X_{ij}/\sqrt{\sum_{l=1}^{k} X_{il}^2}$.

5: Call $\mathscr{F}$ with input of the eigenvectors to obtain the classification result.

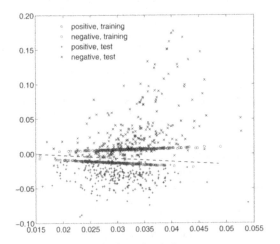

Fig. 15.1 Projected data of *rec* vs *talk* in 2-dimensional eigen-space.

15.3.5 Case Study

Figure 15.1 plots the *rec* vs *talk* data (data details will be presented in Section 15.4.1) represented by the two smallast eigenvectors using our algorithm CDSC. The data points in the figure are sufficiently separated for classification since the eigenvectors contain the needed structural information. Moreover, the training and test data are similar in terms of Euclidean distance. In this way, the approximate decision boundary can be easily detected (the dashed line) and, as a result, good performance is obtained using our method.

15.4 Experiments

Our method is evaluated extensively on several data sets with the training and test data from different domains. As we will show later, our method outperforms several state-of-the-art classifiers in all the tasks.

	Data Set		Positive (250 in all)	Negative (250 in all)
SRAA	auto vs aviation	train	sim-auto	sim-aviation
		test	real-auto	real-aviation
	real vs simulated	train	real-aviation	sim-aviation
		test	real-auto	sim-auto
20NG	rec vs talk	train	rec.{autos, motorcycles}	talk.{politics.guns, politics.misc}
		test	rec.{sport.baseball, sport.hockey}	talk.{politics.mideast, religion.misc}
	rec vs sci	train	rec.{autos, sport.baseball}	sci.{med, space}
		test	rec.{motorcycles, sport.hockey}	sci.{crypt, electronics}
	comp vs talk	train	comp.{graphics, windows.x, sys.mac.hardware}	talk.{politics.mideast, religion.misc}
		test	comp.{os.ms-windows.misc, sys.ibm.pc.hardware}	talk.{politics.guns, politics.misc}
	comp vs sci	train	comp.{graphics, os.ms-windows.misc}	sci.{crypt, electronics}
		test	comp.{sys.mac.hardware, windows.x, sys.ibm.pc.hardware}	sci.{med, space}
	comp vs rec	train	comp.{graphics, sys.mac.hardware, sys.ibm.pc.hardware}	rec.{motorcycles, sport.hockey}
		test	comp.{os.ms-windows.misc, windows.x}	rec.{autos, sport.baseball}
	sci vs talk	train	sci.{electronics, med}	talk.{politics.misc, religion.misc}
		test	sci.{crypt, space}	talk.{politics.guns, politics.mideast}
Reuters	orgs vs places	train	orgs.{...}	places.{...}
		test	orgs.{...}	places.{...}
	people vs places	train	people.{...}	places.{...}
		test	people.{...}	places.{...}
	orgs vs people	train	orgs.{...}	people.{...}
		test	orgs.{...}	people.{...}

Table 15.1 The composition of all the data sets. Since there are too many subcategories in Reuters-21578, we omit the composition details of last three data sets here.

15.4.1 Data Sets

The cross-domain data sets are generated in specific strategies using 20 Newsgroups[1], Reuters-21578[2] and SRAA[3]. The basic idea of our design is utilizing the hierarchy of the data sets to distinguish domains. Specifically, the task is defined as top-category classification. Each top category is split into two disjoint parts with different sub-categories, one for training and the other for test. Because the training and test data are in different subcategories, they are across domains as a result. To reduce the computational burden, we sampled 500 training and 500 test examples for each task.

15.4.1.1 20 Newsgroups

The 20 Newsgroups is a text collection of approximately 20,000 newsgroup documents, partitioned across 20 different newsgroups nearly evenly. Six different data sets are generated for evaluating cross-domain classification algorithms. For each data set, two top categories[4] are chosen, one as positive and the other as negative. Then, the data are split based on sub-categories. Different sub-categories can be considered as different domains, while the task is defined as top category classification. The splitting strategy ensures the domains of labeled and unlabeled data related, since they are under the same top categories. Besides, the domains are also ensured to be different, since they are drawn from different sub-categories. Table 15.1 shows how the data sets are generated in our experiments.

---

[1] http://people.csail.mit.edu/jrennie/20Newsgroups/

[2] http://www.daviddlewis.com/resources/testcollections/

[3] http://www.cs.umass.edu/~mccallum/data/sraa.tar.gz

[4] Three top categories, *misc*, *soc* and *alt* are removed, because they are too small.

Data Set	Verification of Data Set			Traditional Classification				Cross-Domain Classification		
	$\mathcal{D}_{in}-\mathcal{D}_{out}$	$\mathcal{D}_{out}$-CV	$\mathcal{D}_{in}$-CV	SVM	TSVM	SGT	SC	CoCC	KDE	CDSC
real vs simulated	0.330	0.032	0.030	0.330	0.316	0.276	0.278	0.250	0.330	**0.188**
auto vs aviation	0.252	0.033	0.048	0.252	0.188	0.208	0.160	0.142	0.248	**0.120**
comp vs sci	0.380	0.012	0.016	0.380	0.334	0.428	0.270	0.192	0.380	**0.098**
rec vs talk	0.316	0.003	0.002	0.316	0.118	0.190	0.428	**0.092**	0.324	0.092
rec vs sci	0.234	0.007	0.003	0.234	0.162	0.160	0.192	0.160	0.234	**0.124**
sci vs talk	0.198	0.009	0.006	0.198	0.148	0.114	0.362	0.100	0.194	**0.044**
comp vs rec	0.142	0.008	0.003	0.142	0.104	0.044	0.086	0.090	0.142	**0.042**
comp vs talk	0.098	0.005	0.005	0.098	**0.024**	0.030	0.042	0.042	0.100	**0.024**
orgs vs people	0.306	0.106	0.020	0.306	0.294	0.288	0.276	**0.232**	0.298	**0.232**
orgs vs places	0.428	0.085	0.093	0.428	0.424	0.456	0.386	0.400	0.418	**0.318**
people vs places	0.262	0.113	0.017	0.262	0.256	0.216	0.230	0.226	0.262	**0.202**
average	0.268	0.038	0.022	0.268	0.215	0.219	0.246	0.175	0.266	**0.135**

Table 15.2 The error rate given by each classifier. Under the column "Verification of Data Set", "$\mathcal{D}_{in}-\mathcal{D}_{out}$" means training on in-domain $\mathcal{D}_{in}$ and testing on out-of-domain $\mathcal{D}_{out}$; "$\mathcal{D}_{out}$-CV" and "$\mathcal{D}_{in}$-CV" means 10-fold cross-validation on out-of-domain $\mathcal{D}_{out}$ and in-domain $\mathcal{D}_{in}$. Note that, the experimental results given by CoCC here are somewhat different from those presented in the original paper, since we sampled only 500 examples from each original data set.

15.4.1.2 Reuters-21578

Reuters-21578 is one of the most famous test collections for evaluation of automatic text categorization techniques. It contains 5 top categories. Among these categories, *orgs*, *people* and *places* are three big ones. For the category *places*, all the documents about the USA are removed to make the three categories nearly even, because more than a half of the documents in the corpus are in the USA sub-categories. Reuters-21578 corpus also has hierarchical structure. We generated three data sets *orgs vs people*, *orgs vs places* and *people vs places* for cross-domain classification in a similar way as what have been done on the 20 Newsgroups. Since there are too many sub-categories, the detailed description cannot be listed here.

15.4.1.3 SRAA

SRAA is a Simulated/Real/Aviation/Auto UseNet data set for document classification. 73,218 UseNet articles are collected from four discussion groups about simulated autos (*sim-auto*), simulated aviation (*sim-aviation*), real autos (*real-auto*) and real aviation (*real-aviation*). Consider the task that aims to predict labels of instances between *real* and *simulated*. The documents in *real-auto* and *sim-auto* are used as in-domain data, while *real-aviation* and *sim-aviation* as out-of-domain data. Then, the data set *real vs sim* is generated as shown in Table 15.1. Therefore all the data in the in-domain data set are about *auto*, while all the data in the out-of-domain set are about *aviation*. The *auto vs aviation* data set is generated in the similar way as shown in Table 15.1.

15.4.1.4 Verification of Data Sets

To verify our data design, the error rates are recorded using the SVM classifier in the scenario of cross-domain learning ($\mathcal{D}_{in}-\mathcal{D}_{out}$) as well as the single-domain classification case within the out-of-domain and within the in-domain, respectively. Under the column "SVM" in Table 15.2, the three groups of classification results are displayed in the sub-columns. The column "$\mathcal{D}_{in}-\mathcal{D}_{out}$" means that the classifier is trained on in-domain data and tested on out-of-domain data. The next two columns "$\mathcal{D}_{out}$-CV" and "$\mathcal{D}_{in}$-CV" show the best results by the SVM classifier obtained during 10-fold cross validation. In these two experiments, the training and test data are extracted from the same domain, out-of-domain $\mathcal{D}_{out}$ and in-domain $\mathcal{D}_{in}$ respectively. Note that the error rates under the $\mathcal{D}_{in}-\mathcal{D}_{out}$ column is much worse than the ones under $\mathcal{D}_{out}$–CV and $\mathcal{D}_{in}$–CV. This implies that our data sets are not applicable for traditional classification.

15.4.2 Evaluation Metric

The test error rate metric is chosen to demonstrate the performance of our method. It measures the accuracy of the classification result on test data. The lower the value is, the more accurate our method seems. Denote $c(d)$ to be the true label of d and $h(d)$ is the classification result. The test error rate ε is

$$\varepsilon = \frac{|\{d|d \in S_{out} \text{ and } c(d) \neq h(d)\}|}{|S_{out}|} .$$

15.4.3 Comparison Methods

To verify the effectiveness of our classifier, the supervised learner SVM is set as the baseline method. Our method is also compared to several semi-supervised classifiers, including Transductive SVM (TSVM) [20], Spectral Graph Transducer (SGT) [21] and Spectral Classifier (SC) [22]. Note that [22] is approximately a special case CDSC with $\lambda = 0$. We also compare to the co-clustering based classification (CoCC) [10] as the state-of-the-art cross-domain learning algorithm and one representative selection bias correction (KDE) [29]. CoCC builds connection between in-domain and out-of-domain through feature clustering, and is formulated under the co-clustering framework. KDE corrects the domain bias in the in-domain, and then adapts the in-domain classification model to out-of-domain. We use test error rate as the evaluation measure.

15.4.4 Implementation Details

On the textual data designed in Section 15.4.1, we have conducted preprocessing procedures including tokenizing text into bag-of-words, converting text into low-case words, stop-word removal and stemming using the Porter stemmer [26]. Each document $\mathbf{d}_i$ in S is represented by a feature vector using *Vector Space Model*. Each feature represents a term, which is weighted by its *tf-idf* value. Feature selection is carried out by thresholding Document Frequency [34]. In our experiments, Document Frequency threshold is set to 3, and the final result is not sensitive to it. The cosine similarity measure $\frac{\mathbf{x}_i \cdot \mathbf{x}_j}{|\mathbf{x}_i||\mathbf{x}_j|}$ is adopted when constructing the similarity matrix.

The comparison methods are implemented by SVM^{light}[1] and SGT^{light}[2]. All parameters are set default by the software. The Spectral Classifier (SC) is implemented according to [22]. CoCC uses the same initialization and parameters in [10]. KDE is implemented according to [29, 35].

---

[1] Software available at http://svmlight.joachims.org.

[2] Software available at http://sgt.joachims.org.

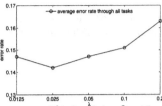

Fig. 15.2 The average error rate curve of λ when fixing β at 15.

15.4.5 Experimental Results

15.4.5.1 Performance

By comparing with the traditional supervised classifier, it is observed that the cross-domain data present much difficulty in classification, where SVM (training on in-domain $\mathscr{D}_{in}$ and testing on out-of-domain $\mathscr{D}_{out}$) made more than 20% average prediction errors. In Table 15.2, we observe that the TSVM and SGT always outperformed the supervised classifier SVM. The semi-supervised classifiers worked better since they used the unlabeled data in the classification process, so that they captured more information in the out-of-domain. However, semi-supervised learning still works under the identical-domain assumption, and thus its improvement is limited. The situations are similar in SC. CoCC improves a lot over the traditional classification algorithm, since CoCC is a cross-domain classification algorithm, and it effectively transfers knowledge across different domains. KDE shows few improvement against SVM in our experiments, although it can effectively correct selection bias between two different domains. In our opinion, KDE fails to improve much in cross-domain learning because the domain difference may be affected by the selection bias very few. In general, our algorithm CDSC is a spectral cross-domain learning method, and achieves the best performance against all the comparison methods. Compared to the state-of-the-art cross-domain learning algorithm CoCC, CDSC also shows superiority in this experiments. We believe, it is because the data size in our experiment is not so large, and spectral learning is much more superior in learning with small data than many other learning methods.

However, in some data sets the performance is not satisfactory. For example, this can be observed in *orgs* vs *places*. This can be attributed to less common knowledge between in-domain and out-of-domain data. Our method requires that the in-domain and out-of-domain should be related, namely that they share some knowledge. If this condition cannot be satisfied, the quality of transferred knowledge will not be guaranteed. As to the tasks derived from the 20 Newsgroups, the in-domain and out-of-domain data may share a large amount of common knowledge which leads to better performance, despite the fact that other methods failed in most cases. In general, our algorithm can alleviate the classification difficulty better when the in-domain and out-of-domain are not the same albeit related.

15.4.5.2 Parameter Tuning

There are two parameters in our method: β adjusts the enforcement of supervisory constraints; λ represents the trade-off of transferring knowledge into the target domain. We tested 5 different values of β when λ is fixed. λ is enumerated from 0.0125 to 0.2 with 5 log-scale values with fixing β. We use the average error rate through 11 tasks for evaluation. From Figure 15.2, it can be seen that, empirically the best λ is between $[0.0125, 0.05]$, and we set $\lambda = 0.025$ in our experiments. From Figure 15.3, the performance of CDSC is not very sensitive to β, and we set $\beta = 15$ in the experiments.

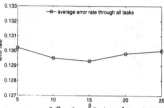

Fig. 15.3 The average error rate curve of β when fixing λ at 0.025.

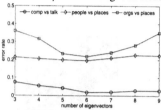

Fig. 15.4 The error rates against the number of eigenvectors.

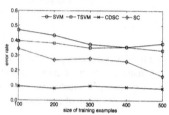

Fig. 15.5 The error rate curve on the data set *comp* vs *sci* against different sizes of training examples.

15.4.5.3 Eigenvectors

The eigenvectors obtained in the classification process represent the original information approximately in a different feature space. In this work, the optimal number is found by enumerating the number of used eigenvectors empirically. Figure 15.4 illustrates the error rates of several data sets against different numbers of eigenvectors used for classification. From the figure, it can be seen that, generally, the classification on 6 eigenvectors shows the best performance.

15.4.5.4 Varying the Size of the Training Data

We have also investigated the influence by the size of training examples. Take *comp* vs *sci* data set for example (Figure 15.5). We chose a portion of examples in the training data randomly ranging from 100 examples to all of the samples (500). We observe that SVM, TSVM and SC often performed, in general, increasingly worse when the number of training examples decreases. In contrast to these baselines, the error rate curve of our algorithm is generally stable. This indicates our algorithm CDSC can better deal with the data sparsity problem. More importantly, CDSC tops the performance over almost all trials.

15.4.5.5 Similarity Pattern

Spectral methods promise to draw the similar data points nearer by representing the original data in the eigen-space. But how does this projection work on cross-domain data? To answer this question,

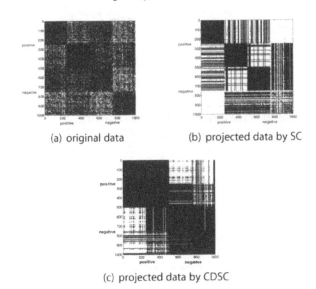

(a) original data   (b) projected data by SC

(c) projected data by CDSC

Fig. 15.6 The similarity pattern on the data set *rec vs talk*. The data are indexed firstly by category and secondly by training and test, namely positive training, positive test, negative training and negative test in order. The document-document similarity matrix of the original data valued by the cosine measure, which has a threshold by the mean of this matrix.

we illustrate the similarity pattern of the original data, the projected data in Spectral Classifier (SC) [22] and the projected data in our method (CDSC). Take the data set *rec vs talk* for example. The data are indexed firstly by category and secondly by training and test, namely positive training, positive test, negative training and negative test in order. Figure 6(a) displays the document-document similarity matrix of the original data valued by the cosine measure, which has a threshold by the mean of this matrix. The latter two patterns are similarly thresholded. In Figure 6(b), it is shown that SC fails to draw the data within the same category more similar. Figure 6(c) plots the similarity matrix of the projected data using our method. The projected data show more obvious block-like behavior within the same category. On the contrary to the SC pattern, the data from same category become similar while the data from different categories become dissimilar although the whole data are across domains. It is mainly attributed to our novel objective function, which also considers the out-of-domain separation. This block-like behavior indicates that the supervisory knowledge from another domain can be used directly and effectively. In this way, the classifier will find the decision boundary more easily and more accurately and hence perform better.

15.5 Related Work

15.5.1 Spectral Methods

Spectral clustering is theoretically based on spectral graph theory [9]. Its main idea is to find the optimal partition that satisfies certain criterion. However, regular cut minimization often leads to trivial partition (one against the rest). To avoid this problem, several improved partition criteria were introduced, e.g., Ratio Cut [8], Normalized Cut [28], Min-Max Cut [15]. The intra-cluster similarity is maximized and the inter-cluster connection is optionally minimized, turning the clustering task into an optimization problem. Since finding a discrete-valued solution is NP-hard, a common approach is to relax the problem into an approximate real-valued solution with the help of Rayleigh Quotient's property [16]. As to the discretization, linear order search [28] and other variant search methods (e.g. linkage differential order [?]) are commonly used to derive the cluster membership. Another approach was proposed in [25] which first normalizes the eigenvectors and then applies the K-Means clustering method.

In addition to these unsupervised learning methods (described in Section 15.2), [19] developed a semi-supervised spectral clustering algorithm by incorporating the prior knowledge. In a supervised manner, [22] designs a spectral learning framework for classification. To represent the supervisory knowledge, the similarity between two same-label data points is set to 1. An one-nearest-neighbor classifier is applied to the data represented by eigenvectors. [22] also showed how to make spectral classification to achieve better performance by adding more labeled and unlabeled data. Compared to these methods in [25, 19], our method is derived from spectral clustering, but the eigenvectors are used for classification instead of clustering. A difference from [22] is that our method classifies the unlabeled data based on the label information from a different domain, while [22] focuses on learning within a single domain.

15.5.2 Transfer Learning

Transfer learning has been introduced to handle the learning problem where learning and prediction are in different scenarios. The idea of transfer learning is inspired by the intuition that humans often learn better when they have learned well in related domains. For instance, a good checker player may find it easier to learn to play chess. Previous works in transfer learning include "learning how to learn" [27] ,"learning one more thing" [30] and "multi-task learning" [7], which laid the initial foundations. [2] presented the notion of relatedness between learning tasks, which provided theoretical justifications for transfer learning. In our problem setting, we aim to accomplish the same task (i.e. learn with the same label set) in different domains, which is called *multi-domain* or *cross-domain learning* – a special case of transfer learning.

The cross-domain learning can be classified into two categories according to whether the out-of-domain supervision is given. [32] investigated how to exploiting auxiliary data in k-Nearest-Neighbors and SVM algorithm. They used the term "auxiliary data" to refer to the in-domain data and their experiments have demonstrated that the learning performance can be significantly improved with the help of auxiliary data. [14] utilized additional "in-domain" labeled data to train a statistical classifier under the *Conditional Expectation-Maximization* framework. Those "in-domain" data play a role as auxiliary data in tackling the scarcity of "out-of-domain" training data. In these works [32, 23, 14, 13, 12], auxiliary data serve as a supplement to the ordinary training data. In contrast to these works, our work focuses on the second category of cross-domain learning, where the problem is classification *without* any training examples in the *out-of-domain*. Note that, in our problem, the in-domain and out-of-domain data are assumed to be relevant, in order to make the cross-domain learning feasible. In the past, [10] proposed a co-clustering based algorithm to overcome the domain difference. In this paper, we use both in-domain supervision and out-of-domain structural information to handle the cross-domain problem through spectral learning. As we showed in the experiments, our algorithm shows superiority over [10], when the data size is not sufficiently large. Other work includes *Covariate shift* [29] (or *sample selection bias* [35]) is a similar problem which occurs when samples are selected non-randomly. Originated from the Nobel-prize work in 2000, [17] made his contributions on correction of *sample selection bias* in econometrics. Recent researches on covariate shift used the instance weighting method to correct the bias. Although correcting sample selection bias [35] can solve the classification when training and test data are governed by different selection bias, it still mainly focuses on learning within a single domain. Our experiments in Section 15.4 show that correcting sample selection bias can only improve very little in cross-domain learning.

Covariate shift [29] (or *sample selection bias* [35]) is a similar problem which occurs when samples are selected non-randomly. Originated from the Nobel-prize work in 2000, [17] made his contributions on correction of *sample selection bias* in econometrics. Recent researches on covariate shift include [35, 29, 18, 4, 3]. They used the instance weighting method to correct the bias. Although correcting sample selection bias [35] can solve the classification when training and test data are governed by different selection bias, it still mainly focuses on learning within a single domain. Our experiments in Section 15.4 show that correcting sample selection bias can only improve very little in cross-domain learning.

15.6 Conclusion and Future Work

In this paper, a novel spectral classification based method CDSC is presented where an objective function is proposed for cross-domain learning. In the cross-domain setting, the labeled data from the in-domains are available for training and the unlabeled data from out-of-domains are to be classified. Based on the normalized cut cost function, supervisory knowledge is transferred through a constraint matrix, and the regularized objective function (see Equation (15.10)) finds the consistency between the in-domain supervision and the out-of-domain intrinsic structure. The original data are then represented by a set of eigenvectors, to which a linear classifier is applied to get the final predictions. Several cross-domain learning tasks are used to evaluate our learning method, where experimental results justify that our method is effective on handling this cross-domain classification problem.

There are several directions for future work. The CDSC is given in batch style in this paper. In the future, we would like to extend CDSC to an online cross-domain classifier. It is also important to speed up our algorithm to cope with the large-scale data sets.

Acknowledgments

Qiang Yang would like to thank the support of Hong Kong RGC Grant 621307. Gui-Rong Xue would like to thank Microsoft Research Asia for their support to the MSRA-SJTU joint lab project "Transfer Learning and its application on the Web". We also thank the anonymous reviewers for their valuable comments.

References

1. S. Ben-David, J. Blitzer, K. Crammer, and F. Pereira. Analysis of representations for domain adaptation. In *NIPS*, 2007.
2. S. Ben-David and R. Schuller. Exploiting task relatedness for multiple task learning. In *COLT*, 2003.
3. S. Bickel, M. Brückner, and T. Scheffer. Discriminative learning for differing training and test distributions. In *ICML*, 2007.
4. S. Bickel and T. Scheffer. Dirichlet-enhanced spam filtering based on biased samples. In *NIPS*, 2007.
5. J. Blitzer, K. Crammer, A. Kulesza, F. Pereira, and J. Wortman. Learning bounds for domain adaptation. In *NIPS*, 2008.

6. J. Blitzer, R. McDonald, and F. Pereira. Domain adaptation with structural correspondence learning. In *EMNLP*, 2006.
7. R. Caruana. Multitask Learning. *Machine Learning*, 28(1):41–75, 1997.
8. C.-K. Cheng and Y.-C. A. Wei. An improved two-way partitioning algorithm with stable performance [VLSI]. *IEEE Transactions on Computer-Aided Design of Integrated Circuits and Systems*, 10(12):1502–1511, 1991.
9. F. R. K. Chung. *Spectral Graph Theory*. American Mathematical Society, 1997.
10. W. Dai, G.-R. Xue, Q. Yang, and Y. Yu. Co-clustering based classification for out-of-domain documents. In *SIGKDD*, 2007.
11. W. Dai, G.-R. Xue, Q. Yang, and Y. Yu. Transferring naive bayes classifiers for text classification. In *AAAI*, 2007.
12. W. Dai, Q. Yang, G.-R. Xue, and Y. Yu. Boosting for transfer learning. In *ICML*, 2007.
13. H. Daumé III. Frustratingly easy domain adaptation. In *ACL*, 2007.
14. H. Daumé III and D. Marcu. Domain adaptation for statistical classifiers. *JAIR*, 1:1–15, 2006.
15. C. Ding, X. He, H. Zha, M. Gu, and H. Simon. Spectral min-max cut for graph partitioning and data clustering. In *ICDM*, 2001.
16. G. H. Golub and C. F. Van Loan. *Matrix Computation*. The Johns Hopkins University Press Baltimore, 1996.
17. J. J. Heckman. Sample selection bias as a specification error. *Econometrica*, 47(1):153–162, 1979.
18. J. Huang, A. J. Smola, A. Gretton, K. Borgwardt, and B. Schölkopf. Correcting sample selection bias by unlabeled data. In *NIPS*, 2007.
19. X. Ji and W. Xu. Document clustering with prior knowledge. In *SIGIR*, 2006.
20. T. Joachims. Transductive inference for text classification using support vector machines. In *ICML*, 1999.
21. T. Joachims. Transductive learning via spectral graph partitioning. In *ICML*, 2003.
22. S. D. Kamvar, D. Klein, and C. D. Manning. Spectral learning. In *IJCAI*, 2003.
23. X. Liao, Y. Xue, and L. Carin. Logistic regression with an auxiliary data source. In *ICML*, 2005.
24. M. Meila and J. Shi. A random walks view of spectral segmentation. In *Proceedings of the 8th International Workshop on Artificial Intelligence and Statistics*, 2001.
25. A. Y. Ng, M. I. Jordan, and Y. Weiss. On spectral clustering: Analysis and an algorithm. In *NIPS*, 2001.
26. M. Porter. An algorithm for suffix stripping program. *Program*, 14(3):130–137, 1980.
27. J. Schmidhuber. On learning how to learn learning strategies. Technical Report FKI-198-94, Fakultat fur Informatik, 1994.
28. J. Shi and J. Malik. Normalized cuts and image segmentation. *IEEE Transactions on Pattern Analysis and Machine Intelligence*, 22(8):888–905, 2000.
29. H. Shimodaira. Improving predictive inference under covariate shift by weighting the log-likelihood function. *Journal of Statistical Planning and Inference*, 90(2):227–244, 2000.
30. S. Thrun and T. Mitchell. Learning one more thing. In *IJCAI*, 1995.
31. K. Wagstaff and C. Cardie. Clustering with instance-level constraints. In *ICML*, 2000.
32. P. Wu and T. G. Dietterich. Improving SVM accuracy by training on auxiliary data sources. In *ICML*, 2004.
33. D. Xing, W. Dai, G.-R. Xue, and Y. Yu. Bridged refinement for transfer learning. In *PKDD*, 2007.
34. Y. Yang and J. O. Pedersen. A comparative study on feature selection in text categorization. In *ICML*, 1997.
35. B. Zadrozny. Learning and evaluating classifiers under sample selection bias. In *ICML*, 2004.